Eugen von Böhm-Bawerk

Karl Marx and the Close of his System

Eugen von Böhm-Bawerk

Karl Marx and the Close of his System

ISBN/EAN: 9783743625013

Printed in Europe, USA, Canada, Australia, Japan

Cover: Foto ©Suzi / pixelio.de

Manufactured and distributed by brebook publishing software (www.brebook.com)

Eugen von Böhm-Bawerk

Karl Marx and the Close of his System

KARL MARX

AND THE CLOSE OF HIS SYSTEM

BY Eugen von Böhm-Bawerk

&

BÖHM-BAWERK'S

CRITICISM OF MARX

BY Rudolf Hilferding

Together with an Appendix consisting of an Article by
Ladislaus von Bortkiewicz on the Transformation of Values
into Prices of Production in the Marxian System

Edited with an introduction
by PAUL M. SWEEZY

AUGUSTUS M. KELLEY
NEW YORK 1949

Printed in the United States of America
by H. WOLFF, New York

CONTENTS

Tʜɪs volume brings together two of the most important items in the large literature concerned with criticizing and evaluating the economic doctrines of Karl Marx. Böhm-Bawerk's contribution, in its English translation, has been out of print and very difficult to obtain for many years. Hilferding's answer to Böhm-Bawerk was brought out in translation by an obscure socialist publisher in Glasgow and never acquired wide circulation in either Britain or this country. In view of the recent growth of interest in Marxism, I believe the time has come to make these works available to a larger English-reading public; and I also believe that each gains in value through being presented side by side with the other.

As an appendix there is included an article by the German statistician-economist Bortkiewicz. This article, bearing on one of the central points at issue between Böhm-Bawerk and Hilferding, has achieved considerable fame; but hitherto it has not been translated into English, and I have seen no evidence that it has been read by more than a handful of specialists. I believe that serious students of Marxian economics, whether hostile or friendly, will be glad to have it made readily available for study and reference.

In this introduction I shall discuss these three works in the hope of illuminating the point of view from which their authors wrote and of placing them in the development of the literature of which they form a part.

BÖHM-BAWERK'S CRITICISM OF MARX

BÖHM-BAWERK'S WORK was first published in 1896, under the title *Zum Abschluss des Marxschen Systems,* in a volume of essays in honor of Karl Knies.[1] It appeared in Russian the following year and in English (in both London and New York) in 1898.

The original English title is retained here because it is by this title that the work is now widely known. At the same time it is necessary to point out that this title is not strictly accurate and has given rise to misunderstandings. "Karl Marx and the Close of His System" sounds like an obituary for Marx and his theories;[2] but, though the spirit of an obituary is not lacking from Böhm-Bawerk's writing, it would be mistaken to assume that this is what he intended to convey by the title. The third and final volume of *Capital* was published by Engels in 1894, and Böhm-Bawerk's work was in the nature of an extended review. The German title means simply "On the Conclusion of the Marxian System," and this describes the work as accurately as a brief title can.

It was quite natural, one might almost say inevitable, that Böhm-Bawerk should write this book. In his well-known history of theories of capital and interest,[3] he had devoted a whole

---

[1] O. v. Boenigk, ed., *Staatswissenschaftliche Arbeiten: Festgaben für Karl Knies,* Berlin, 1896. It appeared in separate covers during the same year and was reprinted in Franz X. Weiss, ed., *Böhm-Bawerk's Kleinere Abhandlungen über Kapital und Zins,* Vienna and Leipzig, 1926.

[2] For example, this seems to be the sense in which William Blake interprets it. See *An American Looks at Karl Marx* (1939), pp. 414-415, 424.

[3] *Geschichte und Kritik der Kapitalzins-Theorien,* first edition, 1884. Published in English (translation by William Smart) as *Capital and Interest,* 1890. The second and third editions, each with much new material, appeared in 1900 and 1914. They have not been translated into English. The fourth edition appeared in 1921 and is merely a reprint of the third.

chapter to criticism of the theories of value and surplus value expounded in the first volume of *Capital*. There he had noted that Marx was aware that commodities do not in fact sell at their values under developed capitalist conditions. He also noted that Marx promised to solve this problem in a later volume, a promise which Böhm-Bawerk was convinced Marx could not keep.[1] Hence, when the third volume finally appeared with Marx's detailed treatment of this question, Böhm-Bawerk doubtless felt duty bound to examine it with all possible care and to pronounce his verdict.

In *Karl Marx and the Close of His System*, Böhm-Bawerk took over the main arguments of his chapter on Marx from the first edition of *Capital and Interest;* and in subsequent editions of the latter he incorporated the substance of the criticism of the third volume of *Capital* from *Karl Marx and the Close of His System*. Nevertheless, the latter is far more detailed and elaborate; not only does it stand on its own feet but it contains all that is important in Böhm-Bawerk's writings on Marxian economics.

If we are to understand the significance of *Karl Marx and the Close of His System* it is necessary to identify Böhm-Bawerk and to recognize his place in the development of modern economic theory.

The relevant facts of his career can be briefly told. Eugen von Böhm-Bawerk was born (1851) into one of the aristocratic-bureaucratic families which were the real rulers of Imperial Austria, his father being at the time a high official in Moravia. When he was still very young his father died and the family moved to Vienna where, except for nine years of teaching at the University of Innsbruck (1880-1889), he spent most of the rest

---

[1] "It is singular," Böhm-Bawerk wrote, "that Marx himself became aware of the fact that there was a contradiction here, and found it necessary for the sake of his solution to promise to deal with it later on. But the promise was never kept, and indeed could not be kept." *Capital and Interest*, p. 390.

of his life. After taking a course of law at the University of Vienna he entered the Finance Ministry in 1872. In 1875 he took a three-year leave of absence to study economics with some of the outstanding German professors of the day. From this time on, his career was a mixture of government service and university teaching. He served as Finance Minister in three different cabinets (1895, 1897-1898, 1900-1904). From 1904 until his death in 1914 he held a chair in political economy at the University of Vienna.

As an economist, Böhm-Bawerk was from the first a champion of the new subjective value or marginal utility theory which his somewhat older contemporary, Carl Menger, had been the first to enunciate in Austria. Böhm-Bawerk, along with Menger and Friedrich Wieser (whose sister he married in 1880), was thus one of the founders of the so-called Austrian school. His two major works, *Capital and Interest* and *The Positive Theory of Capital*, were published in 1884 and 1889 respectively, before he was forty years old; and as the subjective value theory spread geographically and gained in popularity, Böhm-Bawerk's fame grew by leaps and bounds. Outside of his own country he came to be much better known than Menger or Wieser, and by the turn of the century it is probable that his international reputation was greater than that of any other living economist, with the possible exception of Alfred Marshall. Only in Britain, where the authority of Marshall and Edgeworth (at Cambridge and Oxford respectively) was virtually unchallenged, did Böhm-Bawerk fail to attract a substantial following; while in countries as widely separated as Sweden, the United States, and Japan his influence upon academic economics was profound.

It is against this background that we must evaluate Böhm-Bawerk's critique of the theories of Marx. Organized socialism in Europe experienced a rapid growth in the last three decades of the nineteenth century, and it was also during this period that within the continental socialist movement Marxism won out over rival schools and doctrines.[1] Hence, while the original re-action of the academic world had been to ignore Marx, it became increasingly difficult to maintain this attitude; as time went on it became more and more urgent to organize a counter-attack.

The publication of the third volume of *Capital* offered the perfect opportunity, and Böhm-Bawerk was a "natural" to take the lead. He had already, in *Capital and Interest*, established himself as a formidable opponent of Marxism by his attacks on what he called the "exploitation theory" of interest; his inter-national reputation insured that whatever he wrote would re-ceive a wide and respectful hearing. It is therefore not surprising that when *Karl Marx and the Close of His System* was published in 1896 it was an immediate success and soon became what might almost be called the official answer of the economics pro-fession to Marx and the Marxian school.

It would not be fruitful to trace in detail the influence of Böhm-Bawerk's critique on orthodox economics, especially since a large part of that influence was never formally acknowledged and hence would be practically impossible to document. Franz X. Weiss, the editor of Böhm-Bawerk's collected papers, un-doubtedly expressed the view of most continental academic economists when he wrote that *Karl Marx and the Close of His System* "is rightly regarded as the best criticism of the Marxian theories of value and surplus value." [2]

So far as the United States is concerned, all the serious criti-cisms of Marxian economics with which I am acquainted recog-nize the authority, if not the primacy, of Böhm-Bawerk in this

[1] Engels summed up these developments in his triumphal appearance before the Zurich Congress of the Second International (1893). "From the little sects of those days [the 1840's]," he told the cheering delegates, "socialism has now developed into a powerful party before which the whole world of officialdom trembles. Marx is dead; but if he were still alive, there would be no man in Europe or America who could look back on his lifework with better reason for pride." Quoted in Gustav Mayer, *Friedrich Engels* (1934), pp. 322-323.
[2] Biographical introduction to *Gesammelte Schriften von Eugen von Böhm-Bawerk* (1924), pp. vii-viii.

field; [1] while the similarity of the anti-Marxian arguments in the average textbook to those of Böhm-Bawerk is too striking to be easily accounted a coincidence.

From the Marxian camp the testimony to Böhm-Bawerk's pre-eminence as an opponent is at least as striking. Louis B. Boudin, in the economic chapters of his important survey of the Marxian system and its critics, pays most attention to Böhm-Bawerk's arguments: "First because Böhm-Bawerk is so far superior to his comrades in arms and his authority is acknowledged by them to such an extent, that it can hardly be claimed to be unfair to these critics, to pick Böhm-Bawerk as an example of them all. Second, because there seems to be quite a good deal of unanimity among these critics on this particular point [value theory], and the arguments advanced by the others are either directly borrowed from Böhm-Bawerk, very often with an acknowledgment of receipt, or are variations on the same tune deserving no particular attention." [2] The situation did not change greatly in this respect in the following decades. William Blake, writing in 1939, could say: "Böhm-Bawerk anticipated nearly all the attacks on Marxism from the viewpoint of those who hold political economy to center on a subjective theory of value. On the whole, little has been added to his case by other critics; their important contributions are outside the theories he chose to contest." [3]

[1] See, for example, O. D. Skelton's *Socialism: A Critical Analysis* (1911), which is perhaps the ablest anti-socialist book by an American. Skelton refers to *Karl Marx and the Close of His System* as a "classic analysis," and his own thought is obviously strongly influenced by it. In his well-known textbook, the late Professor Taussig devoted two chapters to socialism; in his bibliography to these chapters he lists Böhm-Bawerk first among "the innumerable discussions and refutations of the Marxian doctrines." *Principles of Economics,* 3rd ed. (1921), Vol. II, p. 502. It would be easy to multiply examples.
[2] *The Theoretical System of Karl Marx* (1907), p. 85.
[3] *Op. cit.,* p. 415. I may perhaps also be allowed to quote what I wrote myself at about the same time: "By far the best statement of this point of view [i.e. that the alleged contradiction between Volumes I and III of *Capital* proves the uselessness of the labor theory of value] is that of Böhm-Bawerk, *Karl Marx and the Close of His System.* It is hardly an exaggeration to say

It has been necessary to stress the historical importance of Böhm-Bawerk's criticism of Marx, but this should not lead us into the error of falsely evaluating the work itself. The truth is that in its essentials *Karl Marx and the Close of His System* is not a particularly remarkable performance. It is obviously the work of a skilled debater, but its intellectual content is largely confined to applications of the elementary principles of the marginal utility theory. Böhm-Bawerk's line of reasoning was thoroughly familiar in academic economic circles, and any number of his contemporaries could have produced a critique of Marx which would have differed from Böhm-Bawerk's only in matters of emphasis and detail. The examples of Wicksteed [1] in England and Pareto [2] in the Latin countries prove this, if indeed proof is required. We do not need to assume, therefore, that things would have been much different if *Karl Marx and the Close of His System* had never been written. Some other economist would have come forward to do the job which Böhm-Bawerk did; or perhaps Pareto's critique, since it bore the

that subsequent critiques of Marxian economics have been mere repetitions of Böhm's arguments. The one great exception is the critique of Ladislaus von Bortkiewicz." *The Theory of Capitalist Development* (1942), p. 70n. I discuss Bortkiewicz later in the present introduction.

[1] P. H. Wicksteed, *Das Kapital: A Criticism*, first published in the socialist magazine *Today*, October, 1884; reprinted in *The Common Sense of Political Economy* (1933), Vol. II, pp. 705ff. In my judgment Wicksteed's criticism, despite its brevity, is in many respects a better piece of work than the virtually simultaneous chapter on Marx in Böhm-Bawerk's *Capital and Interest*. It is interesting to note that Wicksteed's review appeared at a time when Marxism seemed to be making real headway in Britain. Later on, when the British labor movement had definitely turned away from Marxism, no top-flight British economist showed any interest in the subject until Mrs. Joan Robinson's very interesting *Essay on Marxian Economics* (1942).

[2] Pareto's criticism of Marx is divided into two parts, separated by nearly a decade. First, his introduction to *Karl Marx: Le capital, extraits faits par M. Paul Lafargue* (1893); second, two chapters entitled "L'économie marxiste" and "La théorie matérialiste de l'histoire et la lutte des classes" (totaling 133 pages) in *Les systèmes socialistes* (2 vols., 1902). Both of these, written in Pareto's characteristically arrogant and superficial manner, I consider definitely inferior to Böhm-Bawerk. A useful commentary on Pareto is Erwin Schuler, *Pareto's Marx-Kritik* (written before 1933, published 1935).

authoritative stamp of the Lausanne school, might have assumed
the pre-eminent position that Böhm-Bawerk's actually occu-
pied.[1] Marx had to be refuted, and history, in casting her eyes
over the possible candidates, selected Böhm-Bawerk as best
fitted for the assignment. But if he had refused or fallen down
on the job, some one else would have been ready to take his
place. Here is a case, I think, where we can clearly accept Engels' dictum: "That such and such a man and precisely that man
arises at that particular time in that given country is of course
pure accident. But cut him out and there will be a demand for a
substitute, and this substitute will be found, good or bad, but in
the long run he will be found."[2]

It is not my purpose in this introduction to discuss the details of Böhm-Bawerk's case against Marx. The reader can follow these through for himself. But I think it is necessary to say
something about the attitude which Böhm-Bawerk adopts toward Marx and the scope of the criticism which follows from
this attitude.

Böhm-Bawerk was writing at a time when subjective value
theory had scored its greatest triumphs and was the accepted
basis of serious academic economics. He, in common with its
other exponents, was completely convinced that economics had
at last attained to the coveted status of a genuine science; and
he took it for granted as requiring no argument that the problems which he and his colleagues (both in Austria and abroad)
were working on were *the* problems which the young science
must attempt to solve. In keeping with this attitude, Böhm-
Bawerk implicitly, and no doubt unconsciously, assumed that
Marx had been engaged in the same enterprise and could legiti-

[1] It could be argued that Pareto did in fact occupy this position in the Latin
countries. I do not know the relevant literature well enough to form an
opinion on this; but I do know that Pareto's criticisms of Marx were never
translated and exerted no significant influence in German- or English-speaking
countries.
[2] Marx-Engels, *Selected Correspondence* (1935), p. 518.

mately be judged by the same standards as might be applied, for example, to Marshall or J. B. Clark.

What were these problems which economics was trying to solve? They all centered around and were really dependent upon the problem of value, in the sense of exchange ratios established upon the market. ("Price" as the money expression of value was regarded as the proper subject of monetary as opposed to "pure" theory.) Indeed, all the phenomena of economics—such as wages, rent, interest, and profits—were in the last analysis special cases of the problem of value, *derived from* and *regulated by* the operations of commodity markets in a more or less complex fashion.

Given this starting point, the subjective value theorist has hardly any choice when he undertakes to evaluate a systematic body of economic doctrine such as that of Marx. He must first test the value theory. Does it explain the phenomena of exchange ratios as they are found in typical, concrete market situations? If so, he can proceed to the rest of the theory. If not, then the rest of the theory must necessarily be wrong and there is no sense in wasting time on it. It is like a problem in arithmetic: if you find an error in the first line, you know that the answer must be wrong and that the subsequent calculations are worthless.

It was entirely within the framework of this approach that Böhm-Bawerk carried out his examination of Marxian theory. After a brief introduction, he devotes two chapters to setting out Marx's theories of value, surplus value, average rate of profit, and price of production—"for the sake of connection," as he says.[1] On the basis of this exposition he concludes that Marx had not one but two theories of value (one in Volume I of *Capital* and another in Volume III) in Böhm-Bawerk's sense of the term, that is, market exchange ratios. Moreover, according to Böhm-Bawerk, these two theories lead to different results, not occasionally or exceptionally but regularly and as a matter of

[1] Below, p. 3 ff.

principle. Hence, Böhm-Bawerk "cannot help himself"; he is forced to the conclusion that there is a contradiction between Volume I and Volume III of *Capital.* He next proceeds to analyze at length—more than a third of the whole critique is devoted to this—the arguments by which, according to Böhm-Bawerk, Marx seeks to prove that the contradiction is only apparent and that the theory of Volume I is valid, after all. Having disposed of these arguments one by one, Böhm-Bawerk is at last ready to deal with the heart of the matter, "the error in the Marxian system," for it is by now clear that error there must be. Naturally, he finds that the error lies in the fact that Marx started from the old-fashioned and exploded labor theory of value instead of pushing his way through to the new and scientifically correct subjective theory of value. This error ramifies throughout the system and vitiates it from top to bottom.

This, then, is the form and substance of Böhm-Bawerk's case against Marx. It is particularly important to recognize that it is not a personal attack on Marx.[1] Nor is it simply one theorist's dissection of the work of another, though this is undoubtedly what Böhm-Bawerk was aiming at. It is rather a systematic exposition of why subjective value theory, the "new economics" of half a century ago, rejected the Marxian system root and branch. It is this fact, rather than any special brilliance or originality in the work itself, which constitutes the importance of Böhm-Bawerk's critique.

HILFERDING'S REPLY TO BÖHM-BAWERK

Das Finanzkapital by Rudolf Hilferding is certainly one of the best-known works in the field of Marxian economics since

---

[1] Franz Weiss says, with justice, that "Böhm-Bawerk's criticism of Marx contrasts favorably with much that has since been written, both for and against Marx, by its dispassionate tone. Standing in complete opposition to Marx's teachings, Böhm-Bawerk was extremely careful to be fair to him as a person." *Gesammelte Schriften von Eugen von Böhm-Bawerk,* pp. xiii-xiv.

Capital itself.[1] The author is less well-known than the book, however, and it may be interesting as well as useful for our present purpose to review Hilferding's career before taking up his reply to Böhm-Bawerk, which was one of the earliest, if not actually the first, of his published writings.[2]

Hilferding was born in Vienna in 1877 of a well-to-do Jewish mercantile family. He studied medicine at the University of Vienna, but even during his student days his interests seem to have run more to the social sciences. He soon became a socialist and organized, along with Otto Bauer (later leader of the Austrian Socialists) and others, the first student socialist society.

Intellectually brilliant and personally attractive, Hilferding was not slow to gain the favorable attention of the leaders of the German-speaking socialist movement. In 1902 Kautsky invited him to become a regular contributor to *Die Neue Zeit*, the theoretical organ of the German Social Democratic Party. In 1906 he was asked by Bebel to go to Berlin to serve as an instructor in the party school there. He remained in this position about a year and then was chosen to be the foreign editor of *Vorwärts*, chief German Social Democratic newspaper. From this period on, he was prominent in the affairs of the German party, serving on its Central Committee and playing a leading part in its Reichstag delegation.

Meanwhile, in 1904, Hilferding and Max Adler had published in Vienna the first volume in a series entitled *Marx Studien* which was to provide an outlet for the younger Viennese socialist intellectuals. This first volume contained three studies, the second and third being by Josef Karner [3] and Max Adler.[4] The

[1] A translation of *Das Finanzkapital* is now in preparation and will be published by Augustus M. Kelley.
[2] For details and dates I have relied on Alexander Stein, *Rudolf Hilferding und die deutsche Arbeiterbewegung: Gedenkblätter*, published by the German Social Democratic Party in 1946.
[3] "Die Soziale Funktion der Rechtsinstitute." Josef Karner was a pen name used by Karl Renner, first Premier and later President of the Austrian Government after World War II.
[4] "Kausalität und Teleologie im Streite um die Wissenschaft."

first was Hilferding's *Böhm-Bawerk's Marx-Kritik* which is reproduced in this volume in the English of the well-known translators Eden and Cedar Paul.[1]

Hilferding's next and most substantial work, *Das Finanzkapital*, was likewise published as one of the *Marx Studien*
series. It appeared in 1910; but, as Hilferding tells us in a preface (dated Christmas, 1909), it was finished in its main outlines
"already four years ago"—that is to say as early as 1905. Hailed
by Otto Bauer as "the book for which we have long been waiting," *Das Finanzkapital* won for its author the reputation of
being the leading economist of the German-speaking socialist
movement. Nor was recognition of the importance of Hilferding's book confined to Germany and Austria. Lenin was much
influenced by *Das Finanzkapital;* and on the first page of
Imperialism, he refers to it in the following terms: "In spite of
the author's mistake regarding the theory of money, and in spite
of a certain inclination to reconcile Marxism and opportunism,
this work affords a very valuable theoretical analysis of 'the
latest phase of capitalist development,' as the subtitle of Hilferding's book reads."

Entirely thought out and largely written before he had
reached the age of thirty, *Das Finanzkapital* was Hilferding's
last important contribution to socialist literature. He never
wrote another book, and what he did produce during the last
three decades of his life was mainly of a journalistic nature,
possessing little lasting interest. When he undertook a more
general theoretical analysis, as in his contribution to a two-

---

[1] *Böhm-Bawerk's Criticism of Marx,* by Rudolf Hilferding, translated from
the German by Eden and Cedar Paul, Socialist Labour Press, Glasgow, no
date. William Blake dates the English edition 1920 (*An American Looks at
Karl Marx,* p. 672); and though I cannot confirm this date, I think it is
probably correct. An advertisement in the back refers to "the late Karl Lieb-
knecht," and this proves that it cannot have been published before 1919. The
long translators' footnote (p. 143 below) indicates, on the other hand, that it
was published before communication had been re-established between British
and German socialists after the interruption of wartime.

volume symposium on capitalism in 1931,[1] he simply repeated, with hardly any change, the ideas of *Das Finanzkapital*.

When war broke out in 1914, Hilferding's strong pacifist and humanitarian leanings caused him to vote with the left wing of the German Social Democratic Party against war credits. The following year, however, he was drafted into the Austrian Army and spent most of the rest of the war years as a doctor on the Italian front, a fact which precluded his playing an active political role between 1914 and the Revolution of 1918. When he returned to Germany after the war he cast his lot with the Independent Social Democratic Party which had been formed in April, 1917, as a result of a split between the left and center socialists on the one hand and the right socialists on the other. Hilferding quickly rose to a position of leadership among the Independents, filling the important post of editor-in-chief of their newspaper *Freiheit*. He was never a real leftist, however, and when the issue of joining the new Communist International came up before the Halle Congress of the Independents (1920), he was one of the leaders of the minority which opposed the move. The Independents now split, the majority forming the bulk of the German Communist Party and the minority seeking to rejoin the Social Democratic Party. In 1922, after negotiations in which Hilferding took a prominent part, what remained of the Independent Party returned to the parent organization.

During the last ten years of the Weimar Republic Hilferding found his spiritual home in the right wing of the Social Democratic Party. He was generally considered the Party's leading thinker, edited its theoretical journal *Die Gesellschaft*, and twice held the post of Finance Minister in the Reich Government—once under Stresemann in 1923 and again under Müller in 1928-29. Looked at from any point of view, his record, like that of the Social Democratic Party itself, was one of unbroken failure. As Finance Minister he was equally ineffective in deal-

[1] "Die Eigengesetzlichkeit der kapitalistischen Entwicklung," in Volume I of B. Harms, ed., *Kapital und Kapitalismus*, Berlin, 1931.

ing with inflation in 1923 and with impending depression in 1929. But far more important than these specific failures was his general misjudgment of the post-war situation and his gross underestimation of the Nazi danger. As late as January, 1933, he wrote in *Die Gesellschaft* that the primary aim of the socialists was to fight the communists. Hilferding's attitude in these tragic days is dramatically illustrated by the following account, written by an acquaintance who was in contact with him at the time:

> I remember distinctly having spoken to him a few days after Hitler was appointed Chancellor and asking him whether he thought that the time was ripe for the unions to call a general strike. Even then, in the first days of February 1933, he was sitting in a comfortable easy chair with warm felt slippers on his feet and remarked with a benign smile that I was a young firebrand and that political skill consists of waiting for the right moment. After all, he said, Hindenburg is still the President, the government is a coalition government, and while Hitlers come and go, the ADGB [the German trade union federation] is an organization that should not risk its entire existence for a fleeting political purpose. It was only a few days later that he was hiding at some friend's house being already sought by the Gestapo.[1]

Franz Neumann has justly remarked that "it was the tragedy of the Social Democratic Party and trade unions to have had as leaders men with high intellectual qualities but completely devoid of any feeling for the condition of the masses and without any insight into the great social transformations of the post-war period."[2] To none of the leaders does this apply with greater force than to Hilferding himself.

Hilferding escaped from the Gestapo in 1933, but unfortunately not for good. He went via Denmark to Switzerland, where

[1] From a personal letter, the writer of which prefers to remain anonymous.
[2] Franz Neumann, *Behemoth* (1942), p. 32.

he stayed until 1938, and then to Paris. When the Nazis took
Paris he fled south and early in 1941 had completed arrange-
ments to come to the United States. But just as he was about to
board a boat at Marseilles he was picked up by the Vichy police
and handed over to the Germans. The end came a few days later.
One report says that he committed suicide in a prison cell,
another that he was tortured to death by the Gestapo.

Looking at Hilferding's career as a whole, we can see that its
creative phase was relatively short, being bounded by *Böhm-
Bawerk's Criticism of Marx* at one end and *Das Finanzkapital*
at the other. He was a person with the greatest of natural gifts
whose vision was clouded and whose energies were stultified by
easy success. But the ultimate tragedy of Hilferding's life—and
surely the failure to fulfill great promise is always an individual
as well as a social tragedy—must not be allowed to obscure the
outstanding merit of the work which he did accomplish. His
answer to Böhm-Bawerk and his study of finance capital will
always remain among the classics of Marxian literature.

The significance of *Böhm-Bawerk's Criticism of Marx* is twofold. On the one hand, it was the only full-scale reply to Böhm-
Bawerk from the Marxian camp; [1] and on the other hand it is
probably the clearest statement we have of the fundamental
difference in outlook between Marxian economics and modern
orthodox economics. I shall not deal here with Hilferding's refutations of Böhm-Bawerk's specific arguments, beyond pointing
out that he gives a good account of himself and shows that even
at the age of twenty-five [2] he could stand up and trade punches
with so experienced and inveterate a polemicist as Böhm-

[1] Louis B. Boudin, *op. cit.,* answered some of Böhm-Bawerk's arguments but
not in the systematic way that Hilferding did. Bukharin's *The Economic
Theory of the Leisure Class* (originally published in 1919, English translation
1927) is an attack on the Austrian school rather than an answer to Böhm-
Bawerk's attack on Marx.

[2] *Böhm-Bawerk's Criticism of Marx* was published in 1904 when Hilferding
was twenty-seven, but the preface of the volume of *Marx Studien* in which it
appeared explains that the manuscript was completed before the end of 1902.

Bawerk (it would hardly be unfair, I think, to describe *Capital and Interest* as one sustained polemic against all earlier theorists of capital and interest and also against all of Böhm-Bawerk's contemporaries who did not agree with him.) But I do want to call attention to what seems to me the most important contribution of Hilferding's work, its recognition and explicit statement of what divides the Marxist from the marginal-utility theorist; and I want to emphasize that Hilferding, by making his whole analysis turn around this difference in outlook, was in fact illustrating the difference in a concrete way.

Hilferding's work is divided into three parts: "Value as an Economic Category," "Value and Average Profit," and "The Subjective Outlook." While the first two parts are necessary to a full understanding of the third, it is in this last that he states the essentials of his case with greatest force and clarity. The crucial question, in Hilferding's view, is whether the individual or society is made the starting point of economics. If we start from the individual, as Böhm-Bawerk does, we are led naturally to consider the individual's wants in relation to the objects which satisfy them instead of "the social relationships of human beings one with another" (p. 133 below). "Such an outlook," according to Hilferding, "is unhistorical and unsocial. Its categories are natural and eternal categories" (p. 133 below). Marx, on the other hand, starts from society and is therefore led to consider labor as "the constitutive element in human society, as the element whose development determines in the final analysis the development of society" (p. 133). Thus it is "because labor is the bond uniting an atomized society, and not because labor is the matter most technically relevant, that labor is the principle of value and that the law of value is endowed with reality" (p. 134). Closely related to these different starting points is the fact that "in striking contrast with Böhm-Bawerk, Marx looks on the theory of value, not as the means for ascertaining prices, but as the means for discovering the laws of motion of capitalist society" (p. 139). Hence for Marx, again in striking contrast with Böhm-Bawerk, the assumption that commodities exchange at their values "merely constitutes the theoretical starting point for a subsequent analysis" (p. 188). Hilferding's argument is excellently summed up in the following passage:

> Whereas for Böhm-Bawerk, labor seems merely one of the determinants in personal estimates of value, in Marx's view the degree of productivity of labor and the method of organization of labor determine the character of social life. Since labor, viewed in its social function as the total labor of society of which each individual labor forms merely an aliquot part, is made the principle of value, economic phenomena are subordinated to objective laws independent of the individual will and controlled by social relationships, relationships of production, wherein commodities play the part of intermediaries, the social relationships being reproduced by these intermediate processes or undergoing a gradual transformation until they demand a new type of intermediation (p. 186).

It is characteristic of the marginal utility school that "Böhm-Bawerk has never become aware of this contrast of outlooks" [1] (p. 186). The closest he comes to such an awareness is in his discussion of the "objective" and "subjective" methods in economics; but in reality, according to Hilferding, "we are not concerned at all with two different methods, but with contrasted and mutually exclusive outlooks upon the whole of social life" (p. 187).

In my opinion this fundamental difference in outlooks cer-

---

[1] It should be added that Hilferding's criticism made no impression on Böhm-Bawerk in this or in any other respect. The only reference to Hilferding in the third edition of *Capital and Interest* (in German) occurs in a footnote in which Böhm-Bawerk says that "Hilferding's subsequently published [i.e., subsequent to *Karl Marx and the Close of His System*] apologetic counter-criticism has in no way caused me to change my views" (p. 396n).

tainly does exist; and the fact that Böhm-Bawerk does not, while Hilferding does, recognize its existence is itself a consequence of the difference. From Böhm-Bawerk's unhistorical and unsocial standpoint there is only one possible way of regarding economic phenomena. Hence, as I pointed out above, he takes it for granted that Marx must be trying to do the same things that he, Böhm-Bawerk, is trying to do. On the other hand, from Hilferding's historical and social standpoint it is quite natural that the defenders of capitalism should look at the system, which they consider to be the only possible system, differently from its critics who proceed on the assumption that all social systems have a transitory character.

This situation, it must be admitted, makes it extraordinarily difficult for the two schools of economics to communicate intelligently with each other. One holds firmly to the view that their respective theories must be judged by the same standards, while the other is equally insistent that they cannot be. Thus, Böhm-Bawerk regards Marxian theory as simply wrong, while Hilferding regards Böhm-Bawerkian theory as irrelevant to the crucial developmental tendencies of the capitalist system.

I doubt whether this difficulty can be overcome; but it can at least be recognized, and those who recognize it should be better able to clarify their own position to themselves and to others. It is certainly not the least merit of Hilferding's work that it not only expounds the Marxian view but also states the difference between the Marxian and the orthodox views with unexampled lucidity.

BORTKIEWICZ ON THE TRANSFORMATION PROBLEM

Both Böhm-Bawerk and Hilferding devote much attention to the relation between the first and third volumes of *Capital*. Böhm-Bawerk argues that the theory of value in the first volume is in flat contradiction to the theory of "price of production" in the third, while Hilferding holds that price of production is merely a *modification* of value and hence that the two theories are logically related and in no sense contradictory. The nature of their views and of the disagreement between them was such that neither Böhm-Bawerk nor Hilferding was moved to examine critically the actual procedure which Marx used in transforming values into prices of production. Böhm-Bawerk believed that the mere fact of a difference between value and price of production was enough to deprive the whole operation of any interest, while Hilferding was concerned to answer Böhm-Bawerk's argument and not to defend Marx's procedure. And yet there is a very real problem here.

According to the theory of Volume I, commodities exchange in proportion to the quantity of labor (stored-up and living) embodied in them. Surplus value (or profit), however, is a function of the quantity of living labor alone. Hence, of two commodities of equal value one with relatively more living labor will contain more surplus value than one with relatively more stored-up labor; and this implies that equal investments of capital will yield different rates of profit depending on whether more or less is put into wages (living labor) on the one hand or material accessories (stored-up labor) on the other. But this theory contradicts the obvious fact that under capitalism equal investments, regardless of their composition, tend to yield equal profits.

In the first two volumes, Marx ignores differences in the composition of different capitals; in effect, he assumes that such differences do not exist. But in Volume III he drops this assumption and, recognizing the tendency to general equality in the rates of profit, inquires how the resulting "prices of production" are related to the values of Volume I.

Marx works this relation out by starting from a value scheme in which the composition of capitals varies, with a consequent multiplicity of profit rates. He now takes the average of these profit rates and calculates prices of production by the following formula:

$$c+v+(c+v)p=\text{price of production}$$

where c represents the investment in plant and materials, v the investment in wages, and p the average rate of profit.

Now there is undoubtedly a flaw in this method. The two items c and v are taken over from the value scheme and remain unchanged in the price of production scheme. In other words, input is measured in values while output is measured in prices of production. Obviously this is not right. A large part of today's output becomes tomorrow's input, and it is clear that, to be consistent, they must be measured in the same terms. Marx himself was aware of the difficulty,[1] and it is not unlikely that he would have dealt with it if he had lived to complete the third volume. But, as it stands, the treatment of the relation between the values and prices of production is not logically satisfactory.

Böhm-Bawerk obviously did not see this problem at all. It is true that he regarded the whole operation of transforming values into prices of production as pointless, but a skilled debater does not ignore a detected weakness in his opponent's argument simply because he considers the argument to be futile. Hilferding, on the other hand, seems never to have questioned the soundness of Marx's procedure. Indeed this is not surprising. Earlier Marxist writers had taken it for granted, and no hostile critic had called it in question.

It was left for Bortkiewicz, in the paper included as an appendix to this volume, to take up the problem and to attempt to solve it within the framework of the Marxian theory of value and surplus value.

Ladislaus von Bortkiewicz is known primarily as a statistician. In an obituary which appeared in the *Economic Journal* (June, 1932), Professor Schumpeter called him "by far the most

[1] See my book *The Theory of Capitalist Development*, pp. 115-116.

eminent German statistician since Lexis," [1] and I think nothing has occurred in the meanwhile to make this judgment less
valid today than it was in 1932. In the opinion of Oscar Anderson, himself a mathematical statistician of distinction, Bortkiewicz was "one of the few really great men in the field of
mathematical statistics." [2] This high reputation as a statistician
has not unnaturally tended to divert attention from Bortkiewicz's contributions to economics; and an additional reason
for his relative obscurity as an economist lies in the fact that the
most significant of these contributions took the form of critiques
of the theories of others. But if it be granted that the function
of criticism is important in its own right, then it can hardly be
denied that Bortkiewicz deserves a place among the top-flight
economists of the early twentieth century.[3]

It is not easy to classify Bortkiewicz's economics. Professor
Schumpeter says that Bortkiewicz professed "the Marshallian
creed," but this probably refers to the later period of his life
and to his teaching rather than to his writing. At any rate there
is little evidence of Marshallian influence in his papers on
Marx,[4] and it is with these that we are primarily concerned.

[1] Wilhelm Lexis (1837-1914) was Bortkiewicz's teacher. It is not strictly
accurate to call Bortkiewicz a German though he lived more than half his life
in Germany and did all his scientific work there. He was born in St. Petersburg in 1868 of a Russified Polish family and attended the University of St.
Petersburg. He went to Germany to do advanced work and stayed on as a
teacher. He was appointed to a position at the University of Berlin in 1901
and remained there until his death in 1931. He was always a rather distant
and isolated figure, remaining somewhat of a foreigner even after thirty years'
residence in Germany.

[2] Obituary in the *Zeitschrift für Nationalökonomie,* Vol. III, No. 2 (1932).
This obituary contains the only comprehensive bibliography of Bortkiewicz's
works with which I am acquainted.

[3] Aside from his papers on the Marxian system, about which more will be
said presently, Bortkiewicz produced notable critiques of Pareto and Böhm-
Bawerk. (All the relevant articles are listed in the obituary by Oscar Anderson,
cited in the preceding footnote; they can be readily identified by their titles.)
In my opinion, Bortkiewicz delivered the *coup de grâce* to Böhm-Bawerk's
celebrated theory of interest.

[4] Nor, I might add, in his analyses of Pareto and Böhm-Bawerk.

Judging from these papers, it seems to me that Bortkiewicz must be described as a modern Ricardian. The powerful impress of Ricardo's thought is evident throughout, and Bortkiewicz was at great pains to defend Ricardo against what he considered to be unjustified criticism.

A faithful Ricardian in Bortkiewicz's time could not but have an ambivalent attitude toward both of the important contemporary schools of economic thought. In fundamental social outlook and aims he was in agreement with the subjective value school and opposed to the Marxian school. On the other hand, acceptance of the labor theory of value necessarily brought him into conflict with many of the most important doctrines of the subjective value theorists and gave him much in common with Marxian ideas. This peculiar mixture of sympathies and antipathies is altogether characteristic of Bortkiewicz's economic writings and goes far, I suspect, to explain their strikingly original and stimulating quality.[1]

Bortkiewicz's attitude toward Marx had four facets. Where Marx agreed with Ricardo, Bortkiewicz tended to approve. Where Marx disagreed with Ricardo, Bortkiewicz tended to defend Ricardo. Where Marx departed altogether from Ricardo, as in the whole theory of capitalist development, Bortkiewicz was either uninterested or uncomprehending. And finally, where Marx pushed further along trails which Ricardo had blazed, Bortkiewicz was a sympathetic and constructive critic. It is in this last connection that Bortkiewicz took up the problem of value and price in the Marxian system.

The Ricardian system involves a highly original and at the same time paradoxical line of reasoning. Starting from the labor theory of value, Ricardo stumbled upon the theory that profit is a deduction from the product of labor. But given the existence

[1] It probably also has a good deal to do with his neglect as an economist. Both schools tended to regard him as an unfriendly outsider. Under the circumstances no one was interested in disseminating his ideas or in building up his reputation.

of profit, and assuming capitals of different durability or turn-over time, Ricardo proceeded at once to demonstrate that the result is exchange ratios (prices) which no longer conform to the requirements of the labor theory of value. In other words, the labor theory of value forms the starting point for a chain of reasoning which leads to conclusions at variance with the labor theory of value.

Now the question at once arises: Is this a legitimate pro-cedure? Does it lead to valid results, or is it self-defeating? Ricardo never attempted to answer these questions; he was con-tent to take the validity of his results for granted.

For a strict logician like Bortkiewicz this must have been a very unsatisfactory state of affairs. He was convinced of the cor-rectness of Ricardo's theory of profit (which he called the "de-duction theory"), but he could not help recognizing that the reasoning which supported it was incomplete and unsatisfactory. There was no rational explanation in the Ricardian system of the relation of "values" to "prices" or of the role of profit in mediating between them. Under these circumstances, it is quite understandable that Marx's explicit posing of this problem and attempt to solve it in Volume III of *Capital* claimed Bort-kiewicz's careful attention and even seemed to him to be Marx's outstanding contribution to economic theory.[1]

Bortkiewicz wrote two papers on Marxian economics: "Wert-rechnung und Preisrechnung"[2] and the article which is printed below, "On the Correction of Marx's Fundamental Theoretical

---

[1] "It must not be overlooked," he wrote, "that the originality of the [Marx-ian] system consists primarily in the juxtaposition of value calculation and price calculation, and in the derivation of prices from values and of profit from surplus value; by comparison the other peculiar features of the system are of secondary importance." "Wertrechnung und Preisrechnung im Marx-schen System," Part III, *Archiv für Sozialwissenschaft und Sozialpolitik,* September, 1907, p. 481. This is the final installment of a long paper. The first two parts appeared in the same journal for July 1906 and July 1907. It will be referred to in the text as "Wertrechnung und Preisrechnung."
[2] See preceding footnote. I hope to be able to publish an English translation of this work sometime in the future.

Construction in the Third Volume of *Capital*." It is obvious from
the titles that both are centered around the problem of the relation between values and prices, and it is also clear from their
respective publication dates that they were, so to speak, joint
products of a period of intensive study of Marx and his critics.[1]
The fact that they were published separately and in different
journals, however, shows that Bortkiewicz regarded them as
independent works each of which could stand on its own feet.

"Wertrechnung und Preisrechnung" is much the more ambi-
tious and general of the two. It includes an elaborate examination of earlier criticisms of Marx (from which, incidentally, the
critics, including Böhm-Bawerk, emerge with little glory), a
discussion of the flaw in Marx's method of transforming values
into prices of production, and a reconsideration of this problem
in terms of an equational system (attributed by Bortkiewicz to
the Russian economist W. K. Dmitrieff) which conforms to
Ricardian theory more closely than to Marxian theory. It does
not, however, attempt to solve the transformation problem as
Marx himself presented it. It was to this task that the article
included in the present volume was specifically directed.

It is not my purpose in this introduction to analyze the
method which Bortkiewicz substitutes for Marx's. Whatever
may be thought of it today, and of the corollaries which Bortkiewicz drew from it, there can be no question that it was the
first attempt to solve the problem and thus forms the actual
starting point for all subsequent work on the subject. Moreover
—and this is something which many Marxists tend to overlook
—the aim of the article, and in my judgment its effect as well,
was not to attack Marxian theory but to vindicate it. Most
previous (and, for that matter, subsequent) critics considered
the theory of value and surplus value to be the Achilles' heel of
the Marxian system. Bortkiewicz almost alone regarded it as
Marx's most important contribution. By eliminating relatively

[1] The article included below appeared in July 1907, the same month in which
Part II of "Wertrechnung und Preisrechnung" was published.

superficial errors he hoped to be able to show that the core of the system was sound. No serious student of classical-Marxian political economy can, I submit, afford to neglect Bortkiewicz's reasoning.

I do not want to be interpreted as making extravagant claims for Bortkiewicz. When I undertook to write a general introduction to Marxian economics,[1] I found Bortkiewicz's treatment of the transformation problem to be the most complete and satisfactory available. In order to show that the error in Marx's method is without importance for the theoretical system as a whole, I reproduced in summary form Bortkiewicz's solution of the problem. For the rest I discussed the *significance* of the problem rather than the *method* of solving it. My discussion fortunately called the problem to the attention of others better equipped than I to deal with its mathematical aspects. Their work, some of which has been published [2] (with more, I hope, to follow), has convinced me that Bortkiewicz's method of transforming values into prices, while unobjectionable as far as it goes, is mathematically clumsy and is based on unnecessarily restrictive assumptions. I also suspect that most of Bortkiewicz's corollaries are connected in one way or another with assumptions of this kind or, as Kenneth May suggests, flow from a confusion on Bortkiewicz's part between the failure of certain relations to appear in his mathematical formulas and their absence from the real phenomena which the formulas only partially reflect.

[1] *The Theory of Capitalist Development* (1942).
[2] Maurice Dobb, in a review in *Science and Society* (Summer, 1943), was the first to raise questions. It was Dobb also who stimulated J. Winternitz to a mathematical reconsideration of the transformation problem. A very brief summary of Winternitz's results appeared in the *Economic Journal* for June 1948 under the title: "Values and Prices: a Solution of the so-called Transformation Problem." I hope the entire paper on which this summary is based will eventually be published. A valuable commentary on Winternitz, which throws new light on several aspects of the controversy, appeared in the December 1948 issue of the *Economic Journal:* "Value and Price of Production: a Note on Winternitz' Solution," by Kenneth May.

It is to be hoped that the discussion which has now been begun will lead to a more or less definitive solution of the transformation problem and its implications. If the publication in English, and in readily available form, of Bortkiewicz's original essay on the subject contributes to that end I shall regard it as fully justified.

As editor of these works I have in general confined my efforts to making them more readable and more usable to present-day teachers and students of the social sciences. Style and spelling have been rendered uniform throughout. All quotations from *Capital* now refer to the Kerr edition, though the wording (except in the case of Hilferding's quotations from Volume III) remains that of the translators of these works. The translations themselves have been altered in a few places which were unclear, or ambiguous, or dated, by checking back to the German originals. For example, Miss Macdonald's translation of *Arbeitskraft* as "working powers" has everywhere been replaced by the more familiar "labor power." All references in Hilferding to Böhm-Bawerk have been given the page numbers of the present volume. Several of Eden and Cedar Paul's translators' notes to Hilferding remain and are identified by their initials. (See especially the long note on pp. 143-144 where the Pauls enter into a debate with Hilferding; in my judgment, Hilferding is perfectly correct in his interpretation of Marx at this point, but he did overlook a change in wording between the second and third editions which should have been taken into account.)

PAUL M. SWEEZY

April 10, 1949.
Wilton, N. H.

KARL MARX
AND THE CLOSE OF HIS SYSTEM

BY Eugen von Böhm-Bawerk

As an author Karl Marx was enviably fortunate. No one will affirm that his work can be classed among the books which are easy to read or easy to understand. Most other books would have found their way to popularity hopelessly barred if they had labored under an even lighter ballast of hard dialectic and wearisome mathematical deduction. But Marx, in spite of all this, has become the apostle of wide circles of readers, including many who are not as a rule given to the reading of difficult books. Moreover, the force and clearness of his reasoning were not such as to compel assent. On the contrary, men who are classed among the most earnest and most valued thinkers of our science, like Karl Knies, had contended from the first, by arguments that it was impossible to ignore, that the Marxian teaching was charged from top to bottom with every kind of contradiction both of logic and of fact. It could easily have happened, therefore, that Marx's work might have found no favor with any part of the public—not with the general public because it could not understand his difficult dialectic, and not with the specialists because they understood it and its weaknesses only too well. As a matter of fact, however, it has happened otherwise.

Nor has the fact that Marx's work remained a torso during the lifetime of its author been prejudicial to its influence. We are usually, and rightly, apt to mistrust such isolated first volumes of new systems. General principles can be very prettily put forward in the "General Sections" of a book, but whether they really possess the convincing power ascribed to them by their author can only be ascertained when in the construction of the system they are brought face to face with all the facts in detail. And in the history of science it has not seldom happened that a promising and imposing first volume has never been followed by a second, just because, under the author's own more searching scrutiny, the new principles had not been able to stand the test of concrete facts. But the work of Karl Marx has not suffered in this way. The great mass of his followers, on the strength of his first volume, had unbounded faith in the yet unwritten volumes.

This faith was, moreover, in one case put to an unusually severe test. Marx had taught in his first volume that the whole value of commodities was based on the labor embodied in them, and that by virtue of this "law of value" they must exchange in proportion to the quantity of labor which they contain; that, further, the profit or surplus value falling to the capitalist was the fruit of extortion practiced on the worker; that, nevertheless, the amount of surplus value was not in proportion to the whole amount of the capital employed by the capitalist, but only to the amount of the "variable" part—that is, to that part of capital paid in wages—while the "constant capital," the capital employed in the purchase of the means of production, added no surplus value. In daily life, however, the profit of capital is in proportion to the *total* capital invested; and, largely on this account, the commodities do not as a fact exchange in proportion to the amount of work incorporated in them. Here, therefore, there was a contradiction between system and fact which hardly seemed to admit of a satisfactory explanation. Nor did the obvious contradiction escape Marx himself. He says with reference to it, "This law" (the law, namely, that surplus value is in proportion only to the variable part of capital), "clearly contradicts all prima facie experience." [1] But at the same time he declares the contradiction to be only a seeming one, the solution of which requires many missing links, and will be postponed to later volumes of his work.[2] Expert criticism thought it might venture to prophesy with certainty that Marx would never redeem this promise, because, as it sought elaborately to prove, the contradiction was insoluble. Its reasoning, however, made no impression at all on the mass of Marx's followers. His simple promise outweighed all logical refutations.

The suspense grew more trying when it was seen that in the second volume of Marx's work, which appeared after the master's death, no attempt had been made towards the announced solution (which, according to the plan of the whole work, was reserved for the third volume), nor even was the slightest intimation given of the direction in which Marx proposed to seek for the solution. But the preface of the editor, Friedrich Engels, not only contained the reiterated positive assertion that the solution was given in the manuscript left by Marx, but contained also an open challenge, directed chiefly to the followers of Rodbertus, that, in the interval before the appearance of the third volume, they should from their own resources attempt to solve the problem "how, not only without contradicting the law of value but even by virtue of it, an equal average rate of profit can and must be created."

I consider it one of the most striking tributes which could have been paid to Marx as a thinker that this challenge was taken up by so many persons, and in circles so much wider than the one to which it was chiefly directed. Not only followers of Rodbertus, but men from Marx's own camp, and even economists who did not give their adherence to either of these heads of the socialist school, but who would probably have been called by Marx "vulgar economists," vied with each other in the attempt to penetrate into the probable nexus of Marx's lines of

[1] *Capital*, Vol. I, p. 335.
[2] Vol. I, pp. 335, 572n.

thought, which were still shrouded in mystery. There grew up between 1885, the year when the second volume of Marx's *Capital* appeared, and 1894 when the third volume came out, a regular prize essay competition on the "average rate of profit" and its relation to the "law of value." [1] According to the view of Friedrich Engels—now, like Marx, no longer living—as stated in his criticism of these prize essays in the preface to the third volume, no one succeeded in carrying off the prize.

Now at last, however, with the long-delayed appearance of the conclusion of Marx's system, the subject has reached a stage when a definite decision is possible. For of the mere promise of a solution each one could think as much or as little as he liked. Promises on the one side and arguments on the other were, in a sense, incommensurable. Even successful refutations of attempted solutions by others, though these attempts were held by their authors to have been conceived and carried out in the spirit of the Marxian theory, did not need to be acknowledged by the adherents of Marx, for they could always appeal from the faulty likeness to the promised original. But now at last this latter has come to light, and has procured for thirty years' struggle a firm, narrow, and clearly defined battle-ground within which both parties can take their stand in order and fight the matter out, instead of on the one side contenting

---

[1] From an enumeration of Loria's, I draw up the following list ("L'opera postuma di Carlo Marx," *Nuova Antologia*, Vol. I, February 1895, p. 18), which contains some essays unknown to me: Lexis, *Jahrbücher für National-ökonomie*, new series, Vol. XI (1885), pp. 452-465; Schmidt, *Die Durch-schnittsprofitrate auf Grund des Marxschen Wertgesetzes*, Stuttgart, 1889; a discussion of the latter work by myself in the *Tübinger Zeitschrift für die gesamte Staatswissenschaft*, 1890, pp. 590 ff.; Loria in the Jahrbücher für *Nationalökonomie*, new series, Vol. XX (1890), pp. 272 ff.; Stiebling, *Das Wertgesetz und die Profitrate*, New York, 1890; Wolf, "Das Rätsel der Durchschnittsprofitrate bei Marx," *Jahrbücher für Nationalökonomie*, third series, Vol. II (1891), pp. 352 ff.; Schmidt, *Die Neue Zeit*, 1892-3, Nos. 4 and 5; Landé, *Ibid.*, Nos. 19 and 20; Fireman, "Kritik der Marxschen Werttheorie," *Jahrbücher für Nationalökonomie*, third series, Vol. III (1892), pp. 793 ff.; finally, Lafargue, Soldi, Coletti, and Graziadei in the *Critica Sociale* from July to November, 1894.

themselves with the hope of future revelations, or on the other passing Proteus-like from one shifting, unauthentic interpretation to another.

Has Marx himself solved his own problem? Has his completed system remained true to itself and to facts, or not? To inquire into this question is the task of the following pages.

Chapter One

THE THEORY OF VALUE AND SURPLUS VALUE

THE pillars of the system of Marx are his conception of value and his law of value. Without them, as Marx repeatedly asserts, all scientific knowledge of economic facts would be impossible. The mode in which he arrives at his views with reference to both has been described and discussed times without number. For the sake of connection I must recapitulate briefly the most essential points of his argument.

The field of research which Marx undertakes to explore in order "to come upon the track of value" (I, 55) he limits from the beginning to *commodities,* by which, according to him, we are not to understand all economic goods, but only those *products of labor* which are made for the market.[1] He begins with the "Analysis of a Commodity" (I, 41). A commodity is, on one side, a useful thing, which by its properties satisfies human wants of some kind; and on the other, it forms the material medium of exchange value. He then passes to an analysis of this latter. "Exchange value presents itself in the

[1] Vol. I, pp. 47, 49, 83, 121, and often. Compare also Adler, *Grundlagen der Karl Marxschen Kritik der bestehenden Volkswirtchaft,* Tübingen, 1887, pp. 210 and 213.

first instance as the quantitative relation, the proportion, in which values in use of one kind are exchanged for values in use of another kind, a relation which constantly changes with time and place." Exchange value, therefore, appears to be something accidental. And yet there must be in this changing relation something that is stable and unchanging, and this Marx undertakes to bring to light. He does it in his well-known dialectical manner. "Let us take two commodities, wheat and iron, for example. Whatever may be their relative rate of exchange it may always be represented by an equation in which a given quantity of wheat is equal to a given quantity of iron: for example, 1 quarter wheat = 1 cwt. iron. What does this equation tell us? It tells us that there exists a common factor of the same magnitude in two different things, in a quarter of wheat and in a cwt. of iron. The two things are therefore equal to a third which is in itself neither the one nor the other. Each of the two, so far as it is an exchange value, must therefore be reducible to that third."

"This common factor," Marx goes on, "cannot be a geometrical, physical, chemical or other natural property of the commodities. Their physical properties come into consideration for the most part only in so far as they make the commodities useful, and so make them values in use. But, on the other hand, the exchange relation of commodities is obviously determined without reference to their value in use. Within this relation one value in use is worth just as much as any other, if only it is present in proper proportion. Or, as old Barbon says, 'One sort of wares are as good as another, if the value be equal. There is no difference or distinction in things of equal value.' As values in use commodities are above everything of different qualities; as exchange values they can only be of different quantities, and they can, therefore, contain no atom of value in use.

"If then we abstract from the value in use of commodities, there remains to them only one common property, that of being products of labor. But even as products of labor they have already, by the very process of abstraction, undergone a change under our hands. For if we abstract from the value in use of a commodity, we at the same time abstract from the material constituents and forms which give it a value in use. It is no longer a table, or a house, or yarn, or any other useful thing. All its physical qualities have disappeared. Nor is it any longer the product of the labor of the carpenter, or the mason, or the spinner, or of any other particular productive industry. With the useful character of the labor products there disappears the useful character of the labors embodied in them, and there vanish also the different concrete forms of these labors. They are no longer distinguished from each other, but are all reduced to identical human labor—abstract human labor.

"Let us examine now the residuum. There is nothing but this ghostly objectivity, the mere cellular tissue of undistinguishable human labor, that is, of the output of human labor without regard to the form of the output. All that these things have now to show for themselves is that human labor has been expended in their production—that human labor has been stored up in them; and as crystals of this common social substance they are— values."

With this, then, we have the conception of value discovered and determined. It is in dialectical form not identical with exchange value, but it stands, as I would now make plain, in the most intimate and inseparable relation to it. It is a kind of logical distillation from it. It is, to speak in Marx's own words, "the common element that manifests itself in the exchange relation, or exchange value, of commodities"; or again conversely, "the exchange value is the only form in which the value of commodities can manifest itself or be expressed" (I, 45).

After establishing the conception of value Marx proceeds to describe its measure and its amount. As labor is the substance of value so the amount of the value of all goods is measured by the quantity of labor contained in them, which is, in its turn, measured by its duration—but not by that particular duration, or working time, which the individual who made the commodity has happened to need, but by the working time that is socially necessary. Marx defines this last as the "working time required to produce a value in use under the normal conditions of production, and with the degree of skill and intensity of labor prevalent in a given society" (I, 46). "It is only the quantity of socially necessary labor, or the working time socially necessary for the production of a value in use, which determines the amount of the value. The single commodity is here to be regarded as an average specimen of its class. Commodities, therefore, in which equal quantities of labor are embodied, or which can be produced in the same working time, have the same value. The value of one commodity is related to the value of any other commodity as the working time necessary for the production of the one is to that necessary for the production of the other. As values, all commodities are only specific quantities of crystallized working time."

From all this is derived the subject matter of the great "law of value," which is "immanent in the exchange of commodities" (I, 176, 184), and governs exchange relations. It states, and must state, after what has gone before, that commodities are exchanged in proportion to the socially necessary working time incorporated in them (I, 86). Other modes of expressing the same law are that "commodities exchange according to their values" (I, 177, 217; III, 221), or that "equivalent exchanges with equivalent" (I, 184, 217). It is true that in isolated cases according to momentary fluctuations of supply and demand prices occur which are over or under the values. But these "constant oscillations of market prices . . . compensate and cancel each other, and reduce themselves to the average price as their inner law" (I, 184n). In the long run "the socially necessary working time always asserts itself by main force, like an overruling natural law, in the accidental and ever fluctuating exchange relations" (I, 86). Marx declares this law to be the "eternal law of the exchange of commodities" (I, 215), and "the rational element" and "the natural law of equilibrium" (III, 221). The inevitably occurring cases already mentioned in which commodities are exchanged for prices which deviate from their values are to be looked upon, in regard to this rule, as "accidental" (I, 184n), and he even calls the deviation "a breach of the law of the exchange of commodities" (I, 177).

On these principles of the theory of value Marx founds the second part of the structure of his teaching, his renowned doctrine of surplus value. In this part he traces the source of the gain which capitalists obtain from their capital. Capitalists lay down a certain sum of money, convert it into commodities, and then—with or without an intermediate process of production—convert these back again into more money. Whence comes this increment, this increase in the sum drawn out as compared with the sum originally advanced? or whence comes "the surplus value" as Marx calls it?[1]

Marx proceeds to mark off the conditions of the problem in his own peculiar way of dialectical exclusion. He first declares that the surplus value cannot originate either in the fact that the capitalist, as buyer, buys commodities regularly under their value, nor in the fact that the capitalist, as seller, sells them regularly over their value. So the problem presents itself in the following way: "The owner of money must buy the commodities at their value, then sell them at their value, and yet at the end of the process must draw out more money than he put in. Such are the conditions of the problem. *Hic Rhodus, hic salta!*" (I, 185 ff.).

The solution Marx finds in this, that there is one commodity whose value in use possesses the peculiar property of being a source of exchange value. This commodity is the capacity of

[1] I gave at the time in another place (*Geschichte und Kritik der Kapitalzinstheorieen*, 1884, pp. 421 ff.; English translation by William Smart, 1890, pp. 367 ff.) an exhaustive account of this part of his doctrine. I make use of this account now, with numerous abridgments, such as the present purpose demands.

labor, labor power. It is offered for sale in the market under the twofold condition that the laborer is personally free, for otherwise it would not be his labor power only that would be for sale, but his whole person as a slave; and that the laborer is destitute of "all the means necessary for the realizing of his labor power," for otherwise he would prefer to produce on his own account and to offer for sale his products rather than his labor power. It is by trading in this commodity that the capitalist obtains the surplus value; and he does so in the following way: the value of the commodity, "labor power," is regulated like any other commodity by the working time necessary for its reproduction; that is, in this case, by the working time which is needed to create so much means of subsistence as is required for the maintenance of the worker. If, for example, a working time of six hours is required in a given society for the production of the necessary means of subsistence for one day, and, at the same time, as we will suppose, this working time is embodied in three shillings of money, then the labor power of one day can be bought for three shillings. If the capitalist has concluded this purchase, the value in use of the labor power belongs to him and he realizes it by causing the laborer to work for him. But if he made him work only so many hours a day as are embodied in the labor power itself, and as must have been paid for in the buying of the same, no surplus value would arise. For, according to the assumption, six hours of labor could not put into the products in which they are embodied a greater value than three shillings, and so much the capitalist has paid as wages. But this is not the way in which capitalists act. Even if they have bought the labor power for a price which only corresponds to six hours' working time, they yet make the laborer work the whole day for them. And now in the product made during this day there are incorporated more hours of labor than the capitalist was obliged to pay for. He has, therefore, a greater value than the wages he has paid, and the difference is "surplus value," which falls to the capitalist.

Let us take an example: suppose that a worker can spin ten pounds of cotton into yarn in six hours; and suppose this cotton has required twenty hours of labor for its own production and possesses accordingly a value of ten shillings; and suppose, further, that during the six hours of spinning the spinner uses up so much of his tools as corresponds to the labor of four hours and represents consequently a value of two shillings; then the total value of the means of production consumed in the spinning will amount to twelve shillings, corresponding to twenty-four hours' labor. In the spinning process the cotton "absorbs" another six hours of labor. Therefore the yarn that has been spun is, as a whole, the product of thirty hours of labor, and will have accordingly a value of fifteen shillings. On the supposition that the capitalist has made the hired laborer work only six hours in the day, the production of the yarn has cost him at least fifteen shillings: ten shillings for cotton, two shillings for wear and tear of tools, three shillings for wages of labor. Here there is no surplus value.

It is quite a different thing, however, if the capitalist makes the laborer work twelve hours a day. In twelve hours the laborer works up twenty pounds of cotton in which forty hours of labor have been previously embodied, and which are, therefore, worth twenty shillings. He further uses up in tools the product of eight hours' labor, of the value of four shillings. But during a day he adds to the raw material twelve hours' labor, that is, a new value of six shillings. And now the balance sheet stands as follows: the yarn produced during a day has cost in all sixty hours' labor, and has, therefore, a value of thirty shillings. The outlay of the capitalist amounted to twenty shillings for cotton, four shillings for wear and tear of tools, and three shillings for wages; in all, therefore, only twenty-seven shillings. There remains now a "surplus value" of three shillings.

Surplus value, therefore, according to Marx, is due to the fact that the capitalist makes the laborer work for him a part of the day without paying him for it. In the laborer's working day two portions may be distinguished. In the first part—the "necessary working time"—the worker produces the means necessary for his own support, or the value of those means; and for this part of his labor he receives an equivalent in wages. During the second part—the "surplus working time"—he is exploited, he produces "surplus value" without receiving any equivalent for it (I, 239 ff.). "All surplus value is in substance the embodiment of unpaid working time" (I, 585).

The following definitions of the amount of surplus value are very important and very characteristic of the Marxian system. The amount of surplus value may be brought into relation with various other amounts. The different proportions and proportionate numbers which arise out of this must be clearly distinguished.

First of all there are two elements to be distinguished in the capital which enables the capitalist to appropriate surplus values, each of which elements in relation to the origin of surplus value plays an entirely different part from the other. Really new surplus value can only be created by the living work which the capitalist gets the worker to perform. The value of the means of production which are used is maintained, and it reappears in a different form in the value of the product, but adds no surplus value. "That part of the capital, therefore, which is converted into the means of production, that is, into raw material, auxiliary material, and implements of labor, does not alter the amount of its value in the process of production," for which reason Marx calls it "constant capital." "On the other hand, that part of capital which is converted into labor power does alter its value in the process of production. It reproduces its own equivalent and a surplus in addition," the surplus value. Therefore Marx calls it the "variable part of capital" or "variable capital" (I, 233). Now the proportion in which the surplus value stands to the advanced variable part of capital (in which alone the surplus value "makes good its value") Marx calls the *rate of surplus value*. It is identical with the proportion in which the surplus working time stands to the necessary working time, or the unpaid labor to the paid, and serves Marx, therefore, as an exact expression for the degree of exploitation of labor (I, 241 ff.). If, for instance, the working time necessary for the worker to produce the value of his day's wages of three shillings amounts to six hours, while the actual number of hours he works in the day amounts to twelve, so that during the second six hours, which is surplus working time, he produces another value of three shillings, which is surplus value, then the surplus value is exactly equal to the amount of variable capital paid in wages, and the rate of the surplus value is reckoned at 100 percent.

Totally different from this is the rate of profit. The capitalist calculates the surplus value, which he appropriates, not only upon the variable capital but upon the total amount of capital employed. For instance, if the constant capital be £410, the variable capital £90, and the surplus value also £90, the rate of surplus value will be, as in the case just given, 100 percent, but the rate of profit only 18 percent, that is, £90 profit on an invested capital of £500.

It is evident, further, that one and the same rate of surplus value can and must present itself in very different rates of profit according to the composition of the capital concerned: the greater the variable and the less the constant capital employed (which latter does not contribute to the formation of surplus value, but increases the fund, in relation to which the surplus value, determined only by the variable part of capital, is reckoned as profit) the higher will be the rate of profit. For example, if (which is indeed almost a practical impossibility) the constant capital is nothing and the variable capital is £50, and the surplus value, on the assumption just made, amounts to 100 percent, the surplus value acquired amounts also to £50; and as this is reckoned on a total capital of only £50, the rate of profit would in this case also be fully 100 percent. If, on the other hand, the total capital is composed of constant and variable capital in the proportion of 4 to 1; or, in other words, if to a variable capital of £50 is added a constant capital of £200, the surplus value of £50, formed by the surplus value rate of 100 percent, has to be distributed on a capital of £250, and on this it represents only a profit rate of 20 percent. Finally, if the capital were composed in the proportions of 9 to 1, that is £450 of constant to £50 of variable capital, a surplus value of £50 would be related to a total capital of £500, and the rate of profit would be only 10 percent.

Now this leads to an extremely interesting and important result, in pursuing which we are led to an entirely new stage of the Marxian system, the most important new feature which the third volume contains.

Chapter Two

*THE THEORY OF THE AVERAGE RATE OF
PROFIT AND OF THE PRICE OF
PRODUCTION*

THAT result is as follows: The "organic composition" (III, 172) of the capital is for technical reasons necessarily different in the different "spheres of production." In various industries which demand very different technical manipulations, the quantity of raw material worked up on one working day is very different; or, even, when the manipulations are the same and the quantity of raw material worked up is nearly equal, the value of that material may differ very much, as, for instance in the case of copper and iron as raw materials of the metal industry; or finally the amount and value of the whole industrial apparatus, tools, and machinery, which are utilized by each worker employed, may be different. All these elements of difference when they do not exactly balance each other, as they seldom do, create in the different branches of production a different proportion between the constant capital invested in the means of production and the variable capital expended in the purchase of labor. Every branch of economic production needs consequently a special, a peculiar "organic composition" for the capital invested in it. According to the preceding argument, therefore, given an equal rate of surplus value, every branch of production must show a different, a special rate of profit, on the condition certainly, which Marx has hitherto always assumed, that commodities exchange with each other "according to their values," or in proportion to the work embodied in them.

And here Marx arrives at the famous rock of offense in his theory, so hard to steer past that it has formed the most important point of dispute in the Marxian literature of the last ten years. His theory demands that capitals of equal amount, but of dissimilar organic composition, should exhibit different profits. The real world, however, most plainly shows that it is governed by the law that capitals of equal amount, without regard to possible differences of organic composition, yield equal profits. We will let Marx explain this contradiction in his own words.

"We have thus shown that in different branches of industry varying rates of profit are obtained according to the differences in the organic composition of the capitals, and also, within given limits, according to their periods of turnover; and that, therefore, even with equal rates of surplus value, there is a law (or general tendency), *although only for capitals possessing the same organic composition*—the same periods of turnover being assumed—that the profits are in proportion to the amounts of the capitals, and therefore equal amounts of capital yield in equal periods of time equal amounts of profit. The argument rests on the basis which has hitherto generally been the basis of our reasoning, *that commodities are sold according to their values*. On the other hand, there is no doubt that, in reality, not reckoning unessential, accidental, and self-compensating differences, the difference in the average rate of profit for different branches of industry *does not exist* and could not exist without upsetting the whole system of capitalist production. *It appears therefore that here the theory of value is irreconcilable with the actual movement of things*, irreconcilable with the actual phenomena of production, and that, on this account, the attempt to understand the latter must be given up" (III, 181). How does Marx himself try to solve this contradiction?

To speak plainly his solution is obtained at the cost of the assumption from which Marx has hitherto started, *that commodities exchange according to their values*. This assumption Marx now simply drops. Later on we shall form our critical judgment of the effect of this abandonment on the Marxian system. Meanwhile I resume my summary of the Marxian argument, and give one of the tabular examples which Marx brings forward in support of his view.

In this example he compares five different spheres of production, in each of which the capital employed is of different organic composition, and in making his comparison he keeps at first to the assumption which has been hitherto made, that commodities exchange according to their values. For the clear understanding of the following table, which gives the results of this assumption, it must be remarked that c denotes constant capital and v variable, and in order to do justice to the actual diversities of daily life, let us assume (with Marx) that the constant capitals employed are "worn out" in different lengths of time, so that only a portion, and that an unequal portion, of the constant capital in the different spheres of production is used up in the year. Naturally only the used-up portion of constant capital—*the "used-up* c"—goes into the value of the product, while the whole *"employed* c" is taken into account in reckoning the rate of profit.

We see that this table shows, in the different spheres of production where the exploitation of labor has been the same, very different rates of profit, corresponding to the different organic composition of the capitals. But we can also look at the same facts and data from another point of view. "The aggregate sum of the capital employed in the five spheres is 500; the aggregate sum of the surplus value produced is 110; and the aggregate value of the commodities produced is 610. If we con-

sider the 500 as a single capital of which I to V form only different parts (just as in a cotton mill in the different departments,
in the carding-room, the roving-room, the spinning-room, and
the weaving-room, a different proportion of variable and constant capital exists and the average proportion must be calculated for the whole factory), then in the first place the
average composition of the capital of 500 would be 500 = 390c
+ 110v, or, in percentages, 78c + 22v. Taking each of the
capitals of 100 as being one fifth of the aggregate capital its

Capitals	Surplus Value Rate, Percent	Surplus Value	Profit Rate, Percent	Used-up C	*Value of the Commodities*
I 80c + 20v	100	20	20	50	90
II 70c + 30v	100	30	30	51	111
III 60c + 40v	100	40	40	51	131
IV 85c + 15v	100	15	15	40	70
V 95c + 5v	100	5	5	10	20

composition would be this average one of 78c + 22v; and likewise to every 100 would accrue as average surplus value 22;
therefore the average rate of profit would be 22 percent (III,
183-184). Now at what price must the separate commodities be
sold in order that each of the five portions of capital should
actually obtain this average rate of profit? The following table
shows this. In it has been inserted the heading "Cost Price,"
by which Marx understands that part of the value of commodities which makes good to the capitalists the price of the
consumed means of production and the price of the labor
power employed, but yet does not contain any surplus value or
profit, so that its amount is equal to v + used-up c.

"Taken together," comments Marx on the results of this

table, "the commodities are sold $2 + 7 + 17 = 26$ over their value, and $8 + 18$ under their value, so that the variations in price mutually cancel each other, either through an equal division of the surplus value or by cutting down the average profit of 22 percent on the invested capital to the respective cost prices of the commodities, I to V; in the same proportion *in which one part of the commodities is sold over its value another part will be sold under its value. And now their sale at such prices makes it possible that the rate of profit for I to V should be*

Capitals	Surplus Value	Used-up C.	Value of the Commodities	Cost Price of the Commodities	Price of the Commodities	Profit Rate, Percent	Deviation of the Price from the Value
I 80c + 20v	20	50	90	70	92	22	+ 2
II 70c + 30v	30	51	111	81	103	22	— 8
III 60c + 40v	40	51	131	91	113	22	—18
IV 85c + 15v	15	40	70	55	77	22	+ 7
V 95c + 5v	5	10	20	15	37	22	+17

equal, 22 percent, without regard to the different organic composition of the capital I to V" (III, 185).

Marx goes on to say that all this is not a mere hypothetical assumption, but absolute fact. The operating agent is *competition.* It is true that owing to the different organic composition of the capitals invested in various branches of production "the rates of profit which obtain in these different branches *are originally very different.*" But "these different rates of profit are reduced by competition to a common rate which is the average of all these different rates. The profit corresponding to this common rate, which falls to a given amount of capital, whatever its organic composition may be, is called *average*

profit. That price of a commodity which is equal to its cost
price plus its share of the yearly average profit of the capital
employed (not merely that consumed) in its production (regard
being had to the quickness or slowness of turnover) is its *price
of production*" (III, 186). This is in fact identical with Adam
Smith's natural price, with Ricardo's price of production, and
with the *prix nécessaire* of the physiocrats (III, 233). And the
actual exchange relation of the separate commodities is *no
longer determined by their values but by their prices of production;* or as Marx likes to put it "the values change into
prices of production" (III, 231). Value and price of production
are only exceptionally and accidentally coincident, namely, in
those commodities which are produced by the aid of a capital,
the organic composition of which chances to coincide exactly
with the *average* composition of the whole social capital. In all
other cases value and production price necessarily and in principle part company. And his meaning is as follows: According
to Marx we call "capitals which contain a greater percentage of
constant, and therefore a smaller percentage of variable capital
than the social average capital, capitals of *higher* composition;
and contrariwise those capitals in which the constant capital
fills a relatively smaller, and the variable a relatively larger
space than in the social average capital are called capitals of
lower composition." So in all those commodities which have been
created by the aid of capital of "higher" composition than the
average composition the price of production will be *above* their
value, and in the opposite case it will be *under* the value. Or,
commodities of the first kind will be necessarily and regularly
sold *over* their value and commodities of the second kind *under*
their value (III, 193 ff. and often elsewhere).

   The relation of the individual capitalists to the total surplus
value created and appropriated in the whole society is finally
illustrated in the following manner: "Although the capitalists
of the different spheres of production in selling their commodities get back the value of the capital used up in the pro-

duction of these commodities, they do not thereby recover the
surplus value, and therefore profit, created in their own particular spheres, by the production of these commodities, but only
so much surplus value, and therefore profit, as falls by an equal
division to every aliquot part of the whole capital, from the
total surplus value or total profit which the entire capital of
society has created in a given time, in all the spheres of production taken together. Every 100 of invested capital, whatever its composition, secures in every year, or other period of
time, the profit which, for this period, falls due to a 100 as a
given part of the total capital. So far as profit is concerned, the
different capitalists are in the position of simple members of a
joint stock company, in which the profits are divided into equal
shares on every 100, and therefore for the different capitalists
vary only according to the amount of capital invested by each
in the common undertaking, according to the relative extent of
his participation in the common business, according to the
number of his shares" (III, 186 ff.). Total profit and total surplus value are identical amounts (III, 204). And the average
profit is nothing else "than the total amount of surplus value
divided among the amounts of capital in every sphere of production in proportion to their quantities" (III, 205).

An important consequence arising from this is that the profit
which the individual capitalist draws is clearly shown to arise
not only from the work performed by himself (III, 201), but
often proceeds for the most part, and sometimes entirely (for
example, in the case of mercantile capital), from laborers with
whom the capitalist concerned has no connection whatever.
Marx, in conclusion, puts and answers one more question, which
he regards as the specially difficult question: in what manner
"does this adjustment of profits to a common rate of profit
take place, since it is evidently a result and not a starting
point?"

He first of all puts forward the view that in a condition of
society in which the capitalist system is not yet dominant, and

in which, therefore, the laborers themselves are in possession
of the necessary means of production, commodities are actually
exchanged according to their real value, and the rates of profit
could *not* therefore be equalized. But as the laborers could
always obtain and keep for themselves an equal surplus value
for an equal working time—that is, an equal value over and
above their necessary wants—the actually existing difference in
the profit rate would be "a matter of indifference, just as today
it is a matter of indifference to the hired laborer by what rate
of profit the amount of surplus value squeezed out of him is
represented" (III, 208). Now as such conditions of life in which
the means of production belong to the worker are historically
the earlier, and are found in the old as well as in the modern
world, with peasant proprietors, for instance, and artisans, Marx
thinks he is entitled to assert that it is "quite in accordance with
facts to regard the values of commodities as, not only theoretically but also historically, prior to the prices of production"
(III, 209).

In societies organized on the capitalist system, however, this
changing of values into prices of production and the equalization
of the rates of profit which follows certainly do take place.
There are some long preliminary discussions, in which Marx
treats of the formation of market value and market price with
special reference to the production of separate parts of commodities produced for sale under conditions of varying advantage. And then he expresses himself as follows very clearly and
concisely on the motive forces of this process of equalization
and on its mode of action: "If commodities are . . . sold
according to their values . . . very different rates of profit are
obtained. . . . Capital withdraws itself, however, from a sphere
with a low rate of profit, and throws itself into another which
yields a higher profit. By this continual interchange, or, in a
word, by its apportionment between the different spheres, as
the rate of profit sinks here and rises there, such a relation of
supply to demand is created as to make the average profit in

the different spheres of production the same, and thus values are changed into prices of production" (III, 230). [1]

[1] W. Sombart in the classical, clear, and comprehensive account of the concluding volume of the Marxian system which he lately gave in the *Archiv für Soziale Gesetzgebung* (Vol. VII, 1895, pp. 255 ff.), also regards the passages quoted in the text as those which contain the strict answer to the problem given (*Ibid.*, p. 564). We shall have to deal later more at large with this important and ingenious, but critically, I think, unsatisfactory essay.

Chapter Three

THE QUESTION OF THE CONTRADICTION

MANY years ago, long before the above-mentioned prize essays on the compatibility of an equal average rate of profit with the Marxian law of value had appeared, the present writer had expressed his opinion on this subject in the following words: "Either products do actually exchange in the long run in proportion to the labor attaching to them—in which case an equalization of the gains of capital is impossible; or there is an equalization of the gains of capital—in which case it is impossible that products should continue to exchange in proportion to the labor attaching to them." [1]

From the Marxian camp the actual incompatibility of these two propositions was first acknowledged a few years ago by Conrad Schmidt. [2] Now we have the authoritative confirmation of the master himself. He has stated concisely and precisely that an equal rate of profit is only possible when the conditions of sale are such that some commodities are sold above their value, and others under their value, and thus are not exchanged in proportion to the labor embodied in them. And neither has he

[1] *Capital and Interest*, p. 362.
[2] See his work, *Die Durchschnittsprofitrate auf Grundlage des Marxschen Wertgesetzes*, Stuttgart, 1889, especially section 13; and my review of this work in the *Tübinger Zeitschrift für die gesamte Staatswissenschaft*, 1890, pp. 590 ff.

left us in doubt as to which of the two irreconcilable propositions conforms in his opinion to the actual facts. He teaches, with a clearness and directness which merit our gratitude, that it is the equalization of the gains of capital. And he even goes so far as to say, with the same directness and clearness, that the several commodities do not actually exchange with each other in proportion to the labor they contain, but that they exchange in that varying proportion to the labor which is rendered necessary by the equalization of the gains of capital.

In what relation does this doctrine of the third volume stand to the celebrated law of value of the first volume? Does it contain the solution of the seeming contradiction looked for with so much anxiety? Does it prove "how not only without contradicting the law of value, but even by virtue of it, an equal average rate of profit can and must be created"? Does it not rather contain the exact opposite of such a proof, namely, the statement of an actual irreconcilable contradiction, and does it not prove that the equal average rate of profit can only manifest itself if, and because, the alleged law of value does not hold good?

I do not think that any one who examines the matter impartially and soberly can remain long in doubt. In the first volume it was maintained, with the greatest emphasis, that all value is based on labor and labor alone, and that values of commodities were in proportion to the working time necessary for their production. These propositions were deduced and distilled directly and exclusively from the exchange relations of commodities in which they were "immanent." We were directed "to start from the exchange value, and exchange relation of commodities, in order to come upon the track of the value concealed in them" (I, 55). The value was declared to be "the common factor which appears in the exchange relation of commodities" (I, 45). We were told, in the form and with the emphasis of a stringent syllogistic conclusion, allowing of no exception, that to set down two commodities as equivalents in exchange implied that "a common factor of *the same magnitude*" existed in both, to which each of the two *"must* be reducible" (I, 43). Apart, therefore, from temporary and occasional variations which "appear to be a breach of the law of the exchange of commodities" (I, 177), commodities which embody the same amount of labor *must* on principle, in the long run, exchange for each other. And now in the third volume we are told briefly and dryly that what, according to the teaching of the first volume, *must* be, is not and never can be; that individual commodities do and must exchange with each other in a proportion different from that of the labor incorporated in them, and this not accidentally and temporarily, but of necessity and permanently.

I cannot help myself; I see here no explanation and reconciliation of a contradiction, but the bare contradiction itself. Marx's third volume contradicts the first. The theory of the average rate of profit and of the prices of production cannot be reconciled with the theory of value. This is the impression which must, I believe, be received by every logical thinker. And it seems to have been very generally accepted. Loria, in his lively and picturesque style, states that he feels himself forced to the "harsh but just judgment" that Marx "instead of a solution has presented a mystification." He sees in the publication of the third volume "the Russian campaign" of the Marxian system, its "complete theoretical bankruptcy," a "scientific suicide," the "most explicit surrender of his own teaching" (*l'abdicazione più esplicita alla dottrina stessa*), and the "full and complete adherence to the most orthodox doctrine of the hated economists." [1]

And even a man who is so close to the Marxian system as Werner Sombart says that a "general head shaking" best represents the probable effect produced on most readers by the third volume. "Most of them," he says, "will not be inclined to regard

[1] "L'opera postuma di Carlo Marx," *Nuova Antologia*, February 1895, pp. 20, 22, 23.

'the solution' of 'the puzzle of the average rate of profit' as a 'solution'; they will think that the knot has been cut, and by no means untied. For, when suddenly out of the depths emerges a 'quite ordinary' theory of cost of production, it means that the celebrated doctrine of value has come to grief. For, if I have in the end to explain the profits by the cost of production, wherefore the whole cumbrous apparatus of the theories of value and surplus value?" [1] Sombart certainly reserves to himself another judgment. He attempts to save the theory in a way of his own, in which, however, so much of it is thrown overboard that it seems to me very doubtful if his efforts have earned the gratitude of any person concerned in the matter. I shall later examine more closely this attempt, which is in any case interesting and instructive. But, before the posthumous apologist, we must give the master himself the careful and attentive hearing which so important a subject deserves.

Marx himself must, of course, have foreseen that his solution would incur the reproach of being no solution at all, but a surrender of his law of value. To this prevision is evidently due an anticipatory self-defense which, if not in form yet in point of fact, is found in the Marxian system; for Marx does not omit to interpolate in numerous places the express declaration that, in spite of exchange relations being directly governed by prices of production, which differ from the values, all is nevertheless moving within the lines of the law of value and this law, "in the last resort" at least, governs prices. He tries to make this view plausible by several inconsequent observations and explanations. On this subject he does not use his customary method of a formal close line of reasoning, but gives only a series of running, incidental remarks which contain different arguments, or turns of expression which may be interpreted as such. In this case it is impossible to judge on which of these

[1] "Zur Kritik des Ökonomischen Systems von Karl Marx," *Archiv für soziale Gesetzgebung,* Vol. VII (1895), pp. 571 ff. Subsequently referred to as "Zur Kritik."

arguments Marx himself intended to place the greatest weight,
or what was his conception of the reciprocal relations of these
dissimilar arguments. However that may be, we must, in justice
to the master as well as to our own critical problem, give each
of these arguments the closest attention and impartial consideration.

The running remarks appear to me to contain the following
four arguments in favor of a partly or wholly permanent
validity of the law of value.

First argument: even if the *separate* commodities are being
sold either above or below their values, these reciprocal fluctuations cancel each other, and in the community itself—taking
into account all the branches of production—the *total of the
prices of production* of the commodities produced still remains
equal to the sum of their values (III, 188).

Second argument: the law of value governs the *movement of
prices,* since the diminution or increase of the requisite working
time makes the prices of production rise or fall (III, 208, 211).

Third argument: the law of value, Marx affirms, governs
with undiminished authority the exchange of commodities in
certain "primary" stages, in which the change of values into
prices of production has not yet been accomplished.

Fourth argument: in a complicated economic system the law
of value regulates the prices of production at least *indirectly and
in the last resort,* since the total value of the commodities, determined by the law of value, determines the total surplus value.
The latter, however, regulates the amount of the average profit,
and therefore the general rate of profit (III, 212).

Let us test these arguments, each one on its own merits.

FIRST ARGUMENT

IT IS admitted by Marx that separate commodities exchange
with each other either over or under their value according as

the share of constant capital employed in their production is above or below the average. Stress is, however, laid on the fact that these individual deviations which take place in opposite directions compensate or cancel each other, so that the sum total of all prices paid corresponds exactly with the sum of all values. "In the same proportion in which one part of the commodities is sold above its value another part will be sold under its value" (III, 185). "The aggregate price of the commodities I to V [in the table given by Marx as an example] would therefore be equal to their aggregate values, and would therefore be, in fact, a money expression of the aggregate amount of labor, both past and recent, contained in the commodities I to V. And in this way in the community itself—when we regard the total of all the branches of production—the sum of the prices of production of the commodities manufactured is equal to the sum of their values" (III, 188). From this, finally, the argument is more or less clearly deduced that at any rate for the sum of all commodities, or for the community as a whole, the law of value maintains its validity. "Meanwhile it resolves itself into this—that by as much as there is too much surplus value in one commodity there is too little in another, and therefore the *deviations from value* which lurk in the prices of production *reciprocally cancel each other.* In capitalist production as a whole '*the general law maintains itself as the governing tendency,*' only in a very complex and approximate manner, as the constantly changing average of perpetual fluctuations" (III, 190).

This argument is not new in Marxian literature. In similar circumstances it was maintained, a few years ago, by Conrad Schmidt, with great emphasis, and perhaps with even greater clearness of principle than now by Marx himself. In his attempt to solve the riddle of the average rate of profit Schmidt also, while he employed a different line of argument from Marx, arrived at the conclusion that separate commodities *cannot* exchange with each other in proportion to the labor attaching to them. He too was obliged to ask the question whether, in face of this fact, the validity of Marx's law of value could any longer be maintained, and he supported his affirmative opinion on the very argument that has just been given.[1]

I hold the argument to be absolutely untenable. I maintained this at the time against Conrad Schmidt, and I have no occasion today in relation to Marx himself to make any alteration in the reasoning on which I founded my opinion then. I may content myself now with simply repeating it word for word. In opposing Conrad Schmidt, I asked how much or how little of the celebrated law of value remained after so much had practically been given up, and then continued: "That not much remains will be best shown by the efforts which the author makes to prove that, in spite of everything, the law of value maintains its validity. After he has admitted that the actual prices of commodities differ from their values, he remarks that this divergence only relates to those prices obtained by *separate commodities*, and that it disappears as soon as one considers the *sum* of all separate commodities, the yearly national produce, and that the total price which is paid for the whole national produce taken together does certainly coincide entirely with the amount of value actually embodied in it (p. 51). I do not know whether I shall be able to show sufficiently the bearings of this statement, but I shall at least attempt to indicate them.

"What then, we ask, is the chief object of the 'law of value'? It is nothing else than the elucidation of the exchange relations of commodities as they actually appear to us. We wish to know, for instance, why a coat should be worth as much in exchange as twenty yards of linen, and ten pounds of tea as much as half a ton of iron, etc. It is plain that Marx himself so conceives the explanatory object of the law of value. There can clearly only be a question of an exchange *relation* between different separate commodities *among each other*. As soon, however, as

[1] See his work quoted above, especially section 13.

one looks at all commodities *as a whole* and sums up the prices, one must studiously and of necessity avoid looking at the relations existing inside of this whole. The internal relative differences of price do compensate each other in the sum total. For instance, what the tea is worth more than the iron the iron is worth less than the tea and vice versa. In any case, when we ask for information regarding the exchange of commodities in political economy it is no answer to our question to be told the total price which they bring when taken altogether, any more than if, on asking by how many fewer minutes the winner in a prize race had covered the course than his competitor, we were to be told that all the competitors together had taken twenty-five minutes and thirteen seconds.

"The state of the case is this: to the question of the problem of value the followers of Marx reply first with their law of value, that commodities exchange in proportion to the working time incorporated in them. Then they—covertly or openly—revoke this answer in its relation to the domain of the exchange of separate commodities, the one domain in which the problem has any meaning, and maintain it in full force only for the whole aggregate national produce, for a domain therefore in which the problem, being without object, could not have been put at all. As an answer to the strict question of the problem of value the law of value is avowedly contradicted by the facts, and in the only application in which it is not contradicted by them it is no longer an answer to the question which demanded a solution, but could at best only be an answer to some other question.

"It is, however, not even an answer to another question; it is no answer at all; it is simple tautology. For, as every economist knows, commodities do eventually exchange with commodities—when one penetrates the disguises due to the use of money. Every commodity which comes into exchange is at one and the same time a commodity and the price of what is given in exchange for it. The aggregate of commodities therefore is identical with the aggregate of the prices paid for them; or, the price of the whole national produce is nothing else than the national produce itself. Under these circumstances, therefore, it is quite true that the total price paid for the entire national produce coincides exactly with the total amount of value or labor incorporated in it. But this tautological declaration denotes no increase of true knowledge, neither does it serve as a special test of the correctness of the alleged law that commodities exchange in proportion to the labor embodied in them. For in this manner one might as well, or rather as unjustly, verify any other law one pleased—the law, for instance, that commodities exchange according to the measure of their specific gravity. For if certainly as a 'separate ware' one pound of gold does not exchange with one pound of iron, but with 40,000 pounds of iron; still, the *total price* paid for one pound of gold and 40,000 pounds of iron *taken together* is nothing more and nothing less than 40,000 pounds of iron and one pound of gold. The total weight, therefore, of the total price—40,001 pounds—corresponds exactly to the like total weight of 40,001 pounds incorporated in the whole of the commodities. Is weight consequently the true standard by which the exchange relation of commodities is determined?"

I have nothing to omit and nothing to add to this judgment in applying it now to Marx himself, except perhaps that in advancing the argument which has just been under criticism Marx is guilty of an additional error which cannot be charged against Schmidt. For, in the passage just quoted from page 190 of the third volume, Marx seeks, by a general dictum concerning the way in which the law of value operates, to gain approval for the idea that a certain real authority may still be ascribed to it, even if it does not rule in separate cases. After saying that the "deviations" from value, which are found in the prices of production, cancel each other, he adds the remark that "in capitalist production as a whole the general law maintains itself as the governing tendency, for the most part only in a very complex and approximate manner as the constantly changing *average of perpetual fluctuations."*

Here Marx confounds two very different things: an *average of fluctuations,* and an *average between permanently and fundamentally unequal quantities.* He is so far quite right, that many a general law holds good solely because an average resulting from constant fluctuations coincides with the rule declared by the law. Every economist knows such laws. Take, for example, the law that prices equal costs of production—that apart from special reasons for inequality there is a tendency for wages in different branches of industry, and for profits of capital in different branches of production, to come to a level, and every economist is inclined to acknowledge these laws as "laws," although perhaps there may be no absolutely exact agreement with them in any single case; and therefore even the power to refer to a mode of action operating on the whole, and on the average, has a strongly captivating influence.

But the case in favor of which Marx uses this captivating reference is of quite a different kind. In the case of prices of production which deviate from the "values," it is not a question of fluctuations, but of necessary and permanent divergences.

Two commodities, A and B, which contain the same amount of labor, but have been produced by capitals of different organic composition, do not fluctuate round the same average point, say, for example, the average of fifty shillings; but each of them assumes permanently a different level of price: for instance, the commodity A, in the production of which little constant capital, demanding but little interest, has been employed, the price level of forty shillings; and the commodity B, which has much constant capital to pay interest on, the price level of sixty shillings, allowance being made for fluctuation round each of these deviating levels. If we had only to deal with fluctuations round one and the same level, so that the commodity A might stand at one moment at forty-eight shillings and the commodity B at fifty-two shillings, and at another moment the case were reversed, and the commodity A stood at fifty-two shillings and the commodity B only reached forty-eight, then we might indeed say that in the average the price of both of these commodities was the same, and in such a state of things, if it were seen to obtain universally, one might find, in spite of the fluctuations, a verification of the "law" that commodities embodying the same amount of labor exchange on an equal footing.

When, however, of two commodities in which the same amount of labor is incorporated, one permanently and regularly maintains a price of forty shillings and the other as permanently and regularly the price of sixty shillings, a mathematician may indeed strike an average of fifty shillings between the two; but such an average has an entirely different meaning, or, to be more accurate, has no meaning at all with regard to our law. A mathematical average may always be struck between the most unequal quantities, and when it has once been struck the deviations from it on either side always "mutually cancel each other" according to their amount; by the same amount exactly by which the one exceeds the average the other must of necessity fall short. But it is evident that necessary and permanent differences of prices in commodities of the same cost in labor, but of unequal composition as regards capital, cannot by such playing with "average" and "deviations that cancel each other" be turned into a confirmation of the alleged law of value instead of a refutation. We might just as well try in this way to prove the proposition that animals of all kinds, elephants and May flies included, have the same length of life; for while it is true that elephants live on an average one hundred years and May flies only a single day, yet between these two quantities we can strike an average of fifty years. By as much time as the elephants live longer than the flies, the flies live shorter than the elephants. The deviations from this average "mutually cancel each other," and consequently on the whole and on the average the law that all kinds of animals have the same length of life is established!

Let us proceed.

SECOND ARGUMENT

IN VARIOUS PARTS of the third volume Marx claims for the law of value that it "governs the movement of prices," and he considers that this is proved by the fact that where the working time necessary for the production of the commodities decreases, there also prices fall; and that where it increases prices also rise, other circumstances remaining equal.[1]

This conclusion also rests on an error of logic so obvious that one wonders Marx did not perceive it himself. That in the case of "other circumstances remaining equal" prices rise and fall according to the amount of labor expended proves clearly neither more nor less than that labor is one factor in determining prices. It proves, therefore, a fact upon which all the world is agreed, an opinion not peculiar to Marx, but one acknowledged and taught by the classical and "vulgar economists." But by his law of value Marx had asserted much more. He had asserted that, barring occasional and momentary fluctuations of demand and supply, the labor expended was the sole factor which governed the exchange relations of commodities. Evidently it could only be maintained that *this* law governs the movement of prices if a permanent alteration in prices could not be produced or promoted by any other cause than the alteration in the amount of working time. This, however, Marx does not and cannot maintain; for it is among the results of his own teaching that an alteration in prices must occur when, for instance, the expenditure of labor remains the same, but when, owing to such circumstances as the shortening of the processes of production, the organic composition of the capital is changed. By the side of this proposition of Marx we might with equal justification place the other proposition, that prices rise or fall when, other conditions remaining equal, the length of time during which the capital is

[1] Vol. III, p. 208, and quite similarly in the passage already quoted, Vol. III, p. 211.

invested increases or decreases. If it is impossible to prove by the latter proposition that the length of time during which the capital is invested is the sole factor that governs exchange relations, it is equally impossible to regard the fact that alterations in the amounts of the labor expended affect the movements of prices as a confirmation of the alleged law that labor alone governs the exchange relations.

THIRD ARGUMENT

THIS ARGUMENT has not been developed with precision and clearness by Marx, but the substance of it has been woven into those processes of reasoning, the object of which was the elucidation of the "truly difficult question": "how the adjustment of the profits to the general rate of profit takes place" (III, 205 ff.).

The kernel of the argument is most easily extracted in the following way: Marx affirms, and must affirm, that "the rates of profits are originally very different" (III, 186), and that their adjustment to a general rate of profits is primarily "a result, and cannot be a starting point" (III, 205). This thesis further contains the claim that there exist certain "primitive" conditions in which the change of values into prices of production which leads to the adjustment of the rates of profit has not yet taken place, and which therefore are still under the complete and literal dominion of the law of value. A certain region is consequently claimed for this law in which its authority is perfectly absolute.

Let us inquire more closely what this region is, and see what arguments Marx adduces to prove that the exchange relations in it are actually determined by the labor incorporated in the commodities.

According to Marx the adjustment of the rate of profit is dependent on two assumptions: first, on a capitalist system of production being in operation (III, 206); and secondly, on the leveling influence of *competition* being in *effective action* (III, 187, 204, 212, 230, 231). We must, therefore, logically look for the "primitive conditions" under which the pure regime of the law of value prevails where one or other of these assumed conditions does not exist (or, of course, where both are absent).

On the first of these cases Marx has himself spoken very fully. By a very detailed account of the processes which obtain in a condition of society where capitalist production does not yet prevail, but "where the means of production belong to the worker," he shows the prices of commodities in this stage to be exclusively determined by their values. In order to enable the reader to judge impartially how far this account is really convincing, I must give the full text of it:

"The salient point will be best shown in the following way: Suppose the workers themselves to possess each his own means of production, and to exchange their commodities with each other. These commodities would not then be the product of capital. The value of the tools and raw material employed in the different branches of labor would be different according to the special nature of the work; and also, apart from inequality of value in the means of production employed, different amounts of these means would be required for given amounts of labor, according as one commodity could be finished in an hour and another only in a day, etc. Let us suppose, further, that these laborers work the same time, on an average, allowing for the adjustments which result from differences of intensity, etc., in work. Of any two workers, then, both would, first, in the commodities which represent the produce of their day's labor, have replaced their outlays, that is, the cost prices of the consumed means of production. These would differ according to the technical nature of their branches of industry. Secondly, both would have created the same amount of new value, that is, the value of the day's labor added to the means of production. This would contain their wages plus the surplus value, the surplus work above their necessary wants, of which the result, however, would belong to themselves. *If we express ourselves in capitalistic terms, both receive the same wages plus the same profit,* but also the value, represented, for instance, by the produce of a working day of ten hours. But in the first place the values of their commodities would be different. In commodity I, for example, there would be a larger share of value for the expended means of production than in commodity II. The rates of profit also would be very different for I and II, if we here consider as rates of profit the proportion of the surplus value to the total value of the employed means of production. The means of subsistence which I and II consume daily during the process of production, and which represent the wages of labor, form here that part of the advanced means of production which we usually call variable capital. But the *surplus value would be, for the same working time,* the same for I and II; or, to go more closely into the matter, as I and II, each, receive the value of the produce of one day's work, they receive, after deducting the value of the advanced 'constant' elements, equal values, one part of which may be looked upon as compensation for the means of subsistence consumed during the production, and the other as surplus value—value over and above this. If I has had more outlay it is made up to him by the greater value of his commodity, which replaces this 'constant' part, and he has consequently a larger part of the total value to exchange back into the material elements of this constant part; while if II obtains less he has, on the other hand, the less to exchange back. *Differences in rates of profit would therefore, under this assumption, be a matter of indifference,* just as it is today a matter of indifference to the wage earner by what rate of profit the amount of surplus value squeezed out of him is represented, and just as in international commerce the difference in the rates of profit in the different nations is a matter of indifference for the exchange of their commodities" (III, 206 ff.).

And now Marx passes at once from the hypothetical style of "supposition" with its subjunctive moods to a series of quite positive conclusions. "The exchange of commodities at their values, or approximately at their values, demands, *therefore,* a much lower stage of development than the exchange into prices of production," and "it is, therefore, altogether in keeping with fact to regard the values as not only theoretically but *historically* prior to the prices of production. It holds good for circumstances where the means of production belong to the worker, and these circumstances are found both *in the old and in the modern world,* in the cases of peasants who own land and work it themselves, and in the case of artisans" (III, 208, 209).

What are we to think of this reasoning? I beg the reader above everything to notice carefully that the hypothetical part describes very consistently how exchange would present itself in those primitive conditions of society *if* everything took place according to the Marxian law of value; but that this description contains no shadow of proof, or even of an attempt at proof, *that* under the given assumptions things must so take place. Marx relates, "supposes," asserts, but he gives no word of proof. He consequently makes a bold, not to say naïve jump, when he proclaims as an ascertained result (as though he had successfully worked out a line of argument) that it is, *therefore,* quite consistent with facts to regard values, historically also, as prior to prices of production. As a matter of fact it is beyond question that Marx has not proved by his "supposition" the historical existence of such a condition. He has only hypothetically deduced it from his theory; and as to the credibility of that hypothesis we must, of course, be free to form our own judgment.

As a fact, whether we regard it from within or from without, the gravest doubts arise as to its credibility. It is inherently improbable, and so far as there can be a question here of proof by experience, even experience is against it.

It is inherently altogether improbable. For it requires that it should be a matter of complete indifference to the producers at what time they receive the reward of their activity, and that is economically and psychologically impossible. Let us make this clear to ourselves by considering Marx's own example point by point. Marx compares two workers—I and II. Laborer I represents a branch of production which requires technically a relatively large and valuable means of production resulting from previous labor, raw material, tools, and auxiliary material. Let us suppose, in order to illustrate the example by figures, that the production of the previous material required five years' labor, while the working of it up into finished products was effected in a sixth year. Let us further suppose—what is certainly not contrary to the spirit of the Marxian hypothesis, which is meant to describe very primitive conditions—that laborer I carries on both works, that he both creates the previous material and also works it up into finished products. In these circumstances he will obviously recompense himself for the previous labor of the first years out of the sale of the finished products, which cannot take place till the end of the sixth year. Or, in other words, he will have to wait five years for the payment for the first year's work. For the payment for the second year he will have to wait four years; for the third year, three years, and so on. Or, taking the average of the six years' work, he will have to wait nearly three years after the work has been accomplished for the payment for his labor. The second worker, on the other hand, who represents a branch of production which needs a relatively small means of production resulting from previous labor, will perhaps turn out the completed product, taking it through all its stages, in the course of a month, and will therefore receive his compensation from the yield of his product almost immediately after the accomplishment of his work.

Now Marx's hypothesis assumes that the prices of the commodities I and II are determined exactly in proportion to the amounts of labor expended in their production, so that the product of six years' work in commodity I only brings as much as the total produce of six years' work in commodity II. And further, it follows from this that the laborer in commodity I should be satisfied to receive for every year's work, with an average of three years' *delay* of payment, the *same* return that the laborer in commodity II receives *without any delay;* that therefore delay in the receipt of payment is a circumstance which has no part to play in the Marxian hypothesis, and more especially has no influence on competition, on the crowding or understocking of the trade in the different branches of production, having regard to the longer or shorter periods of waiting to which they are subjected.

I leave the reader to judge whether this is probable. In other respects Marx acknowledges that the special accompanying circumstances peculiar to the work of a particular branch of production, the special intensity, strain, or unpleasantness of a work, force a compensation for themselves in the rise of wages through the action of competition. Should not a year's postponement of the remuneration of labor be a circumstance demanding compensation? And further, granting that all producers *would* as soon wait three years for the reward of their labor, as not at all, *could* they really all wait? Marx certainly assumes that "the laborers should possess their respective means of production"; but he does not and cannot venture to assume that each laborer possesses the amount of means of production which are necessary to carry on that branch of industry which for technical reasons requires the command of the greatest quantity of means of production. The different branches of production are therefore certainly not equally accessible to all producers. Those branches of production which demand the least advance of means of production are the most generally accessible, and the branches which demand larger capital are possible only for an increasingly smaller minority. Has this nothing to do with the circumstance that, in the latter branches, a certain restriction in supply takes place, which eventually forces the price of their products above the proportionate level of those branches in the carrying on of which the odious accompaniment of waiting does not enter and which are therefore accessible to a much wider circle of competitors?

Marx himself seems to have been aware that his case contains
a certain improbability. He notes first of all, as I have done,
though in another form, that the fixing of prices solely in proportion to the amount of labor in the commodities leads in another
direction to a disproportion. He asserts this in the form (which
is also correct) that the "surplus value" which the laborers in
both branches of production obtain over and above their necessary maintenance, calculated on the means of production advanced, shows *unequal rates of profit*. The question naturally
obtrudes itself: why should not this inequality be made to dis-
appear by competition just as in "capitalist" society? Marx feels
the necessity of giving an answer to this, and here only does
something of the nature of an attempt to give proofs instead of
mere assertions come in. Now what is his answer?

The essential point (he says) is that both laborers should receive the same surplus value for the same working time; or, to
be more exact, that for the *same working time* "they should receive the *same values* after deducting the value of the advanced
constant element," and on this assumption the difference in the
rates of profit would be a "matter of indifference, just as it is a
matter of indifference to the wage earner by what rate of profit
the quantity of surplus value squeezed out of him is represented."

Is this a happy simile? If I do not get a thing, then it may
certainly be a matter of indifference to me whether that thing,
which I do not get, estimated on the capital of another person,
represents a higher or lower percentage. But when I get a thing
as a settled right, as the worker, on the non-capitalistic hypothesis, is supposed to get the surplus value as profit, then it certainly is not a matter of indifference to me by what scale that
profit is to be measured or distributed. It may, perhaps, be an
open question whether this profit should be measured and distributed according to the expenditure of labor or to the amount
of the advanced means of production, but the question itself can
certainly not be a merely indifferent matter to the persons inter-

ested in it. And when, therefore, the somewhat improbable fact is affirmed that unequal rates of profit can exist permanently side by side without being equalized by competition, the reason for this certainly cannot be found in the assumption that the height of the rate of profit is a matter of no importance whatever to the persons interested in it.

But are the laborers on the Marxian hypothesis treated alike even as laborers? They obtain for the same working time the same value and surplus value as wages, but they get it at different times. One obtains it immediately after the completion of the work; the other may have to wait years for the remuneration of his labor. Is this really equal treatment? Or does not the condition under which the remuneration is obtained constitute an inequality which cannot be a matter of indifference to the laborers, but which, on the contrary, as experience truly shows, they feel very keenly? To what worker today would it be a matter of indifference whether he received his weekly wages on Saturday evening, or a year, or three years hence? And such marked inequalities would not be smoothed away by competition. That is an improbability for the explanation of which Marx still remains in our debt.

His hypothesis, however, is not only inherently improbable, but it is also contrary to all the facts of experience. It is true that as regards the assumed case, in its full typical purity, we have, after all, no direct experience; for a condition of things in which paid labor is absent and every producer is the independent possessor of his own means of production can now no longer anywhere be seen in its full purity. Still, however, conditions and relationships are found in the "modern world" which correspond at least approximately to those assumed in the Marxian hypothesis. They are found, as Marx himself especially indicates (III, 209), in the case of the peasant proprietor, who himself cultivates his own land, and in the case of the artisan. According to the Marxian hypothesis, it ought to be a matter of observation that the incomes of these persons do not in the least depend on the amounts of capital they employed in production. They should each receive the same amount of wages and surplus value, whether the capital representing their means of production was 10 shillings or 10,000 shillings. I think, however, that my readers will all allow that though indeed in the cases just mentioned there is no such exact bookkeeping as to make it possible to determine proportions with mathematical exactitude, yet the prevailing impression does not confirm Marx's hypothesis, but tends, on the contrary, to the view that in general and as a whole an ampler income is yielded by those branches of industry in which work is carried on with a considerable capital, than by those which have at their disposal only the hands of the producers.

And finally this result of the appeal to fact, which is unfavorable to the Marxian hypothesis, receives not a little indirect confirmation from the fact that in the second case which he instances (a case much easier to test), in which, according to the Marxian theory, the law of value ought to be seen to be completely dominant, no trace of the process alleged by Marx is to be found.

Marx tells us, as we know, that even in a fully developed economy the equalization of the originally different rates of profit can be brought about only through the action of competition. "If the commodities are sold according to their values," he writes in the most explicit of the passages concerning this matter,[1] "very different rates of profit, as has been explained, occur in the different spheres of production, according to the different organic compositions of the amounts of capital invested in them. But capital withdraws itself from a sphere having a lower rate of profit, and throws itself into another which yields a higher profit. By this constant shifting from one sphere to another—in short, by its distribution among the different spheres according as the rate of profit rises in one and sinks in another—it brings

[1] Vol. III, pp. 230 ff. Compare also the shorter statements, Vol. III, pp. 186, 204, 212, and frequently.

about such a proportion between supply and demand that the average profit in the different spheres of production becomes the same."

We should therefore logically expect, wherever this competition of capital was absent, or was at any rate not yet in full activity, that the original mode of forming prices and profits affirmed by Marx would be met with in its full, or nearly its full, purity. In other words, there must be traces of the actual fact that *before* the equalization of the rates of profit the branches of production with the relatively greater amounts of constant capital have won and do win the smallest rates of profit, while those branches with the smaller amounts of constant capital win the largest rates of profit. As a matter of fact, however, there are no traces of this to be found anywhere, either in the historical past or in the present. This has been recently so convincingly demonstrated by a learned professor who is in other respects extremely favorable to Marx, that I cannot do better than simply quote the words of Werner Sombart:

"Development never has and never does take place in the way alleged. If it did it would certainly be seen in operation in the case of at least every new branch of business. If this idea were true, in considering historically the advance of capitalism, one would have to think of it as first occupying those spheres in which living labor preponderated and where, therefore, the composition of capital was under the average (little constant and much variable), and then as passing slowly into other spheres, according to the degree in which prices had fallen in those first spheres in consequence of overproduction. In a sphere having a preponderance of [material] means of production over living labor, capitalism would naturally in the beginning have realized so small a profit, being limited to the surplus value created by the individual, that it would have had no inducement to enter into that sphere. But capitalist production at the beginning of its historical development occurs even to some extent in branches of production of the latter kind, mining, etc. Capital would have had no reason to go out of the sphere of circulation in which it was prospering, into the sphere of production, without a prospect of a 'customary profit' which, be it observed, existed in commercial profit previous to any capitalist production. But we can also show the error of the assumption from the other side. If extremely high profits were obtained in the beginning of capitalist production, in the spheres having a preponderance of living labor, it would imply that all at once capital had made use of the class of producers concerned (who had up to that time been independent), as wage earners, that is, at half the amount of gain they had hitherto procured, and had put the difference in the prices of the commodities, corresponding directly to the values, in its own pocket; and further it supposes, what is an altogether visionary idea, that capitalist production began with declassed individuals in branches of production, some of which were quite new creations, and therefore was able to fix prices according to its own standard.

"But if the assumption of an empirical connection between rates of profit and rates of surplus value is false historically, that is, false as regards the beginning of capitalism, it is even more so as regards conditions in which the capitalist system of production is fully developed. Whether the composition of a capital by means of which a trade is carried on today is ever so high or ever so low, the prices of its products and the calculation (and realization) of the profits are based solely on the outlay of capital.

"If in all times, earlier as well as later, capitals did, as a matter of fact, pass continually from one sphere of production to another, the principal cause of this would certainly lie in the inequality of profits. But this inequality most surely proceeds not from the organic composition of the capital, but from some cause connected with competition. Those branches of production which today flourish more than any others are just those with capitals of very high composition, such as mining, chemical factories, breweries, steam mills, etc. Are these the spheres from which capital has withdrawn and migrated until production has been proportionately limited and prices have risen?" [1]

These statements will provide matter for many inferences against the Marxian theory. For the present I draw only one which bears immediately on the argument, which is the subject of our inquiry: the law of value, which, it is conceded, must give up its alleged control over prices of production in an economy where competition is in full force, has never exercised and could never exercise a real sway even in primitive conditions.

We have now seen, wrecked in succession, three contentions which affirmed the existence of certain reserved areas under the immediate control of the law of value. The application of the law of value to the sum total of all commodities and prices of commodities instead of to their several exchange relations (first argument) has been proved to be pure nonsense. The movement of prices (second argument) does not really obey the alleged law of value, and just as little does it exercise a real influence in "primitive conditions" (third argument). There is only one possibility left. Does the law of value, which has no real immediate power anywhere, have perhaps an indirect control, a sort of suzerainty? Marx does not omit to assert this also. It is the subject of the fourth argument, to which we now proceed.

FOURTH ARGUMENT

THIS ARGUMENT has been often hinted at by Marx, but so far as I can see he has explained it with any approach to fullness in one place only. The essence of it is this: that the "prices of production," which govern the actual formation of prices, are for their

---

[1] "Zur Kritik," pp. 584-586. I am bound, however, to make it clear that in the passage quoted Sombart intended to combat Marx only on the assumption that Marx's doctrines did actually have the meaning attributed to them in the text. He himself ascribes to them, in his "attempt at rescue," already referred to by me, another, and, as I think, a somewhat exotic meaning, which I shall discuss in detail later on.

part in their turn under the influence of the law of value, which
therefore, through the prices of production, governs the actual
exchange relations. The values are "behind the prices of production and determine them in the last resort" (III, 244). The
prices of production are, as Marx often expresses it, only
"changed values" or "changed forms of value" (III, 193, 199,
204 and often). The nature and degree of the influence which
the law of value exercises on the prices of production are more
clearly explained, however, in a passage on pages 211 and 212.
"*The average rate of profit which determines the price of production must,* however, always be approximately equal to the
amount of *surplus value* which falls to a given capital as an
aliquot part of the total social capital. . . . Now, as the total
value of the commodities governs the total surplus value, and
this again determines the amount of the average profit and consequently the general rate of profit—as a general law or a law
governing fluctuation—the *law of value regulates the prices of
production.*"

Let us examine this line of argument point by point.

Marx says at the outset that the average rate of profit determines the prices of production. In Marx's sense this is correct
but not complete. Let us make the connection quite clear.

The price of production of a commodity is first of all composed of the "cost price" to the employer of the means of production and of the average profit on the capital employed. The
cost price of the means of production consists again of two
component parts: the outlay of variable capital, that is, the
money immediately paid in wages, and the outlay for consumed
or used-up constant capital—raw material, machines, and the
like. As Marx rightly explains, on pages 188 ff., 194, and 242, in
a society in which the values have already been changed into
prices of production, the purchase or cost price of these means
of production does not correspond with their value but with the
total amount which has been expended by the producers of
these means of production in wages and material appliances,

plus the average profit on this expenditure. If we continue this analysis we come at last—as does Adam Smith in his *natural price,* with which, indeed, Marx expressly identifies his price of production (III, 233)—to resolve the price of production into two components or determinants: (1) the sum total of the wages paid during the different stages of production, which taken altogether represent the actual cost price of the commodities;[1] and (2) the sum total of the *profits* on all these wage outlays calculated *pro rata temporis,* and according to the average rate of profit.

Undoubtedly, therefore, *one* determinant of the price of production of a commodity is the average profit incidental to its production. Of the other determinant, the total of wages paid, Marx speaks no further in this passage. In another place, however, to which we have alluded, he says in a very general way that "the values stand behind the prices of production," and "that the law of value determines these latter in the last resort." In order to avoid a hiatus, therefore, we must subject this second factor also to our scrutiny and judge accordingly whether it can rightly be said to be determined by the law of value, and, if so, in what degree.

It is evident that the total expenditure in wages is a product of the quantity of labor employed multiplied by the average rate of the wages. Now as, according to the (Marxian) law of value, the exchange relations must be determined solely by the quantity of labor employed, and Marx repeatedly and most emphatically denies that the rate of wages has any influence on the value of the commodities,[2] it is also evident that, of the two components of the factor expenditure in wages, only the amount of labor employed is in harmony with the law of value, while in the second component, rate of wages, a determinant alien to the

---

[1] "The cost price of a commodity refers only to the amount of *paid* labor contained in it" (Vol. III, p. 195).

[2] For instance Vol. III, p. 243, where Marx affirms that "in no circumstances can the rise or fall of wages ever affect the value of the commodities."

law of value enters among the determinants of the prices of production.

The nature and degree of the operation of this determinant may be illustrated, in order to avoid all misunderstanding, by one other example.

Let us take three commodities—A, B, and C—which, to begin with, have the same production price of 100 shillings, but which are of different types of composition as regards the elements of their cost. Let us further suppose that the wages for a day amount at first to five shillings, and the rate of surplus value, or the degree of exploitation, to 100 percent, so that from the total value of the commodities of 300 shillings, 150 falls to wages and another 150 to surplus value; and that the total capital (invested in different proportions in the three commodities) amounts to 1,500 shillings. The average rate of profit would therefore be 10 percent.

The following table illustrates this assumption:

Commodity	Expended Time	Wages	Capital employed	Average profit accruing	Production price
A	10	50s.	500s.	50s.	100s.
B	6	30s.	700s.	70s.	100s.
C	14	70s.	300s.	30s.	100s.
Total	30	150s.	1,500s.	150s.	300s.

Now let us assume a rise in the wages from five to six shillings. According to Marx this can only take place at the expense of the surplus value, other conditions remaining the same.[1] Therefore of the total product of 300 shillings, which remains unaltered, there will fall (owing to a diminution in the degree of exploitation) 180 to wages and only 120 to surplus value, and consequently the average rate of profit on the capital employed falls to 8 percent. The following table shows the changes which take

[1] Compare Vol. III, p. 234 ff.

place, in consequence, in the compositions of the elements of capital and in the prices of production:

Commodity	Expended Time	Wages	Capital employed	Average profit accruing	Production price
A	10	60s.	500s.	40s.	100s.
B	6	36s.	700s.	56s.	92s.
C	14	84s.	300s.	24s.	108s.
Total	30	180s.	1,500s.	120s.	300s.

It appears from this that a rise in wages, when the amount of labor remains the same, brings with it a material alteration in the originally equal prices of production and relations of exchange. The alteration can be partly, but obviously not altogether, traced to the contemporaneous necessary change produced in the average rate of profit by the alteration in the wages. I say "obviously not altogether," because the price of production of commodity C, for example, has really *risen* in spite of the fall in the amount of profit contained in it, therefore this change of price cannot be brought about by the change of profit *only*. I raise this really obvious point merely in order to show that in the rate of wages we have, indisputably, a price determinant which does not exhaust its force in its influence on the rate of profit, but also exerts a special and direct influence; and that therefore we have reason to submit this particular price determinant—which is passed over by Marx in the passage cited above—to a separate consideration. The summary of the results of this consideration I reserve for a later stage, and in the meantime we will examine step by step Marx's assertion concerning the way in which the second determinant of the price of production, the average profit, is regulated by the law of value.

The connection is anything but a direct one. It is effected by the following links in his line of reasoning, some of which are indicated only elliptically by Marx, but which undoubtedly enter into his argument: the *law of value* determines the *aggregate value* of the whole of the commodities produced in the society; [1] the *aggregate value* of the commodities determines the *aggregate surplus value* contained in them; the latter distributed over the total social capital determines the *average rate of profit:* this rate applied to the capital employed in the production of a single commodity gives the *concrete average profit*, which finally enters as an element into the price of production of the commodity in question. In this way the first link in this sequence, the *law of value*, regulates the last link, the *price of production*.

Now for our running commentary on this series of arguments.

(1) We are struck by the fact, which must be kept in mind, that Marx after all does not affirm that there is a connection between the average profit entering into the price of production of the commodities and the values incorporated in single commodities by reason of the law of value. On the contrary, he says emphatically in numerous places that the amount of surplus value which enters into the price of production of a commodity is independent of and indeed fundamentally different from "the surplus value actually created in the sphere in which the separate commodity is produced" (III, 198; similarly III, 195 and often). He therefore does not after all connect the influence ascribed to the law of value with the characteristic function of the law of value, in virtue of which this law determines the exchange relations of the *separate commodities*, but only with another assumed function (concerning the highly problematical nature of which we have already passed an opinion), namely, the determination of the aggregate value *of all commodities taken together*. In this application, as we have convinced ourselves, the law of value has no meaning whatever. If the idea and the law of value are to be brought to bear—and Marx cer-

[1] This link is not expressly inserted by Marx in the passage quoted. Its insertion is nevertheless self-evident.

tainly means that they should—on the exchange relations of goods,[1] then there is no sense in applying the idea and law to an aggregate which as such cannot be subject to those relations. As no exchange of this aggregate takes place, there is naturally neither a measure nor a determinant for its exchange, and therefore it cannot give material for a "law of value." If, however, the law of value has no real influence at all on a chimerical "aggregate value of all commodities taken together," there can be no further application of its influence to other relations, and the whole logical series which Marx endeavored to work out with such seeming cogency hangs therefore in the air.

(2) But let us turn away altogether from this first fundamental defect, and let us independently of it test the strength of the other arguments in the series. Let us assume, therefore, that the aggregate value of the commodities is a real quantity, and actually determined by the law of value. The second argument affirms that this aggregate value of commodities determines the aggregate surplus value. Is this true?

The surplus value, unquestionably, represents no fixed or unalterable quota of the total national product, but is the difference between the "aggregate value" of the national product and the amount of the wages paid to the workers. That aggregate value, therefore, does not in any case rule the amount of the total surplus value by itself alone. It can at the most supply only *one* determinant of its amount, by the side of which stands a second, alien determinant, the rate of wages. But, it may be asked, does not this also, perhaps, obey the Marxian law of value?

In the first volume Marx had still unconditionally affirmed this. "The value of labor," he writes on page 189, "is determined, like that of every other commodity, by the working time necessary to the production, and therefore also reproduction, of this specific article." And on the next page he proceeds to define this

[1] As I have already mentioned, I shall take special notice later of the different view of W. Sombart.

proposition more fully: "For his maintenance the living individual needs a certain amount of means of subsistence. The
working time necessary to the production of the labor power resolves itself, therefore, into the working time necessary to the
production of these means of subsistence, or, the value of the
labor power is the value of the means of subsistence necessary to
the maintenance of its possessor." In the third volume Marx,
however, is forced considerably to modify this statement. Thus,
on page 242 of that volume, he rightly draws attention to the
fact that it is possible that the necessary means of subsistence
of the laborer also can be sold at prices of production which
deviate from that of the necessary working time. In such a case,
Marx says, the variable part of the capital (the wages paid)
may also deviate from its value. In other words, the wages
(apart from purely temporary oscillations) may permanently
deviate from the rate which should correspond to the quantity
of work incorporated in the necessary means of subsistence, or
to the strict requirements of the law of value. Therefore at least
one determinant alien to the law of value is already a factor in
determining the total surplus value.

(3) The factor, aggregate surplus value, thus determined,
"regulates," according to Marx, the average rate of profit, but
obviously only in so far as the aggregate surplus value furnishes
one determinant, while another—the amount of capital existing
in a given society—acts as a second determinant, entirely independent of the first and of the law of value. If, as in the above
table, the total surplus value is 150 shillings, the surplus value
being 100 percent, then, if and because the total capital expended in all its branches of production amounts to 1,500
shillings, the rate of profit amounts to 10 percent. If the total
surplus value remained exactly the same, but the total capital
participating in it amounted to 3,000 shillings, the rate of profit
would obviously amount only to 5 percent; and it would be fully
20 percent if the total capital amounted only to 750 shillings. It

is obvious, therefore, that again a determinant enters into the chain of influence which is entirely alien to the law of value.

(4) We must, therefore, further conclude that the average rate of profit regulates the amount of the concrete average profit which accrues from the production of a special commodity. But this, again, is only true with the same restrictions as in the former arguments of the series. That is to say, the total amount of the average profit which accrues from the production of a separate commodity is the product of two factors: the quantity of invested capital multiplied by the average rate of profit. The quantity of the capital to be invested in the different stages is again determined by two factors, namely, by the quantity of the work to be remunerated (a factor which is of course not out of harmony with Marx's law of value), and also by the rate of wages to be paid; and with this latter factor, as we have just convinced ourselves, a factor alien to the law of value comes into play.

(5) In the next argument of the series we go back again to the beginning: the average profit (defined in the fourth argument) must regulate the price of production of the commodity. This is true with the correction that the average profit is only *one* factor determining prices side by side with the expended wages in which, as we have repeatedly stated, there is an element, which is foreign to Marx's law of value, and which co-operates in determining prices.

Let us sum up. What is the proposition which Marx undertook to prove? It ran thus: "The law of value regulates the prices of production," or as otherwise stated, "the values determine in the last resort the prices of production," or if we formulate the meaning which Marx himself attached to value and law of value in the first volume the statement is: prices of production are governed "in the last resort" by the principle that the quantity of labor is the only condition which determines the exchange relations of commodities.

And what do we find on examining the separate links of the argument? We find that the price of production is, first of all, made up of two components. One, the expended wages, is the product of two factors, of which the first—the quantity of work —is in harmony with the substance of the Marxian "value," and the other—the rate of wages—is not. Marx himself could only affirm of the second component—the total amount of accruing average profit—that it was connected with the law of value by means of a violent perversion of this law, alleging its operation in a domain in which no exchange relations exist at all. But apart from this, the factor "aggregate value of commodities" which Marx wishes to deduce from the law of value must, in any case, co-operate in determining the next link, the aggregate surplus value, along with a factor, "rate of wages," which is no longer homogeneous with the law of value. The "aggregate surplus value" would have to co-operate with a completely foreign element, the mass of social capital, in determining the average rate of profit; and, finally, the latter would have to co-operate with a partially foreign element, expended wages, in determining the accruing total profit.

The factor "aggregate value of all commodities," dubiously regarded as a contribution of the Marxian law of value, consequently co-operates after a triple homeopathic dilution of its influence (and naturally, therefore, with a share of influence diminished in proportion to this dilution) in determining the average profit, and also the prices of production. The following would, therefore, be a sober statement of the facts of the case: The quantity of labor which, according to the Marxian law of value, must entirely and exclusively govern the exchange relations of commodities proves itself as a matter of fact to be only *one* determinant of the prices of production side by side with other determinants. It has a strong, a tolerably direct influence on the one component of prices of production which consists of expended wages; a much more remote, weak, and, for the most part,[1] even problematical influence upon the second component, the average profit.

Now, I ask, do we find in this condition of things a confirmation or a contradiction of the claim that, in the last resort, the law of value determines the prices of production? I do not think that there can be a moment's doubt as to the answer. The law of value maintains that quantity of labor alone determines the exchange relations; facts show that it is *not* only the quantity of labor, or the factors in harmony with it, which determine the exchange relations. These two propositions bear the same relation to each other as Yes to No—as affirmation to contradiction. Whoever accepts the second proposition—and Marx's theory of the prices of production involves this acceptance—contradicts *de facto* the first. And if Marx really could have thought that he did not contradict himself and his first proposition, he allowed himself to be deluded by some strange mistake. He could not have seen that it is very different for one factor involved in a law to have some sort and degree of influence and for the law itself to be in full force.

The most trivial example will perhaps serve best in so obvious a matter. Suppose a discussion on the effect of cannon balls on iron-clad vessels, and someone says that the degree of destructive power in the balls is due solely to the amount of powder with which the cannon is charged. When this statement is questioned and tested by actual experience it is seen that the effect of the shot is due not only to the amount of gunpowder in the charge, but also to the strength of the powder; and, further, to the construction, length, etc., of the barrel of the gun, the form and hardness of the balls, the distance of the object, and last, but

[1] In so far, namely, as it is supposed to be brought about by the factor "aggregate value," which, in my opinion, has nothing to do with the embodied amount of labor. As, however, the factor "expended wages" (in determining which the amount of work to be remunerated certainly co-operates as an element) also appears in the following links, the amount of work always finds a place among the indirect determinants of average profit.

not least, to the thickness and firmness of the plates on the vessel.

And now after all this has been conceded, could it still be said that nevertheless the first statement was true, because it had been proved that the alleged factor, the amount of gunpowder, does exert an important influence on the discharge, and that this was proved by the fact that, other circumstances being equal, the effect of the shot would be greater or less in proportion to the amount of gunpowder used in the charge?

This is what Marx does. He declares most emphatically that nothing can be at the root of exchange relations but quantity of labor alone; he argues strenuously with the economists who acknowledge other determinants of value and price besides the quantity of labor—the influence of which on the exchange value of goods freely reproduced no one denies. From the exclusive position of quantity of labor as the sole determinant of exchange relations he deduces in two volumes the most weighty and practical conclusions—his theory of surplus value and his denunciation of the capitalist organization of society—in order, in the third volume, to develop a theory of prices of production which substantially recognizes the influence of other determinants as well. But instead of thoroughly analyzing these other determinants, he always lays his finger triumphantly on the points where his idol, quantity of labor, either actually, or in his opinion, exerts an influence: on such points as the change in prices when the amount of labor changes, the influence of "aggregate value" on average rate of profit, etc. He is silent about the co-ordinate influence of foreign determinants as well as about the influence of the amount of social capital on the rate of profit, and about the alteration of prices through a change in the organic composition of the capital, or in the rate of wages. Passages in which he recognizes these influences are not wanting in his book. The influence of the rate of wages on prices is, for instance, aptly treated of in pages 234 ff., then in page 242; the influence of the amount of social capital on the height of the average rate of profit in pages 197, 240, 247 ff., 254 ff., 260, and often; the influence of the organic composition of capital on the prices of production in pages 192 ff. It is characteristic that in the passages devoted to the justification of his law of value Marx passes silently over these other influences, and only mentions in a one-sided way the part played by quantity of labor, in order to deduce from the first and un-disputed premise, that quantity of labor co-operates at many points to determine the prices of production, the utterly un-justifiable conclusion that, in the "last resort," the law of value, which proclaims the sole dominion of labor, determines the prices of production. This is to evade the admission of the con-tradiction; it is not to escape from the contradiction itself.

Chapter Four

Section I

THE evidence that an author has contradicted himself may be a necessary stage, but it cannot be the ultimate aim of a fruitful and well-directed criticism. To be aware that there is a defect in a system, which may possibly be accidental only and peculiar to the author, requires a comparatively low degree of critical intelligence. A firmly rooted system can only be effectually overthrown by discovering with absolute precision the point at which the error made its way into the system and the manner in which it spread and branched itself out. As opponents we ought to study the beginning, the development, and the final issue of the error which culminates in self-contradiction as thoroughly, I might almost say as sympathetically, as we would study the connection of a system with which we were in agreement.

Owing to many peculiar circumstances the question of self-contradiction has, in the case of Marx, gained a more than ordinary importance, and consequently I have devoted a considerable space to it. But in dealing with a thinker so important and influential as Marx it is incumbent upon us to apply ourselves to the second and, in this case I think, the actually more fruitful and instructive part of the criticism.

We will begin with a question which will carry us straight to the main point: in what way did Marx arrive at the fundamental proposition of his teaching—the proposition that all value depends solely upon incorporated quantities of labor?

That this proposition is not a self-evident axiom, needing no proof, is beyond doubt. Value and effort, as I have stated at length in another place, are not ideas so intimately connected that one is forced immediately to adopt the view that effort is the basis of value. "That I have toiled over a thing is one fact, that the thing is worth the toil is another and a different fact, and that the two facts do not always go hand in hand is far too firmly established by experience to admit of any doubt. It is proved by all the labor which is daily wasted on valueless results, owing either to want of technical skill, or to bad speculation, or to simple misfortune; and not less by each of the numerous cases in which a very little toil has a result of very great value." [1]

When therefore it is affirmed that a necessary and natural correspondence between value and effort exists in any quarter, it behooves us to give ourselves and our readers some grounds in support of such a statement.

Now Marx himself advances proofs of it in his system; but I think I shall be able to convince my readers that from the outset his line of argument is unnatural and not suited to the character of the problem; and further that the evidence which Marx advances in his system is clearly not the same as that by means of which he himself arrives at his convictions, but was thought out subsequently as an artificial support for an opinion which was previously derived from other sources; and finally—

[1] *Capital and Interest*, p. 377.

and this is the most decisive point—that the reasoning is full of the most obvious faults of logic and method which deprive it of all cogency.

Let us examine this more closely.

The fundamental proposition which Marx puts before his readers is that the exchange value of commodities—for his analysis is directed only to this, not to value in use—finds its origin and its measure in the quantity of labor incorporated in the commodities.

Now it is certain that the exchange values, that is to say the prices of the commodities as well as the quantities of labor which are necessary for their reproduction, are real, external quantities, which on the whole it is quite possible to determine empirically. Obviously, therefore, Marx ought to have turned to experience for the proof of a proposition the correctness or incorrectness of which must be manifested in the facts of experience; or in other words, he should have given a purely empirical proof in support of a proposition adapted to a purely empirical proof. This, however, Marx does not do. And one cannot even say that he heedlessly passes by this possible and certainly proper source of knowledge and conviction. The reasoning of the third volume proves that he was quite aware of the nature of the empirical facts, and that they were opposed to his proposition. He knew that the prices of commodities were not in proportion to the amount of incorporated labor, but to the total cost of production, which comprises other elements besides. He did not therefore accidentally overlook this, the most natural proof of his proposition, but turned away from it with the full consciousness that upon this road no issue favorable to his theory could be obtained.

But there is yet another and perfectly natural way of testing and proving such propositions: the psychological. We can by a combination of induction and deduction, much used in our science, investigate the motives which direct people in carrying on the business of exchange and in determining exchange prices on the one hand, and on the other hand which guide them in their co-operation in production; and from the nature of these motives a typical mode of action may be inferred through which, among other things, it is conceivable that a connection should result between the regularly demanded and accepted prices and the quantity of work necessary for the production of the commodities. This method has often been followed with the best results in exactly similar questions—for instance, the usual justification of the law of supply and demand and of the law of costs of production, and the explanation of ground rents, rest upon it. And Marx himself, in a general way at least, has often made use of it; but precisely in dealing with his fundamental proposition he avoids it. Although, obviously, the affirmed external connection between exchange relations and quantities of work could only be fully understood by the discovery of the psychological links which connect the two, he foregoes all explanation of these internal connections. He even once says, incidentally, that "the deeper analysis" of the two social forces, "demand and supply"—which would have led to this internal connection—"is not apposite here" (III, 223), where the "here" refers only to a digression on the influence of supply and demand on the formation of prices. In reality, however, nowhere in the whole Marxian system is a really "deep" and thorough analysis attempted; and the absence of this analysis is most noticeable where he is preparing the ground for his most important leading idea.

But here again we notice something strange. Marx does not, as might have been expected, pass over this second possible and natural method of investigation with an easy carelessness. He studiously avoids it, and with a full consciousness of what the results of following it would be, and that they would not be favorable to his thesis. In the third volume, for instance, he actually brings forward, under their roughly collective name of "competition," those motives operative in production and exchange, the "deeper analysis" of which he foregoes here and elsewhere, and demonstrates that these motives do not in reality lead to an adjustment of the prices to the quantities of labor incorporated in the commodities, but that, on the contrary, they force them away from this level to a level which implies at least one other co-ordinating factor. Indeed it is competition which, according to Marx, leads to the formation of the celebrated average rate of profit and to the "transfer" of pure labor values into prices of production, which differ from them and contain a portion of average profit.

Now Marx, instead of proving his thesis from experience or from its operant motives—that is, empirically or psychologically —prefers another, and for such a subject somewhat singular line of evidence—the method of a purely logical proof, a dialectic deduction from the very nature of exchange.

Marx had found in old Aristotle the idea that "exchange cannot exist without equality, and equality cannot exist without commensurability" (I, 68). Starting with this idea he expands it. He conceives the exchange of two commodities under the form of an equation, and from this infers that "a common factor of the same amount" must exist in the things exchanged and thereby equated, and then proceeds to search for this common factor to which the two equated things must as exchange values be "reducible" (I, 43).

I should like to remark, in passing, that the first assumption, according to which an "equality" must be manifested in the exchange of two things, appears to me to be very old-fashioned, which would not, however, matter much were it not also very unrealistic. In plain words, it seems to me to be a wrong idea. Where equality and exact equilibrium obtain, no change is likely to occur to disturb the balance. When, therefore, in the case of exchange the matter terminates with a change of ownership of the commodities, it points rather to the existence of some inequality or preponderance which produces the alteration. When composite bodies are brought into close contact with each other

new chemical combinations are produced by some of the constituent elements of one body uniting with those of another
body, not because they possess an exactly equal degree of chemical affinity, but because they have a stronger affinity with each
other than with the other elements of the bodies to which they
originally belonged. And as a matter of fact modern political
economists agree that the old scholastico-theological theory of
"equivalence" in the commodities to be exchanged is untenable.
I will not, however, dwell any longer on this point, but will
proceed to the critical investigation of the logical and systematic
processes of distillation by means of which Marx obtains the
sought-for "common factor" in labor.

It is these processes which appear to me to constitute, as I
have before said, the most vulnerable point in the Marxian
theory. They exhibit as many cardinal errors as there are points
in the arguments—of which there are not a few—and they bear
evident traces of having been a subtle and artificial afterthought
contrived to make a preconceived opinion seem the natural outcome of a prolonged investigation.

Marx searches for the "common factor" which is the characteristic of exchange value in the following way: He passes in
review the various properties possessed by the objects made
equal in exchange, and according to the method of exclusion
separates all those which cannot stand the test, until at last
only one property remains, that of being the product of labor.
This, therefore, must be the sought-for common property.

This line of procedure is somewhat singular, but not in itself
objectionable. It strikes one as strange that instead of sub-
mitting the supposed characteristic property to a positive test
—as would have been done if either of the other methods
studiously avoided by Marx had been employed—Marx tries
to convince us that he has found the sought-for property, by
a purely negative proof, by showing that it is not any of the
other properties. This method can always lead to the desired
end if attention and thoroughness are used—that is to say, if

extreme care is taken that everything that ought to be included is actually passed through the logical sieve and that no mistake has been made in leaving anything out.

But how does Marx proceed?

From the beginning he only puts into the sieve those exchangeable things which contain the property which he desires finally to sift out as "the common factor," and he leaves all the others outside. He acts as one who urgently desiring to bring a white ball out of an urn takes care to secure this result by putting in white balls only. That is to say he limits from the outset the field of his search for the substance of the exchange value to "commodities," and in doing so he forms a conception with a meaning narrower than the conception of "goods" (though he does not clearly define it), and limits it to products of labor as against gifts of nature. Now it stands to reason that if exchange really means an equalization, which assumes the existence of a "common factor of the same amount," this common factor must be sought and found in every species of goods which is brought into exchange, not only in products of labor but also in gifts of nature, such as the soil, wood in trees, water power, coal beds, stone quarries, petroleum reserves, mineral waters, gold mines, etc.[1] To exclude the exchangeable goods which are not products of labor in the search for the common factor which lies at the root of exchange value is, under the circumstances, a great error of method. It is just as though a natural philosopher, desiring to discover a property common to all bodies—weight, for instance—were to sift the properties of a single group of bodies—transparent bodies, for instance—and after passing in review all the properties common to transparent bodies were to declare that transparency must be the cause of

[1] Karl Knies makes the following pertinent objection against Marx: "There is no reason apparent in Marx's statement why the equation, 1 quarter wheat = a cwts. wild-grown wood = b acres of virgin soil = c acres of natural pasture-land, should not be as good as the equation, 1 quarter wheat = a cwts. of forest-grown wood" (*Das Geld,* 1st edition, p. 121, 2nd edition, p. 157).

weight, for the sole reason that he could demonstrate that it could not be caused by any of the other properties.

The exclusion of the gifts of nature (which would never have entered the head of Aristotle, the father of the idea of equality in exchange) is the less to be justified because many natural gifts, such as the soil, are among the most important objects of property and commerce, and also because it is impossible to affirm that in nature's gifts exchange values are always established arbitrarily and by accident. On the one hand, there are such things as accidental prices among products of labor; and on the other hand the prices in the case of nature's gifts are frequently shown to be distinctly related to antecedent conditions or determining motives. For instance, that the sale price of land is a multiple of its rent calculated on an interest usual in the country of sale is as well-known a fact as that the wood in a tree, or the coal in a pit, brings a higher or lower price according to differences of quality or of distance from market, and not by mere accident.

Marx also takes care to avoid mentioning or explaining the fact that he excludes from his investigation a part of exchangeable goods. In this case, as in many others, he manages to glide with dialectic skill over the difficult points of his argument. He omits to call his readers' attention to the fact that his idea of "commodities" is narrower than that of exchangeable goods as a whole. He very cleverly prepares us for the acceptance of the subsequent limitation of the investigation to commodities by placing at the beginning of his book the apparently harmless general phrase that "the wealth of the society in which a capitalist system of production is dominant appears as an immense *collection of commodities.*" This proposition is quite wrong if we take the term "commodity" to mean products of labor, which is the sense Marx subsequently gives to it. For the gifts of nature, inclusive of the soil, constitute a by no means insignificant, but on the contrary a very important element of national wealth. The ingenuous reader easily overlooks this inaccuracy, however, for of course he does not know that later Marx will give a much more restricted meaning to the term "commodity."

Nor is this made clear in what immediately follows. On the contrary, in the first paragraphs of the first chapter we read in turns of a "thing," a "value in use," a "good," and a "commodity," without any clear distinction being made between the last and the three former. "The usefulness of a *thing*," it says on page 42, "makes it a *value in use*"; "the commodity . . . is a *value in use* or *good*." On page 43 we read, "Exchange value appears . . . as the quantitative proportion . . . in which *values in use* of one kind exchange with *values in use* of another kind." And here let it be noticed that it is just the value in use = good which is still directly indicated as the main factor of the exchange phenomenon. And with the phrase "Let us look into the matter more closely," which surely cannot be meant to prepare us for a leap into another and a narrower field of research, Marx continues, "a single *commodity*, a quarter of wheat, for instance, exchanges in the most varying proportions with other *articles*." And "Let us further take two *commodities*," etc. In the same paragraph the term "things" occurs again, and indeed with the application which is most important for the problem, namely, "that a common factor of equal amount exists in two different *things*" (which are made equal to each other in exchange).

On the next page (p. 44), however, Marx directs his search for the "common factor" only to the "exchange value of *commodities*," without hinting, even in the faintest whisper, that he has thereby limited the field of research to a part only of the things possessing exchange value.[1] And immediately, on the next

---

[1] In a quotation from Barbon, in this same paragraph, the difference between commodities and things is again effaced: "One sort of *wares* are as good as another, if the value be equal. There is no difference or distinction in *things* of equal value."

page (p. 45), the limitation is again abandoned and the results just obtained in the narrower area are applied to the wider sphere of values in use, or goods. "A *value in use,* or a *good,* has therefore only a value because abstract human labor is stored up or materialized in it."

If Marx had not confined his research, at the decisive point, to products of labor, but had sought for the common factor in the exchangeable gifts of nature as well, it would have become obvious that work cannot be the common factor. If he had carried out this limitation quite clearly and openly this gross fallacy of method would inevitably have struck both himself and his readers; and they would have been forced to laugh at the naïve juggle by means of which the property of being a product of labor has been successfully distilled out as the common property of a group from which all exchangeable things which naturally belong to it, and which are not the products of labor, have been first of all eliminated. The trick could only have been performed, as Marx performed it, by gliding un-noticed over the knotty point with a light and quick dialectic. But while I express my sincere admiration of the skill with which Marx managed to present so faulty a mode of procedure in so specious a form, I can of course only maintain that the proceeding itself is altogether erroneous.

But we will proceed. By means of the artifice just described Marx has merely succeeded in convincing us that labor can in fact enter into the competition. And it was only by the artificial narrowing of the sphere that it could even have become *one* "common" property of this narrow sphere. But by its side other properties could claim to be as common. How now is the ex-clusion of these other competitors effected? It is effected by two arguments, each of a few words only, but which contain one of the most serious of logical fallacies.

In the first of these Marx excludes all "geometrical, physical, chemical, or other natural properties of the commodities," for "their physical properties only come into consideration in so far as they make the commodities useful—make them values in use, therefore. *On the other hand, the exchange relation of commodities evidently involves our disregarding their values in use*" ; because *"within this relation* [the exchange relation] *one value in use is worth exactly as much as every other, provided only it is present in proper proportions"* (I, 44).

In making clear what this argument involves I may be permitted to quote from my *Capital and Interest* (p. 381) :

"What would Marx have said to the following argument? In an opera company there are three celebrated singers, a tenor, a bass, and a baritone, each with a salary of £2,000. Someone asks, 'What is the common circumstance on account of which their salaries are made equal?' And I answer, 'In the question of salary one good voice counts for just as much as any other, a good tenor for as much as a good bass or a good baritone, provided only it is to be had in proper proportion. Consequently in the question of salary the good voice is evidently disregarded, and the good voice cannot be the common cause of the high salary.' That this argument is false, is clear. But it is just as clear that Marx's syllogism, from which this is copied, is not an atom more correct. Both commit the same fallacy. They confuse abstraction from the genus, and abstraction from the specific forms in which the genus manifests itself. In our illustration the circumstance which is of no account as regards the question of salary is evidently only the special form in which the good voice appears, whether as tenor, bass, or baritone, and by no means the good voice as such. And just so is it with the exchange relation of commodities. The special forms under which the values in use of the commodities may appear, whether they serve for food, shelter, clothing, etc., is of course disregarded, but the value in use of the commodity as such is never disregarded. Marx might have seen that we do not absolutely disregard value in use, from the fact that there can be no exchange value where there is no value in use—a fact which Marx is himself repeatedly forced to admit." [1]

The second step in the argument is still worse: "If the use value of commodities be disregarded"—these are Marx's words —"there remains in them *only one other property, that of being products of labor.*" Is it so? I ask today as I asked twelve years ago: is there only one other property? Is not the property of being scarce in proportion to demand also common to all exchangeable goods? Or that they are the subjects of demand and supply? Or that they are appropriated? Or that they are natural products? For that they are products of nature, just as they are products of labor, no one asserts more plainly than Marx himself, when he declares in one place that "commodities are combinations of two elements, natural material and labor." Or is not the property that they cause expense to their producers —a property to which Marx draws attention in the third volume—common to exchangeable goods?

Why then, I ask again today, may not the principle of value reside in any one of these common properties as well as in the property of being products of labor? For in support of this latter

[1] For example, p. 48: "Lastly, nothing can be a value without also being an object of use. If it is useless, the labor contained in it is also useless; it does not count as labor [*sic!*], and therefore creates no value." Knies has already drawn attention to the logical fallacy animadverted upon in the text (see *Das Geld,* Berlin, 1873, pp. 123 ff.; 2nd edition, pp. 160 ff.). Adler (*Grundlagen der Karl Marxschen Kritik,* Tübingen, 1887, pp. 211 ff.) has strangely misunderstood my argument when he contends against me that good voices are not commodities in the Marxian sense. It did not concern me at all whether "good voices" could be classed as economic goods under the Marxian law of value or not. It only concerned me to present an argument of a logical syllogism which showed the same fallacy as that of Marx. I might for this purpose just as well have chosen an example which was in no way related to the domain of economics. I might, for example, just as well have shown that according to Marx's logic the common factor of *variously colored* bodies might consist in heaven knows what, but not in the blending of various colors. For any *one* combination of colors—for example, white, blue, yellow, black, violet—is as regards variety worth just as much as any other combination, say green, red, orange, sky-blue, etc., if only it is present "in proper proportion"; we therefore apparently abstract from the color and combination of colors!

proposition Marx has not adduced a shred of positive evidence. His sole argument is the negative one, that the value in use, from which we have happily abstracted, is not the principle of exchange value. But does not this negative argument apply equally to all the other common properties overlooked by Marx? And this is not all. On page 44, in which Marx has abstracted from the influence of the value in use on exchange value by arguing that any one value in use is worth as much as any other if only it is present in proper proportion, he writes as follows about products of labor: "But even as the product of labor they have already changed in our hand. For if we abstract from a commodity its value in use, we at the same time take from it the material constituents and forms which give it a value in use. It is no longer a table, or a house, or yarn, or any other useful thing. All its physical qualities have disappeared. *Nor is it any longer the product of the labor of the carpenter, or the mason, or the spinner, or of any other particular productive industry*. With the useful character of the labor products there disappears the useful character of the labor embodied in them, and there vanish also the different concrete forms of those labors. *They are no longer distinguished from each other, but are all reduced to identical human labor—abstract human labor*."

Is it possible to state more clearly or more emphatically that for an exchange relation not only any one value in use, but also any one kind of labor or product of labor is worth exactly as much as any other, if only it is present in proper proportion? Or, in other words, that exactly the same evidence on which Marx formulated his verdict of exclusion against the value in use holds good with regard to labor? Labor and value in use have a qualitative side and a quantitative side. As the value in use is different qualitatively as table, house, or yarn, so is labor as carpentry, masonry, or spinning. And just as one can compare different kinds of labor according to their quantity, so one can compare values in use of different kinds according to the amount of the value in use. It is quite impossible to understand why the very same evidence should result in the one competitor being excluded and in the other getting the crown and the prize. If Marx had chanced to reverse the order of the examination, the same reasoning which led to the exclusion of the value in use would have excluded labor; and then the reasoning which resulted in the crowning of labor might have led him to declare the value in use to be the only property left, and therefore to be the sought-for common property, and value to be "the cellular tissue of value in use." I think it can be maintained seriously, not in jest, that, if the subjects of the two paragraphs on page 44 were transposed (in the first of which the influence of value in use is thought away, and in the second labor is shown to be the sought-for common factor), the seeming justness of the reasoning would not be affected, that "labor" and "products of labor" could be substituted everywhere for "value in use" in the otherwise unaltered structure of the first paragraph, and that in the structure of the second paragraph "value in use" could be substituted throughout for "labor."

Of such a nature are the reasoning and the method employed by Marx in introducing into his system his fundamental proposition that labor is the sole basis of value. In my opinion it is quite impossible that this dialectical hocus-pocus constituted the ground and source of Marx's own convictions. It would have been impossible for a thinker such as he was (and I look upon him as an intellectual force of the very highest order) to have followed such tortuous and unnatural methods had he been engaged, with a free and open mind, in really investigating the actual connections of things, and in forming his own conclusions with regard to them; it would have been impossible for him to fall successively by mere accident into all the errors of thought and method which I have described, and to arrive at the conclusion that labor is the sole source of value as the natural outgrowth, not the desired and predetermined result, of such a mode of inquiry.

I think the case was really different. That Marx was truly and honestly convinced of the truth of his thesis I do not doubt. But the grounds of his conviction are not those which he gives in his system. They were in reality opinions rather than thought-out conclusions. Above all they were opinions derived from authority. Smith and Ricardo, the great authorities, as was then at least believed, had taught the same doctrine. They had not *proved* it any more than Marx. They had only postulated it from certain general confused impressions. But they explicitly contradicted it when they examined things more closely and in quarters where a closer examination could not be avoided. Smith, in the same way as Marx in his third volume, taught that in a developed economic system values and prices gravitate towards a level of costs which besides labor comprises an average profit of capital. And Ricardo, too, in the celebrated fourth section of the chapter "On Value," clearly and definitely stated that by the side of labor, mediate or immediate, the amount of capital invested and the duration of the investment exercise a determining influence on the value of the goods. In order to maintain without obvious contradiction their cherished philosophical principle that labor is the "true" source of value, they were obliged to beat a retreat to mythical times and places in which capitalists and landed proprietors did not exist. There they could maintain it without contradiction, for there was nothing to restrain them. Experience, which does not support the theory, was not there to refute them. Nor were they restrained by a scientific, psychological analysis, for like Marx they avoided such an analysis. They did not seek to prove—they postulated, as a "natural" state, an idyllic state of things where labor and value were one.[1]

[1] The position which is taken by Smith and Ricardo towards the doctrine that value is wholly labor I have discussed exhaustively in the *Geschichte und Kritik*, pp. 428 ff. and have there also shown especially that no trace of a proof of this thesis is to be found in the so-called classical writers. Compare also Knies, *Der Kredit*, 2nd section, pp. 60 ff.

It was to tendencies and views of this kind, which had acquired from Smith and Ricardo a great but not undisputed authority, that Marx became heir, and as an ardent socialist he willingly believed in them. It is not surprising that he did not take a more skeptical attitude with regard to a view which was so well adapted to support his economic theory of the world than did Ricardo, to whom it must have gone sorely against the grain. It is not surprising, too, that he did not allow those views of the classical writers which were against him to excite any critical doubts in his own mind on the doctrine that value is wholly labor, but considered that they were only attempts on their part to escape in an indirect way from the unpleasant consequences of an inconvenient truth. In short, it is not surprising that the same material on which the classical writers had grounded their half-confused, half-contradictory, and wholly unproved opinions should have served Marx as foundation for the same assumption, believed in unconditionally and with earnest conviction. For himself he needed no further evidence. Only for his system he needed a formal proof.

It is clear that he could not rely simply on the classical writers for this, as they had not proved anything; and we also know that he could not appeal to experience, or attempt an economico-psychological proof, for these methods would have straightway led him to a conclusion exactly opposite to the one he wished to establish. So he turned to dialectical speculation, which was, moreover, in keeping with the bent of his mind. And here it was a question of using any means at hand. He knew the result that he wished to obtain, and must obtain, and so he twisted and manipulated the long-suffering ideas and logical premises with admirable skill and subtlety until they actually yielded the desired result in a seemingly respectable syllogistic form. Perhaps he was so blinded by his convictions that he was not aware of the monstrosities of logic and method which had necessarily crept in, or perhaps he was aware of them and thought himself justified in making use of them simply as formal supports, to give a suitable systematic dress to a truth which, according to his deepest convictions, was already substantially proved. Of that I cannot judge, neither is it now possible for any one else to do so. What I will say, however, is that no one, with so powerful a mind as Marx, has ever exhibited a logic so continuously and so palpably wrong as he exhibits in the systematic proof of his fundamental doctrine.

Section II

THIS WRONG thesis he now weaves into his system with admirable tactical skill. Of this we have a brilliant example in the next step he takes. Although he has carefully steered clear of the testimony of experience and has evolved his doctrine entirely "out of the depths of his mind," yet the wish to apply the test of experience cannot be altogether suppressed. If Marx himself would not do it, his readers would certainly do it on their own account. What does he do? He divides and distinguishes. At one point the disagreement between his doctrine and experience is flagrant. Taking the bull by the horns he himself seizes upon this point. He had stated as a consequence of his fundamental principle that the value of different commodities is in proportion to the working time necessary to their production (I, 46). Now it is obvious even to the casual observer that this proposition cannot maintain itself in the face of certain facts. The day's product of a sculptor, of a cabinetmaker, of a violin-maker, of an engineer, etc., certainly does not contain an equal value but a much higher value than the day's product of a common workman or factory hand, although in both the same amount of working time is "embodied." Marx himself, with a masterly dialectic, now brings these facts up for discussion. In considering them he seeks to suggest that they do not contain a contradiction of his fundamental principle, but are only a slightly different reading of it which still comes within the limits of the rule, and that all that is needed is some explanation or more exact definition of the latter. That is to say he declares that labor in the sense of his proposition means the "expenditure of simple [unskilled] labor power, an average of which is possessed in his physical organism by every ordinary man, without special cultivation"; or in other words *"simple average labor"* (I, 51, and also previously in I, 46).

"Skilled labor," he continues, *"counts only as concentrated or rather multiplied unskilled labor,* so that a small quantity of skilled labor is equal to a larger quantity of unskilled labor. *That this reduction is constantly made experience shows.* A commodity may be the product of the most highly skilled labor, but *its value makes it equal to the product of unskilled labor, and represents therefore only a definite quantity of unskilled labor.* The different proportions in which different kinds of labor are reduced to unskilled labor as their unit of measure are fixed by a social process beyond the control of the producers, and therefore seem given to them by tradition."

This explanation may really sound quite plausible to the hasty reader, but if we look at it coolly and soberly we get quite a different impression.

The fact with which we have to deal is that the product of a day's or an hour's skilled labor is more valuable than the product of a day's or an hour's unskilled labor; that, for instance, the day's product of a sculptor is equal to the five days' product of a stone-breaker. Now Marx tells us that things made equal to each other in exchange must contain "a common factor of the same amount," and this common factor must be labor and working time. Does he mean labor in general? Marx's first statements up to page 45 would lead us to suppose so; but it is evident that something is wrong, for the labor of five days is obviously not "the same amount" as the labor of one day. Therefore Marx, in the case before us, is no longer speaking of labor as such but of unskilled labor. The common factor must therefore be the possession of an equal amount of labor of a particular kind, namely, unskilled labor.

If we look at this dispassionately, however, it fits still worse, for in sculpture there is no "unskilled labor" at all embodied, much less therefore unskilled labor equal to the amount in the five days' labor of the stone-breaker. The plain truth is that the two products embody *different kinds* of labor in *different amounts,* and every unprejudiced person will admit that this means a state of things exactly contrary to the conditions which Marx demands and must affirm, namely, that they embody labor of the *same kind* and of the *same amount !*

Marx certainly says that skilled labor "counts" as multiplied unskilled labor, but to "count as" is not "to be," and the theory deals with the being of things. Men may naturally consider one day of a sculptor's work as equal in some respects to five days of a stone-breaker's work, just as they may also consider a deer as equal to five hares. But a statistician might with equal justification maintain, with scientific conviction, that there were one thousand hares in a cover which contained one hundred deer and five hundred hares, as a statistician of prices or a theorist about value might seriously maintain that in the day's product of a sculptor five days of unskilled labor are embodied, and that this is the true reason why it is considered in exchange to be equal to five days' labor of a stone-breaker. I will presently attempt to illustrate, by an example bearing directly on the problem of value, the multitude of things we might prove if we resorted to the verb "to count" whenever the verb "to be" landed us in difficulties. But I must first add one other criticism.

Marx makes an attempt in the passages quoted to justify his maneuver of reducing skilled labor to common labor, and to justify it by experience.

"That this reduction is constantly made experience shows. A commodity may be the product of the most highly skilled labor, but its value makes it equal to the product of unskilled labor, and represents therefore only a definite quantity of unskilled labor."

Good! We will let that pass for the moment and will only inquire a little more closely in what manner and by what means we are to determine the standard of this reduction, which, according to Marx, experience shows is constantly made. Here we stumble against the very natural but for the Marxian theory the very compromising circumstance that the standard of reduction is determined solely *by the actual exchange relations themselves*. But in what proportions skilled is to be translated into terms of simple labor in the valuation of their products is not determined, nor can it be determined a priori by any property inherent in the skilled labor itself, but it is the actual result alone which decides the actual exchange relations. Marx himself says "their value makes them equal to the product of unskilled labor," and he refers to a "social process beyond the control of the producers which fixes the proportions in which different kinds of labor are reduced to unskilled labor as their unit of measure," and says that these proportions therefore *"seem to be given by tradition."*

Under these circumstances what is the meaning of the appeal to "value" and "the social process" as the determining factors of the standard of reduction? Apart from everything else it simply means that Marx is arguing in a complete circle. The real subject of inquiry is the exchange relations of commodities: why, for instance, a statuette which has cost a sculptor one day's labor should exchange for a cart of stones which has cost a stone-breaker five days' labor, and not for a larger or smaller quantity of stones, in the breaking of which ten or three days' labor have been expended. How does Marx explain this? He says the exchange relation is this, and no other—because one day of sculptor's work is reducible exactly to five days of unskilled work. And why is it reducible to exactly five days? Because experience shows that it is so reduced by a social process. And what is this social process? The same process that has to be explained, that very process by means of which the product of one day of sculptor's labor has been made equal to the value of the product of five days of common labor. But if as a matter of fact it were exchanged regularly against the product of only three days of simple labor, Marx would equally bid us accept the rate of reduction of 1:3 as the one derived from experience, and would found upon it and explain by it the assertion that a statuette must be equal in exchange to the product of exactly three days of a stone-breaker's work—not more and not less. In short, it is clear that we shall never learn in this way the actual reasons why products of different kinds of work should be exchanged in this or that proportion. They exchange in this way, Marx tells us, though in slightly different words, because, according to experience, they do exchange in this way!

I remark further in passing that the followers of Marx, having perhaps recognized the circle I have just described, have made the attempt to place the reduction of complicated to simple work on another, a real, basis.

"It is no fiction but a fact," says Grabski,[1] "that an hour of skilled labor contains several hours of unskilled labor." For "in order to be consistent, we must also take into account the labor which was used in acquiring the skill." I do not think it will need many words to show clearly the complete inadequacy also of this explanation. I have nothing to say against the view that to labor in actual operation should be added the quota due to the acquirement of the power to labor. But it is clear that the difference in value of skilled labor as opposed to unskilled labor could only then be explained by reference to this additional quota if the amount of the latter corresponded to the amount of that difference. For instance, in the case we have given, there could only be actually five hours of unskilled labor in one hour of skilled labor, if four hours of preparatory

[1] *Deutsche Worte,* Vol. XV (March, 1895), p. 155.

labor went to every hour of skilled labor; or, reckoned in greater units, if out of fifty years of life which a sculptor devotes to the learning and practicing of his profession, he spends forty years in educational work in order to do skilled work for ten years. But no one will maintain that such a proportion or anything approaching to it is actually found to exist. I turn therefore again from the obviously inadequate hypothesis of the disciple to the teaching of the master himself in order to illustrate the nature and range of its errors by one other example, which I think will bring out most clearly the fault in Marx's mode of reasoning.

With the very same reasoning one could affirm and argue the proposition that the quantity of material contained in commodities constitutes the principle and measure of exchange value—that commodities exchange in proportion to the *quantity of material incorporated in them*. Ten pounds of material in one kind of commodity exchange against ten pounds of material in another kind of commodity. If the natural objection were raised that this statement was obviously false because ten pounds of gold do not exchange against ten pounds of iron but against 40,000 pounds, or against a still greater number of pounds of coal, we may reply after the manner of Marx that it is the amount of *common average material* that affects the formation of value, that acts as unit of measurement. Skillfully wrought costly material of special quality *counts* only as compound or rather multiplied common material, so that a small quantity of material fashioned with skill is equal to a larger quantity of common material. *That this reduction is constantly made experience shows.* A commodity may be of the most exquisite material; its *value* makes it equal to commodities formed of common material, and *therefore represents only a particular quantity of common material.* A "social process," the existence of which cannot be doubted, is persistently reducing the pound of raw gold to 40,000 pounds of raw iron, and the

pound of raw silver to 1,500 pounds of raw iron. The working up
of the gold by an ordinary goldsmith or by the hand of a great
artist gives rise to further variations in the character of the
material to which use, in conformity with experience, does justice by means of special standards of reduction. If one pound
of bar gold, therefore, exchanges against 40,000 pounds of bar
iron, or if a gold cup of the same weight, wrought by Benvenuto
Cellini, exchanges against 4,000,000 pounds of iron, it is not a
violation but a confirmation of the proposition that commodities
exchange in proportion to the "average" material they contain!

I think the impartial reader will easily recognize once more
in these two arguments the two ingredients of the Marxian
recipe—the substitution of "to count" for "to be," and the
explanation in a circle which consists in obtaining the standard
of reduction from the actually existing social exchange relations
which themselves need explanation. In this way Marx has settled his account with the facts that most glaringly contradict
his theory with great dialectical skill, certainly, but, as far as
the matter itself is concerned, naturally and inevitably in a
quite inadequate manner.

But there are, besides, contradictions with actual experience
rather less striking than the foregoing; those, namely, which
spring from the part that the *investment of capital* has in determining the actual prices of commodities, the same which
Ricardo—as we have already noticed—treats of in the fourth
section of the chapter "On Value." Towards them Marx adopts
a change of tactics. For a time he completely shuts his eyes to
them. He ignores them, by a process of abstraction, through the
first and second volumes, and pretends that they do not exist;
that is to say, he proceeds throughout the whole detailed exposition of his doctrine of value, and likewise throughout the
development of his theory of surplus value, on the "assumption"—in part tacitly maintained, in part clearly asserted—
that commodities really exchange according to their values,

which means exactly in proportion to the labor embodied in them.[1]

This hypothetical abstraction he combines with an uncommonly clever dialectical move. He gives certain actual deviations from the law, from which a theorist may really venture to abstract, namely, the accidental and temporary fluctuations of the market prices round their normal fixed level. And on the occasions when Marx explains his intention to disregard the deviations of the prices from the values he does not fail to direct the reader's attention to those "accidental circumstances" which have to be ignored as "the constant oscillations of the market prices," whose "rise and fall compensate each other," and which "reduce themselves to an average price as their inner law." [2] By this reference he gains the reader's approval of his abstraction, but the fact that he does not abstract merely from accidental fluctuations but also from regular, permanent, typical "deviations," whose existence constitutes an integral part of the rule to be elucidated, is not made manifest to the reader who is not closely observant, and he glides unsuspectingly over the author's fatal error of method.

For it is a fatal error of method to ignore in scientific investigation the very point that demands explanation. Now Marx's theory of surplus value aims at nothing else than the explanation, as he conceives it, of the profits of capital. But the profits of capital lie exactly in those regular deviations of the prices of commodities from the amount of their mere costs in labor. If, therefore, we ignore those deviations, we ignore just the principal part of what has to be explained. Rodbertus [3] was guilty of the same error of method, and twelve years ago I taxed him, as well as Marx, with it; and I venture now to repeat the concluding words of the criticism I then made:

[1] For example, Vol. I, pp. 176 ff., 184, 185, 191, and often; also in the beginning of the third volume, pp. 65, 176, 177, 181.
[2] For example, Vol. I, p. 184n.
[3] As to Rodbertus, see the exhaustive account in my *Capital and Interest*, pp. 354 ff., 356n.

"They [the adherents of the exploitation theory] maintain the law that the value of all commodities rests on the working time embodied in them in order that the next moment they may attack as 'opposed to law,' 'unnatural,' and 'unjust,' all forms of value that do not harmonize with this 'law' (such as the difference in value that falls as surplus to the capitalist), and demand their abolition. Thus they first ignore the exceptions in order to proclaim their law of value as universal. And after thus assuming its universality they again draw attention to the exceptions in order to brand them as offenses against the law. This kind of argument is very much as if we were to assume that there were many foolish people in the world, and to ignore that there were also many wise ones, and then, coming to the 'universally valid law' that 'all men are foolish,' should demand the extirpation of the wise on the ground that their existence is obviously 'contrary to law.' " [1]

By his maneuver of abstraction Marx certainly gained a great tactical advantage for his own version of the case. He, "by hypothesis," shut out from his system the disturbing real world, and did not therefore, so long as he could maintain this exclusion, come into conflict with it ; and he does maintain it through the greater part of the first volume, through the whole of the second volume, and through the first quarter of the third volume. In this middle part of the Marxian system the logical development and connection present a really imposing closeness and intrinsic consistency. Marx is free to use good logic here because, by means of hypothesis, he has in advance made the facts to square with his ideas, and can therefore be true to the latter without knocking up against the former. And when Marx is free to use sound logic he does so in a truly masterly way. However wrong the starting point may be, these middle parts of the system, by their extraordinary logical consistency, permanently establish the reputation of the author as an intellectual force of

[1] *Ibid.,* p. 388.

the first rank. And it is a circumstance that has served not a little to increase the practical influence of the Marxian system that during this long middle part of his work, which, as far as intrinsic consistency is concerned, is really essentially faultless, the readers who have got happily over the difficulties at the beginning get time to accustom themselves to the Marxian world of thought and to gain confidence in his connection of ideas, which here flow so smoothly, one out of the other, and form themselves into such a well-arranged whole. It is on these readers, whose confidence has been thus won, that he makes those hard demands which he is at last obliged to bring forward in his third volume. For, long as Marx delayed to open his eyes to the facts of real life, he had to do it some time or other. He had at last to confess to his readers that in actual life commodities do not exchange, regularly and of necessity, in proportion to the working time incorporated in them, but in part exchange above and in part below this proportion, according as the capital invested demands a smaller or a larger amount of the average profit; in short that, besides working time, investment of capital forms a co-ordinate determinant of the exchange relation of commodities. From this point he was confronted with two difficult tasks. In the first place he had to justify himself to his readers for having in the earlier parts of his work and for so long taught that labor was the sole determinant of exchange relations; and secondly—what was perhaps the more difficult task—he had also to give his readers a theoretical explanation of the facts which were hostile to his theory, an explanation which certainly could not fit into his labor theory of value without leaving a residuum, but which must not, on the other hand, contradict it.

One can understand that good straightforward logic could no longer be used in these demonstrations. We now witness the counterpart to the confused beginning of the system. There Marx had to do violence to facts in order to deduce a theorem which could not be straightforwardly deduced from them, and he had to do still greater violence to logic and commit the most incredible fallacies into the bargain. Now the situation repeats itself. Now again the propositions which through two volumes have been in undisturbed possession of the field come into collision with the facts with which they are naturally as little in agreement as they were before. Nevertheless the harmony of the system has to be maintained, and it can only be maintained at the cost of the logic. The Marxian system, therefore, presents us now with a spectacle at first sight strange, but, under the circumstances described, quite natural, namely, that by far the greater part of the system is a masterpiece of close and forcible logic worthy of the intellect of its author, but that in two places —and those, alas! just the most decisive places—incredibly weak and careless reasoning is inserted. The first place is just at the beginning when the theory first separates itself from the facts, and the second is after the first quarter of the third volume when facts are again brought within the horizon of the reader. I here refer more especially to the tenth chapter of the third volume (pp. 203-234).

We have already become acquainted with one part of its contents, and we have subjected it to our criticism, the part, namely, where Marx defends himself against the accusation that there is a contradiction between the law of the price of production and the "law of value." [1] It still remains, however, to glance at the second object with which the chapter is concerned, the explanation with which Marx introduces into his system that theory of the price of production which takes account of actual conditions.[2] This consideration leads us also to one of the most instructive and most characteristic points of the Marxian system—the position of *"competition"* in the system.

[1] See above.
[2] Of course I here quite disregard comparatively small differences of opinion. I have especially refrained in the whole of this paragraph from emphasizing or even mentioning the finer shades of difference which obtain in relation to the conception of the "law of costs."

Section III

"COMPETITION," as I have already hinted, is a sort of collective name for all the psychical motives and impulses which determine the action of the dealers in the market, and which thus influence the fixing of prices. The buyer has his motives which actuate him in buying, and which provide him with a certain guide as to the prices which he is prepared to offer either at once or in the last resort. And the seller and the producer are also actuated by certain motives—motives which determine the seller to part with his commodities at a certain price and not at another price, and the producer to continue and even to extend his production when prices reach a certain level, or to suspend it when they are at a different level. In the competition between buyer and seller all these motives and determinants encounter each other, and whoever refers to competition to explain the formation of prices appeals in effect to what under a collective name is the active play of all the psychical impulses and motives which had directed both sides of the market.

Marx is now, for the most part, engaged in the endeavor to give to competition and the forces operating in it the lowest possible place in his system. He either ignores it, or, if he does not do this, he tries to belittle the manner and degree of its influence where and whenever he can. This is shown in a striking way on several occasions.

First of all he does this when he deduces his law that value is wholly labor. Every impartial person knows and sees that that influence which the quantity of labor employed exerts on the permanent level of prices of goods (an influence not really so special and peculiar as the Marxian law of value makes it appear) acts only through the play of supply and demand, that is to say, through competition. In the case of exceptional exchanges, or in the case of monopoly, prices may come into existence which (even apart from the claim of the capital invested) are out of all proportion to the working time incorporated. Marx naturally knows this too, but he makes no reference to it in his deduction of the law of value. If he had referred to it, then he would have been unable to put aside the question in what way and by what intermediate steps working time should come to be the sole influence determining the height of prices among all the motives and factors which play their part under the flag of competition. The complete analysis of those motives, which then could not have been avoided, would inevitably have placed the value in use much more in the foreground than would have suited Marx, and would have cast a different light on many things, and finally would have revealed much to which Marx did not wish to allow any weight in his system.

And so on the very occasion when, in order to give a complete and systematic explanation of his law of value, it would have been his duty to have shown the part which competition plays as intermediary, he passes away from the point without a word. Later on he does notice it, but, to judge from the place and the manner, not as if it were an important point in the theoretical system; in some casual and cursory remarks he alludes to it in a few words as something that more or less explains itself, and he does not trouble himself to go further into it.

I think that the said facts about competition are most clearly and concisely set forth by Marx in page 209 of the third volume, where the exchange of commodities at prices which approximate to their "values" and correspond therefore to the working time incorporated in them is said to be subject to the three following conditions: (1) that the exchange of commodities be not merely an *"accidental or occasional one,"* (2) that commodities "on both sides should be produced in quantities nearly proportionate to the reciprocal demand, *which itself results from the experience of both sides of the market, and which therefore grows as a result out of a sustained exchange itself"*; and (3) *"that no natural or artificial monopoly* should give to either of the contracting parties the power to sell above the value, or should force either of them to sell below the value." And so what Marx demands as a condition of his law of value coming into operation is a brisk competition on both sides which should have lasted long enough to adjust production relatively to the needs of the buyer according to the experience of the market. We must bear this passage well in mind.

No more detailed proof is added. On the contrary, a little later —indeed, just in the middle of those arguments in which, relatively speaking, he treats most exhaustively of competition, its two sides of demand and supply, and its relation to the fixing of prices—Marx expressly declines a "deeper analysis of these two social impelling forces" as "not apposite here." [1]

But this is not all. In order to belittle the importance, for the theoretical system, of supply and demand, and perhaps also to justify his neglect of these factors, Marx thought out a peculiar and remarkable theory which he develops on pages 223-224 of the third volume, after some previous slight allusions to it. He starts by saying that when one of the two factors preponderates over the other, demand over supply, for instance, or vice versa, irregular market prices are formed which deviate from the "market value," which constitutes the "point of equilibrium" for these market prices; that, on the other hand, if commodities should sell at this their normal market value, demand and supply must exactly balance each other. And to that he adds the following remarkable argument: "If demand and supply balance each other *they cease to act.* If two forces act equally in opposite directions they cancel each other—they produce no result, and phenomena occurring under these conditions *must be explained by some other agency than either of these forces.* If supply and demand cancel each other *they cease to explain anything, they do not affect the market value,* and they leave us altogether in the dark as to the reasons why the market value should express itself in just this and no other sum of money."

[1] Vol. III, p. 223. See also above.

The relation of demand to supply can be rightly used to explain the "deviations from the market value" which are due to the preponderance of one force over the other, but not the level of the market value itself.

That this curious theory squared with the Marxian system is obvious. If the relation of supply to demand had absolutely no bearing on the level of permanent prices, then Marx was quite right, in laying down his principles, not to trouble himself further with this unimportant factor, and straightway to introduce into his system the factor which, in his opinion, exercised a real influence on the degree of value, that is, labor.

It is, however, not less obvious, I think, that this curious theory is absolutely false. Its reasoning rests, as is so often the case with Marx, on a play upon words.

It is quite true that when a commodity sells at its normal market value, supply and demand must in a certain sense balance each other : that is to say, at this price, just the same quantity of the commodity is effectively demanded as is offered. But this is not only the case when commodities are sold at a normal market value, but at whatever market value they are sold, even when it is a varying irregular one. Moreover, every one knows quite well, as does Marx himself, that supply and demand are elastic quantities. In addition to the supply and demand which enters into exchange, there is always an "excluded" demand or supply, that is, a number of people who equally desire the commodities for their needs, but who will not or cannot offer the prices offered by their stronger competitors ; and a number of people who are also prepared to offer the desired commodities, only at higher prices than can be obtained in the then state of the market. But the saying that demand and supply "balance each other" does not apply absolutely to the *total* demand and supply, but only to the *successful part of it*. It is well known, however, that the business of the market consists precisely in selecting the successful part out of the total demand and the total supply, and that the most important means to this selection is the fixing of price. More commodities cannot be bought than are sold. Hence, on the two sides, only a certain fixed number of reflectors (reflectors for only a certain fixed number of commodities) can arrive at a focus. The selection of this number is accomplished by the automatic advance of prices to a point which excludes the excess in number on both sides; so that the price is at the same time too high for the excess of the would-be buyers and too low for the excess of the would-be sellers. It is not, therefore, the successful competitors only who take part in determining the level of prices, but the respective circumstances of those who are excluded have a share in it as well; [1] and on that account, if on no other, it is wrong to argue the complete suspension of the action of supply and demand from the equilibrium of the part which comes effectively into the market.

But it is wrong also for another reason. Assuming that it is only the successful part of supply and demand, being in quantitative equilibrium, that affects the fixing of price, it is quite erroneous and unscientific to assume that forces which hold each other in equilibrium therefore "cease to act." On the contrary, the state of equilibrium is precisely the result of their action, and when an explanation has to be given of this state of equilibrium with all its details—one of the most prominent of which is the height of the level in which the equilibrium was found— it certainly cannot be given "in some other way than by the agency of the two forces." On the contrary, it is only by the agency of the forces which maintain the equilibrium that it can be explained. But such abstract propositions can best be illustrated by a practical example.

---

[1] A closer analysis shows that the price must fall between the money estimates of the so-called marginal pairs, that is, between the amounts which the last actual buyer and the first would-be buyer who is excluded from the market are prepared to offer, and the amounts which the last actual seller and the first would-be seller who is excluded are prepared to take in the last resort for the commodities. For further details see my *Positive Theory of Capital*, p. 208.

Suppose we send up an air balloon. Everybody knows that a balloon rises if and because it is filled with a gas which is thinner than the atmosphere. It does not rise indefinitely, however, but only to a certain height, where it remains floating so long as nothing occurs, such as an escape of gas, to alter the conditions. Now how is the degree of altitude regulated, and by what factor is it determined? This is transparently evident. The density of the atmosphere diminishes as we rise. The balloon rises only so long as the density of the surrounding stratum of atmosphere is greater than its own density, and it ceases to rise when its own density and the density of the atmosphere hold each other in equipoise. The less dense the gas, therefore, the higher the balloon will rise, and the higher the stratum of air in which it finds the same degree of atmospheric density. It is obvious, under these circumstances, therefore, that the height to which the balloon rises cannot be explained in any other way than by considering the relative density of the balloon on one side and of the atmosphere on the other.

How does the matter appear, however, from the Marxian point of view? At a certain height both forces, density of the balloon and density of the surrounding air, are in equipoise. They, therefore, "cease to act," they "cease to explain anything," they do not affect the degree of ascent, and if we wish to explain this we must do it by "something else than the agency of these two forces." "Indeed," we say, "by what then?" Or again, when the index of a weighing machine points to 100 pounds when a body is being weighed, how are we to account for this position of the index of the weighing machine? We are *not* to account for it by the relation of the weight of the body to be weighed on the one side and the weights which serve in the weighing machine on the other, for these two forces, when the index of the weighing machine is in the position referred to, hold each other in equipoise; they therefore cease to act, and nothing can be explained from their relationship, not even the position of the index of the weighing machine.

I think the fallacy here is obvious, and that it is not less obvious that the same kind of fallacy lies at the root of the arguments by which Marx reasons away the influence of supply and demand on the level of permanent prices. Let there be no misunderstanding, however. It is by no means my opinion that a really complete and satisfying explanation of the fixing of permanent prices is contained in a reference to the formula of supply and demand. On the contrary, the opinion, which I have elsewhere often expressed at length, is that the elements which can only be roughly comprehended under the term "supply and demand" ought to be closely analyzed, and the manner and measure of their reciprocal influence exactly defined; and that in this way we should proceed to the attainment of the knowledge of those elements which exert a special influence on the state of prices. But the influence of the relation of supply and demand which Marx reasons away is an indispensable link in this further and more profound explanation; it is not a side issue, but one that goes to the heart of the subject.

Let us take up again the threads of our argument. Various things have shown us how hard Marx tries to make the influence of supply and demand retire into the background of his system, and now at the remarkable turn which his system takes after the first quarter of the third volume he is confronted by the task of explaining why the permanent prices of commodities do not gravitate towards the incorporated quantity of labor but towards the "prices of production" which deviate from it.

He declares competition to be the force which causes this. Competition reduces the original rates of profit, which were different for the different branches of production according to the different organic compositions of the capitals, to a common average rate of profit,[1] and consequently the prices must in the long run gravitate towards the prices of production yielding the one equal average profit.

[1] See above.

Let us hasten to settle some points which are important to the understanding of this explanation.

First, it is certain that a reference to competition is in effect nothing else than a reference to the action of supply and demand. In the passage already mentioned, in which Marx describes most concisely the process of the equalization of the rates of profit by the competition of capitals (III, 230), he expressly says that this process is brought about by "such a relation of supply to demand that the average profit is made equal in the different spheres of production, and that therefore values change into prices of production."

Secondly, it is certain that, as regards this process, it is not a question of mere *fluctuations* round the center of gravitation contemplated in the theory of the first two volumes, that is, round the incorporated working time, but a question of a *definitive forcing* of prices to another permanent center of gravitation, the price of production.

And now question follows on question.

If, according to Marx, the relation of supply and demand exerts no influence at all on the level of permanent prices, how can competition, which is identical with this relation, be the power which shifts the level of the permanent prices from the level of "value" to a level so different as that of the price of production?

Do we not rather see, in this forced and inconsistent appeal to competition as the *deus ex machina* which drives the permanent prices from that center of gravitation which is in keeping with the theory of embodied labor to another center, an involuntary confession that the social forces which govern actual life contain in themselves, and bring into action, some elementary determinants of exchange relations which *cannot* be reduced to working time, and that consequently the analysis of the original theory which yielded working time alone as the basis of exchange relations was an incomplete one which did not correspond with the facts?

And further: Marx has told us himself, and we have carefully noted the passage,[1] that commodities exchange approximately to their values only when a brisk competition exists. Thus he, at that time, appealed to competition as a factor which tends to push the prices of commodities towards their "values." And now we learn, on the contrary, that competition is a force which pushes the prices of commodities away from their values and on to their prices of production. These statements, moreover, are found in one and the same chapter—the tenth chapter, destined, it would seem, to an unhappy notoriety. Can they be reconciled? And, if Marx perhaps thought that he could find a reconciliation in the view that one proposition applied to primitive conditions and the other to developed modern society, must we not point out to him that in the first chapter of his work he did not deduce his theory that value was wholly labor from a *Robinsonade,* but from the conditions of a society in which a "capitalist mode of production prevails" and the "wealth" of which "appears as an immense collection of commodities"? And does he not demand of us throughout his whole work that we should view the conditions of our modern society in the light of his theory of labor, and judge them by it? But when we ask where, according to his own statements, we are to seek in modern society for the region in which his law of value is in force, we ask in vain. For either there is no competition, in which case commodities do not at all exchange according to their values, says Marx (III, 209); or competition exists, and precisely then, he states, they still less exchange according to their values, but according to their prices of production (III, 230).

And so in the unfortunate tenth chapter contradiction is heaped upon contradiction. I will not prolong the already lengthy inquiry by counting up all the lesser contradictions and inaccuracies with which this chapter abounds. I think every one who reads the chapter with an impartial mind will get the im-

---

[1] See above, pp. 93 ff.

pression that the writing is, so to speak, demoralized. Instead of the severe, pregnant, careful style, instead of the iron logic to which we are accustomed in the most brilliant parts of Marx's works, we have here an uncertain and desultory manner not only in the reasoning but even in the use of technical terms. How striking, for instance, is the constantly changing conception of the terms "supply" and "demand," which at one time are presented to us, quite rightly, as elastic quantities, with differences of intensity, but at another are regarded, after the worst manner of a long-exploded "vulgar economy," as simple quantities. Or how unsatisfying and inconsistent is the description of the factors which govern the market value, if the different portions of the mass of commodities which come into the market are created under unequal conditions of production, etc.

The explanation of this feature of the chapter cannot be found simply in the fact that it was written by Marx when he was growing old; for even in later parts there are many splendidly written arguments; and even this unfortunate chapter, of which obscure hints were already scattered here and there in the first volume,[1] must have been *thought out* earlier. Marx's writing is confused and vacillating here because he could not venture to write clearly and definitely without open contradiction and retractation. If at the time when he was dealing with actual exchange relations—those manifested in real life—he had pursued the subject with the same luminous penetration and thoroughness with which he followed, through two volumes, the hypothesis that value is labor to its utmost logical conclusion; if at this juncture he had given to the important term "competition" a scientific import, by a careful economico-psychological analysis of the social motive forces which come into action under that comprehensive name; if he had not halted or rested, so long as a link in the argument remained unexplained, or a consequence not carried to its logical conclusion; or so long as one relation

[1] For example, Vol. I, pp. 184n, 244n.

appeared dark and contradictory—and almost every word of this tenth chapter challenges a deeper inquiry or explanation such as this—he would have been driven step by step to the exposition of a system altogether different in purport from that of his original system, nor would he have been able to avoid the open contradiction and withdrawal of the main proposition of the original system. This could only be avoided by confusion and mystification. Marx must often instinctively have felt this, even if he did not know it, when he expressly declined the deeper analysis of the social motive forces.

Herein lies, I believe, the alpha and omega of all that is fallacious, contradictory, and vague in the treatment of his subject by Marx. His system is not in close touch with facts. Marx has not deduced from facts the fundamental principles of his system, either by means of a sound empiricism or a solid economico-psychological analysis; he founds it on no firmer ground than a formal dialectic. This is the great radical fault of the Marxian system at its birth; from it all the rest necessarily springs. The system runs in one direction, facts go in another; and they cross the course of the system sometimes here, sometimes there, and on each occasion the original fault begets a new fault. The conflict of system and facts must be kept from view, so that the matter is shrouded either in darkness or vagueness, or it is turned and twisted with the same tricks of dialectic as at the outset; or where none of this avails we have a contradiction. Such is the character of the tenth chapter of Marx's third volume. It brings the long-deferred bad harvest, which grew by necessity out of the bad seed.

Chapter Five

WERNER SOMBART'S APOLOGY

An apologist of Marx, as intelligent as he is ardent, has lately appeared in the person of Werner Sombart.[1] His apology, however, shows one peculiar feature. In order to be able to defend Marx's doctrines he has first to put a new interpretation upon them.

Let us go at once to the main point. Sombart admits (and even adds some very subtle arguments to the proof)[2] that the Marxian law of value is false if it claims to be in harmony with actual experience. He says (p. 573) of the Marxian law of value that it "is *not* exhibited in the exchange relation of capitalistically produced commodities," that it "does *not* by any means indicate the point towards which market prices gravitate," that "*just as little* does it act as a factor of distribution in the division of the yearly social product," and that "it *never comes into evidence anywhere*" (p. 577). The "outlawed value" has only "one place of refuge left—*the thought of the theoretical economist. . . .* If we want to sum up the characteristics of Marx's value, we would say, *his value is a fact not of experience but of thought*" (p. 574).

What Sombart means by this "existence in thought" we shall

[1] See the already repeatedly mentioned article "Zur Kritik," pp. 555 ff.
[2] See above, pp. 49-51.

see directly; but first we must stop for a moment to consider the admission that the Marxian value has no existence in the world of real phenomena. I am somewhat curious to know whether the Marxists will ratify this admission. It may well be doubted, as Sombart himself had to quote a protest from the Marxian camp, occasioned by an utterance of C. Schmidt and raised in advance against such a view. "The law of value is not a law of our thought merely; . . . the law of value is a law of a very real nature: it is a natural law of human action."[1] I think it also very questionable whether Marx himself would have ratified the admission. It is Sombart himself who again, with noteworthy frankness, gives the reader a whole list of passages from Marx which make this interpretation difficult.[2] For my own part I hold it to be wholly irreconcilable with the letter and spirit of the Marxian teaching.

Let any one read without bias the arguments with which Marx develops his value of theory. He begins his inquiry, as he himself says, in the domain of "capitalistically organized society, whose wealth is an immense collection of commodities," with the analysis of a commodity (I, 41). In order to "get on the track" of value he starts from the exchange relation of the commodity (I, 45). Does he start from an actual exchange relation, I ask, or from an imaginary one? If he had said or meant the latter, no reader would have thought it worth while to pursue so idle a speculation. He does indeed make very decided reference —as was inevitable—to the phenomena of the actual economic world. The exchange relation of two commodities, he says, can always be represented by an equation: thus 1 quarter wheat = 1 cwt. iron. "What does this equation prove? *That a common factor of the same magnitude exists* in both things, and each of the two, *in so far as it is an exchange value, must be* reducible to this third," which third, as we learn on the next page, is labor of the same quantity.

[1] Hugo Landé, *Die Neue Zeit*, Vol. XI, p. 591.
[2] "Zur Kritik," pp. 575, 584 ff.

If you maintain that the same quantity of labor *exists* in things made equal in exchange, and that these things *must* be reducible to equal amounts of labor, you are claiming for these conditions an existence in the real world and not merely in thought. Marx's former line of argument, we must bear in mind, would have been quite impossible if by the side of it he had wished to propound, for actual exchange relations, the dogma that products of *unequal* amounts of labor exchange, on principle, with each other. If he had admitted this notion (and the conflict with facts with which I reproach him lies precisely in his not admitting it), he would certainly have come to quite different conclusions. Either he would have been obliged to declare that the so-called equalization in exchange is no true equation, and does not admit of the conclusion that "a common factor *of equal magnitude*" is present in the exchanged things, or he would have been obliged to come to the conclusion that the sought-for common factor of equal magnitude is *not*, and could not be *labor*. In any case it would have been impossible for him to have continued to reason as he did.

And Marx goes on to say very decidedly on numerous occasions that his "value" lies at the root of exchange relations, so that indeed products of equal amounts of labor are "equivalents," and as such exchange for each other.[1] In many places,

---

[1] For example, Vol. I, p. 58; Equivalent = *Exchangeable*. "It is only as a value that it [linen] can be brought into relation with the coat as possessing an *equal value* or *exchangeability with it*. . . . When the coat as a thing of value is placed on an equality with the linen, the work existing in the former is made equal to the work existing in the latter." See besides pp. 60, 64 (the proportion in which coats and linen are exchangeable depends on the degree of value of the coats), p. 68 (where Marx declares human work to be the "real element of equality" in the house and the beds which exchange with each other), pp. 73, 74, 75, 76, 77, 84, 85, 86, 87 (analysis of the price of commodities [but still of actual prices only!] leads to the determining of the amount of value), p. 94 (exchange value is the social contrivance for *expressing the labor* expended on a thing), p. 114 ("the price is the money name for the work realized in a commodity"), p. 176 ("the same exchange value, that is, the same quantum of realized social work"), p. 208 ("According to the universal law of value, for example, 10 pounds of yarn are an

some of which are quoted by Sombart himself,[1] he claims that his law of value possesses the character and the potency of a *law of nature*, "it forces its way as the law of gravity does when the house comes down over one's head." [2] Even in the third volume he distinctly sets forth the actual conditions (they amount to a brisk competition on both sides) which must obtain "in order that the prices at which commodities exchange with each other should correspond approximately to their value," and explains further that this "naturally only signifies that their value is the center of gravitation round which their prices move" (III, 209-210).

We may mention in this connection that Marx also often quotes with approval older writers who maintained the proposition that the exchange value of goods was determined by the labor embodied in them, and maintained it undoubtedly as a proposition which was in harmony with actual exchange relations.[3]

Sombart himself, moreover, notes an argument of Marx's in which he quite distinctly claims for his law of value an "empirical" and "historical" truth (III, 209, in connection with III, 231 ff.).

And finally, if Marx claimed only a validity in thought and not in things for his law of value, what meaning would there have been in the painful efforts we have described, with which he sought to prove that, in spite of the theory of the price of production, his law of value governed actual exchange relations, because it regulated the movement of prices on the one side, and on the other the prices of production themselves?

In short, if there is any rational meaning in the tissue of logical arguments on which Marx founds his theory of labor

---

equivalent for 10 pounds of cotton and a quarter of a spindle . . . if the same working time is needed to produce both sides of this equation"), and repeatedly in the same sense.

[1] *Ibid.*, p. 575.

[2] Vol. I, p. 86.

[3] For example, Vol. I, p. 46n.

value I do not believe he taught or could have taught it in the more modest sense which Sombart now endeavors to attribute to it. For the rest, it is a matter which Sombart may himself settle with the followers of Marx. For those who, like myself, consider the Marxian theory of value a failure, it is of no importance whatever. For either Marx has maintained his law of value in the literal sense, that it corresponds with reality, and if so we agree with Sombart's view that, maintained in this sense, it is false; or he did not ascribe any real authority to it, and then, in my opinion, it cannot be construed in any sense whatever which would give it the smallest scientific importance. It is practically and theoretically a nullity.

It is true that about this Sombart is of a very different opinion. I willingly accept an express invitation from this able and learned man (who expects much for the progress of science from a keen and kindly encounter of opinions) to reconsider the "criticism of Marx" on the ground of his new interpretation. I am also quite pleased to settle this particular point with him. I do so with the full consciousness that I am no longer dealing with a "criticism of Marx," such as Sombart invited me to revise on the strength of his new interpretation, but am dispensing purely a "criticism of Sombart."

What, then, according to Sombart, does the existence of value as a "fact of thought" mean? It means that the "idea of value is an aid to our thought which we employ in order to make the phenomena of economic life comprehensible." More exactly, the function of the idea of value is "to cause to pass before us, defined by quantity, the commodities which, as goods for use, are different in quality. It is clear that I fulfill this postulate if I imagine cheese, silk, and blacking as nothing but products of human labor in the abstract, and only relate them to each other quantitatively as quantities of labor, the amount of the quantity being determined by a third factor, common to all and measured by units of time." [1]

[1] "Zur Kritik," p. 574.

So far all goes well, till we come to a certain little hitch. For certainly it is admissible in itself, for some scientific purposes, to abstract from all sorts of differences, which things may exhibit in one way or another, and to consider in them only one property, which is common to them all, and which, as a common property, furnishes the ground for comparison, commensurability, etc. In this very way mechanical dynamics, for instance, for the purpose of many of its problems rightly abstracts altogether from the form, color, density, and structure of bodies in motion, and regards them only as masses; propelled billiard balls, flying cannon balls, running children, trains in motion, falling stones, and moving planets, are looked upon simply as moving bodies. It is not less admissible or less to the purpose to conceive cheese, silk, blacking, as "nothing but products of human labor in the abstract."

The hitch begins when Sombart, like Marx, claims for *this* idea the name of the idea of *value*. This step of his—to go closely into the matter—admits conceivably of two constructions. The word "value," as we know it, in its double application to value in use and value in exchange, is already used in scientific as well as in ordinary language to denote definite phenomena. Sombart's nomenclature, therefore, involves the claim either that that property of things, namely, the being a product of labor, which is alone taken into consideration, is the deciding factor for all cases of value in the ordinary scientific sense, and thus represents, for example, the phenomena of exchange value; or, without any *arrière pensée* of this kind, his nomenclature may be a purely arbitrary one; and, unfortunately for nomenclatures of that kind, there is as guide no fixed compulsory law, but only good judgment and a sense of fitness.

If we take the second of the two constructions, if the application of the term "value" to "embodied labor" does not carry with it the claim that embodied labor is the substance of exchange value, then the matter would be very harmless. It would be only a perfectly admissible abstraction, connected, it is true, with a most unpractical, inappropriate, and misleading nomenclature. It would be as if it suddenly occurred to a natural philosopher to give to the different bodies which, by abstraction of form, color, structure, etc., he had conceived of solely as masses, the name of "active forces," a term which we know has already established rights, denoting a function of mass and velocity, that is to say, something very different from mere mass. There would be no scientific error in this, however, only a (practically very dangerous) gross inappropriateness of nomenclature.

But our case is obviously different. It is different with Marx and different with Sombart. And here, therefore, the hitch assumes larger proportions.

My esteemed opponent will certainly admit that we cannot make any abstraction we like to suit any scientific purpose we like. For instance, to start by conceiving the different bodies as "nothing but masses," which is legitimate in certain dynamic problems, would be plainly inadmissible in regard to acoustic or optical problems. Even within dynamics it is certainly inadmissible to abstract from shape and consistency, when setting forth, for instance, the law of wedges. These examples prove that even in science "thoughts" and "logic" cannot wholly depart from facts. For science, too, the saying holds good, *"Est modus in rebus, sunt certi denique fines."* And I think that I may show, without danger of a contradiction from my esteemed opponent, that those "definite limits" consist in this, that in all cases only those peculiarities may be disregarded which are irrelevant to the phenomenon under investigation : and I emphasize, *really, actually* irrelevant. On the other hand, one must leave to the remainder—to the skeleton, as it were—of the conception which is to be subjected to further study everything that is actually relevant on the concrete side. Let us apply this to our own case.

The Marxian teaching in a very emphatic way bases the scientific investigation and criticism of the *exchange relations of commodities* on the conception of commodities as "nothing but products." Sombart endorses this, and in certain rather indefinite statements—which, on account of their indefiniteness, I do not discuss with him—he even goes so far as to view the foundations of the whole *economic existence* of man in the light of that abstraction.[1]

That embodied labor alone is of importance in the first case (exchange), or even in the second case (economic existence), Sombart himself does not venture to affirm. He contents himself with asserting that with that conception the "fact *most important* economically and objectively" is brought into prominence.[2] I will not dispute this statement, only it must certainly not be taken to mean that all the other important facts besides labor are so completely subordinate that they might be almost if not altogether disregarded, from their insignificance. Nothing could be less true. It is in the highest degree important for the economic existence of human beings whether, for instance, the land which they inhabit is like the valley of the Rhone, or the desert of Sahara, or Greenland; and it is also a matter of great importance whether human labor is aided by a previously accumulated stock of goods—a factor which also cannot be referred exclusively to labor. Labor is certainly *not* the objectively most important circumstance for many goods, especially as regards exchange relations. We may mention, as instances, trunks of old oak trees, beds of coal, and plots of land; and even if it be admitted that it is so for the greater part of commodities, still the fact must be emphasized that the influence of the other factors, which are determining factors along with labor, is so important that actual exchange relations diverge considerably from the line which would correspond with the embodied labor by itself.

But if work is not the sole important factor in exchange

1 For example, pp. 576, 577.
2 P. 576.

relations and exchange value, but only *one*, even though the most powerful, important factor among others—a *primus inter pares*, as it were—then, according to what has been already said, it is simply incorrect and inadmissible to base upon labor alone a conception of value which is synonymous with exchange value; it is just as wrong and inadmissible as if a natural philosopher were to base the "active force" on the mass of the bodies alone, and were by abstraction to eliminate velocity from his calculation.

I am truly astonished that Sombart did not see or feel this, and all the more so because in formulating his opinions he incidentally made use of expressions the incongruity of which, with his own premises, is so striking that one would have thought he could not fail to be struck by it. His starting point is that the character of commodities, as products of social labor, represents the economically and objectively most important feature in them, and he proves it by saying that the supply to mankind of economic goods, *"natural conditions being equal,"* is *in the main* dependent on the development of the social productive power of labor, and thence he draws the conclusion that this feature finds its adequate economic expression in the conception of value which rests upon labor alone. This thought he twice repeats on pages 576 and 577 in somewhat different terms, but the expression "adequate" recurs each time unchanged.

Now, I ask, is it not on the contrary evident that the conception of value as grounded upon labor alone is *not* adequate to the premise that labor is merely the most important among several important facts, but goes far beyond it? It would have been adequate only if the premise had affirmed that labor is the only important fact. But this Sombart by no means asserted. He maintains that the significance of labor is very great in regard to exchange relations and for human life generally, greater than the significance of any other factor; and for such a condition of things the Marxian formula of value, according to which labor alone is all-important, is an expression as little adequate as it would be to put down $1 + \frac{1}{2} + \frac{1}{4}$ as equal to 1 only.

Not only is the assertion of the "adequate" conception of value not apposite, but it seems to me that there lurks behind it a little touch of wiliness—quite unintended by Sombart. While expressly admitting that the Marxian value does *not* stand the test of facts, Sombart demanded an asylum for the "outlawed" value in the *thought* of the theoretical economist. From this asylum, however, he unexpectedly makes a clever sally into the concrete world when he again maintains that his conception of value is adequate to the objectively most relevant fact, or, in more pretentious words, that "*a technical fact which objectively governs* the economic existence of human society has found in it its adequate economic expression" (p. 577).

I think one may justly protest against such a proceeding. It is a case of one thing or the other. Either the Marxian value claims to be in harmony with actual facts, in which case it should come out boldly with this assertion and not seek to escape the thorough test of facts by entrenching itself behind the position that it had not meant to affirm any actual fact but only to construct "an aid for our thought"; or else it does seek to protect itself behind this rampart, it does avoid the thorough test of fact, and in that case it ought not to claim by the indirect means of vague assertions a kind of concrete significance which could justly belong to it only if it had stood the testing by facts which it expressly avoided. The phrase "the adequate expression of the *ruling fact*" signifies nothing less than that Marx is *in the main* even *empirically right*. Well and good. If Sombart or any one else wishes to affirm that let him do so openly. Let him leave off playing with the mere "fact of thought" and put the matter plainly to the test of actual fact. This test would show what the difference is between the complete facts and the "adequate expression of the ruling fact." Until then, however, I may content myself with asserting that in regard to Sombart's views we have to deal not with a harmless variation of a per-

missible but merely inappropriately named abstraction, but
with a pretentious incursion into the domain of the actual, for
which all justification by evidence is omitted and even evaded.

There is another inadmissibly pretentious assertion of Marx's
which I think Sombart has accepted without sufficient criticism;
the statement that it is only by conceiving commodities as
"nothing but products" of social labor that it becomes possible
to our thought to bring them into quantitative relation with
each other—to make them "commensurable," and, therefore,
"to render" the phenomena of the economic world "accessible"
to our thought.[1] Would Sombart have found it possible to accept
this assertion if he had subjected it to criticism? Could he really
have thought that it is only by means of the Marxian idea of
value that exchange relations are made accessible to scientific
thought, or not at all? I cannot believe it. Marx's well-known
dialectical argument on page 44 of the first volume can have
had no convincing power for a Sombart. Sombart sees and
knows as well as I do that not only products of labor, but pure
products of nature too, are put into quantitative relation in
exchange, and are therefore practically commensurable with
each other as well as with the products of labor. And yet, according to him, we cannot conceive of them as commensurable
except by reference to an attribute which they do not possess,
and which, though it can be ascribed to products of labor as
far as quality is concerned, cannot be imputed to them in regard
to quantity since, as has also been admitted, products of labor
do *not* exchange in proportion to the labor embodied in them.
Should not that rather be a sign to the unbiased theorist that,
in spite of Marx, the true common denominator—the true common factor in exchange—has still to be sought for, and sought
for in another direction than that taken by Marx?

[1] *Ibid.*, pp. 574, 582. Sombart has not asserted this in so many words in his
own name, but he approves a statement of C. Schmidt to this effect, and of
which he only corrects an unimportant detail (p. 574). He says, moreover,
that Marx's doctrine of value "performs" just this "service" (p. 582), and at
all events he refrains entirely from denying it.

This leads me to a last point on which I must touch in regard to Sombart. Sombart wishes to trace back the opposition which exists between the Marxian system on the one side, and the adverse theoretical systems—especially of the so-called Austrian economists—on the other, to a dispute about method. Marx, he says, represents an extreme objectivity. We others represent a subjectivity which runs into psychology. Marx does not trace out the motives which determine individual subjects as economic agents in their mode of action, but he seeks the objective factors, the "economic conditions," which are *independent* of the will, and, I may add, often also of the knowledge, of the individual. He seeks to discover "what goes on beyond the control of the individual by the power of relations which are *independent* of him." We, on the contrary, "try to explain the processes of economic life in the last resort by a reference to the mind of the economic subject," and "plant the laws of economic life on a psychological basis." [1]

That is certainly one of the many subtle and ingenious observations which are to be found in Sombart's writings; but in spite of its essential soundness it does not seem to me to meet the main point. It does not meet it in regard to the past by explaining the position taken up hitherto by the critics towards Marx, and therefore it does not meet it as regards the future, demanding, as it does, an entirely new era of Marxian criticism, which has still to begin, for which there is "as good as no preparatory work done," [2] and in regard to which it would be necessary to decide first of all what is to be its method. [3]

The state of things appears to me to be rather this: The difference pointed out by Sombart in the method of investigation certainly exists. But the "old" criticism of Marx did not, so far as I personally can judge, attack his choice of method, but his mistakes in the application of his chosen method. As I have

[1] *Ibid.*, pp. 591 ff.
[2] *Ibid.*, p. 556.
[3] Pp. 593 ff.

no right to speak of other critics of Marx I must speak of myself. Personally, as regards the question of method, I am in the position adopted by the literary man in the story in regard to literature: he allowed every kind of literature with the exception of the *"genre ennuyeux."* I allow every kind of method so long as it is practiced in such a way as to produce some good results. I have nothing whatever to say against the objective method. I believe that in the region of those phenomena which are concerned with human action it can be an aid to the attainment of real knowledge. That certain objective factors can enter into systematic connection with typical human actions, while those who are acting under the influence of the connection are not clearly conscious of it, I willingly admit, and I have myself drawn attention to such phenomena. For instance, when statistics prove that suicides are specially numerous in certain months, say July and November, or that the number of marriages rises and falls according as harvests are plentiful or the reverse, I am convinced that most of those who swell the contingent of suicides that occur in the months of July and November never realize that it is July and November; and also that the decision of those who are anxious to marry is not directly affected by the consideration that the means of subsistence are temporarily cheaper.[1] At the same time the discovery of such

[1] Somehow or other indeed an influence proceeding from the objective factor, and having a symptomatic connection with it, must produce effects on the actors; for instance, in the examples given in the test, the effect on the nerves of the heat of July, or the depressing, melancholy autumn weather, may increase the tendency to suicide. Then the influence coming from the "objective factor" issues, as it were, in a more general typical stimulus, such as derangement of the nerves or melancholy, and in this way affects action. I maintain firmly (in opposition to Sombart's observation, p. 593) that conformity to law in outward action is not to be expected without conformity to law in inward stimulus; but at the same time (and this will perhaps satisfy Sombart from the standpoint of his own method) I hold it to be quite possible that we can observe objective conformities to law in human action and fix them inductively without knowing and understanding their origin in inward stimulus. Therefore there is no law-determined action without law-determined stimulus, but yet there is law-determined action without knowledge of the stimulus of it.

an objective connection is undoubtedly of scientific value.

At this juncture, however, I must make several reservations—self-evident reservations, I think. First, it seems clear to me that the knowledge of such an objective connection, without the knowledge of the subjective links which help to form the chain of causation, is by no means the highest degree of knowledge, but that a full comprehension will only be attained by a knowledge of both the internal and external links of the chain. And so it seems to me that the obvious answer to Sombart's question ("whether the objective movement in the science of political economy is justified as exclusive, or as simply complementary?" [1]) is, that the objective movement can be justified only as complementary.

Secondly, I think, but as it is a matter of opinion I do not wish to press the point with opponents, that it is just in the region of economics, where we have to deal so largely with conscious and calculated human action, that the first of the two sources of knowledge, the objective source, can at the best contribute a very poor and, especially when standing alone, an altogether inadequate part of the total of attainable knowledge.

Thirdly—and this concerns the criticism of Marx in particular—I must ask with all plainness that if any use is made of the objective method it should be the right use. If external objective connections are shown to exist, which, like fate, control action with or without the knowledge, with or without the will of the doer, let them be shown to exist in their correctness. And Marx has not done this. He has not proved his fundamental proposition that labor alone governs exchange relations either objectively, from the external, tangible, objective world of facts (with which on the contrary this proposition is in opposition), or subjectively, from the motives of the exchanging parties; but he gives it to the world in the form of an abortive dialectic, more arbitrary and untrue to facts than has probably ever before been known in the history of our science.

[1] *Ibid.*, p. 593.

And one thing more. Marx did not hold fast to the "objective" pale. He could not help referring to the motives of the operators as to an active force in his system. He does this pre-eminently by his appeal to "competition." Is it too much to demand that if he introduces subjective interpolations into his system they should be correct, well founded, and non-contradictory? And this reasonable demand Marx has continually contravened. It is because of these offenses with which, I say again, the choice of method has nothing to do, but which are forbidden by the laws of every method, that I have opposed and do oppose the Marxian theory as a wrong theory. It represents, in my opinion, the one forbidden *genre*—the *genre, wrong* theories.

I am, and have long been, at the standpoint towards which Sombart seeks to direct the future criticism of Marx, which he thinks has still to be originated. He thinks "that a sympathetic study and criticism of the Marxian system ought to be attempted in the following way: is the objective movement in the science of political economy justified as exclusive or as complementary? If an affirmative answer be given, then it may further be asked: is the Marxian method of a quantitative measurement of the economic facts by means of the idea of value as an aid to thought demanded? If so, is labor properly chosen as the substance of the idea of value? . . . If it is, can the Marxian reasoning, the edifice of system erected on it, its conclusions, etc., be disputed?"

In my own mind I long ago answered the first question of method in favor of a justification of the objective method as "complementary." I was, and am, also equally certain that, to keep to Sombart's words, "a quantitative measurement of economic facts is afforded by *an* idea of value as an aid to thought." To the third question, however, the question whether it is right to select labor as the substance of this idea of value, I have long given a decidedly negative answer; and the further question, the question whether the Marxian reasoning, conclusions, etc., can be disputed, I answer as decidedly in the affirmative.

What will be the final judgment of the world? Of that I have no manner of doubt. The Marxian system has a past and a present, but no abiding future. Of all sorts of scientific systems those which, like the Marxian system, are based on a hollow dialectic, are most surely doomed. A clever dialectic may make a temporary impression on the human mind, but cannot make a lasting one. In the long run facts and the secure linking of causes and effects win the day. In the domain of natural science such a work as Marx's would even now be impossible. In the very young social sciences it was able to attain influence, great influence, and it will probably only lose it very slowly, and that because it has its most powerful support not in the convinced intellect of its disciples, but in their hearts, their wishes, and their desires. It can also subsist for a long time on the large capital of authority which it has gained over many people. In the prefatory remarks to this article I said that Marx had been very fortunate as an author, and it appears to me that a circumstance which has contributed not a little to this good fortune is the fact that the conclusion of his system has appeared ten years after his death, and almost thirty years after the appearance of his first volume. If the teaching and the definitions of the third volume had been presented to the world simultaneously with the first volume, there would have been few unbiased readers, I think, who would not have felt the logic of the first volume to be somewhat doubtful. Now a belief in an authority which has been rooted for thirty years forms a bulwark against the incursions of critical knowledge—a bulwark that will surely but slowly be broken down.

But even when this will have happened socialism will certainly not be overthrown with the Marxian system,—neither practical nor theoretical socialism. As there was a socialism before Marx, so there will be one after him. That there is vital force in socialism is shown, in spite of all exaggerations, not only by the renewed vitality which economic theory has undeniably gained by the appearance of the theoretical socialists, but also by the celebrated "drop of social oil" with which the measures of practical statesmanship are nowadays everywhere lubricated, and in many cases not to their disadvantage. What there is, then, of vital force in socialism, I say, the wiser minds among its leaders will not fail in good time to try to connect with a scientific system more likely to live. They will try to replace the supports which have become rotten. What purification of fermenting ideas will result from this connection the future will show. We may hope perhaps that things will not always go round and round in the same circle, that some errors may be shaken off for ever, and that some knowledge will be added permanently to the store of positive attainment, no longer to be disputed even by party passion.

Marx, however, will maintain a permanent place in the history of the social sciences for the same reasons and with the same mixture of positive and negative merits as his prototype Hegel. Both of them were philosophical geniuses. Both of them, each in his own domain, had an enormous influence upon the thought and feeling of whole generations, one might almost say even upon the spirit of the age. The specific theoretical work of each was a most ingeniously conceived structure, built up by a fabulous power of combination, of innumerable storeys of thought, held together by a marvelous mental grasp, but—a house of cards.

BÖHM-BAWERK'S CRITICISM OF MARX

BY Rudolf Hilferding

THE publication of the third volume of *Capital* has made hardly any impression upon bourgeois economic science. We have seen nothing of the "jubilant hue and cry" anticipated by Sombart.[1] No struggle of intellects has taken place; there was no contest *in majorem scientiae gloriam.* For in the *theoretical* field bourgeois economics no longer engages in blithe and joyous fights. As spokesman for the bourgeoisie, it enters the lists only where the bourgeoisie has practical interests to defend. In the economico-political struggles of the day it faithfully reflects the conflict of interests of the dominant cliques, but it shuns the attempt to consider the totality of social relationships, for it rightly feels that any such consideration would be incompatible with its continued existence as *bourgeois* economics. Even where the bourgeois economists, compiling their "systems" or writing their "sketches," must perforce speak of the relationships of the whole, the only whole they succeed in presenting is laboriously pieced together out of its separate parts. They have ceased to deal with principles; they have ceased to be systematic; they have become eclectics and syncretists. Dietzel, author of *Theoretische So-*

---

[1] Werner Sombart, "Zur Kritik des ökonomischen Systems von Karl Marx," *Archiv für Soziale Gesetzgebung und Statistik,* Vol. VII (1894), pp. 555-594.

zialökonomie, is perfectly logical when, making the best of a bad business, he raises eclecticism to the rank of a principle.

The only exception is the psychological school of political economy. The adherents of this school resemble the classical economists and the Marxists in that they endeavor to apprehend economic phenomena from a unitary outlook. Opposing Marxism with a circumscribed theory, their criticism is systematic in character, and their critical attitude is forced upon them because they have started from totally different premises. As early as 1884, in his *Capital and Interest,* Böhm-Bawerk joined issue with the first volume of *Capital,* and soon after the publication of the third volume of that work he issued a detailed criticism [1] the substance of which was reproduced in the second edition of his *Capital and Interest* [German edition 1900].[2] He believes he has proved the untenability of economic Marxism, and confidently announces that "the beginning of the end of the labor theory of value" has been inaugurated by the publication of the third volume of *Capital.*

Since his criticism deals with principles, since he does not attack isolated and arbitrarily selected points or conclusions, but questions and reflects as untenable the very foundation of the Marxist system, possibility is afforded for a fruitful discussion. But since the Marxist system has to be dealt with in its entirety, this discussion must be more detailed than that which is requisite to meet the objections of the eclectics, objections based upon misunderstanding and concerned only with individual details.

[1] Reprinted above. All page references to *Karl Marx and the Close of His System* refer to the present volume.—Ed.
[2] All Hilferding's subsequent references to this book are from the second German edition (1900), and it is therefore impossible for us to refer the reader to Smart's English translation, made from the first German edition (1884). A third German edition was published in 1914.—E. & C. P.

Chapter One

VALUE AS AN ECONOMIC CATEGORY

THE analysis of the commodity constitutes the starting point of the Marxist system. Böhm-Bawerk's criticism is primarily leveled against this analysis.

Böhm-Bawerk contends that Marx fails to adduce either an empirical or a psychological proof of his thesis that the principle of value is to be sought in labor. He "prefers another, and for such a subject somewhat singular line of evidence—the method of a purely logical proof, a dialectic deduction from the very nature of exchange." [1]

Marx had found in Aristotle the idea that exchange cannot exist without equality, and equality cannot exist without commensurability. Starting with this idea, he conceives the exchange of two commodities under the form of an equation, and from this infers that a common factor of the same amount must exist in the things exchanged and thereby equated, and then proceeds to search for this common factor to which the two equated things must, as exchange values, be reducible. Now according to Böhm-Bawerk the most vulnerable point in the Marxist theory is to be found in the logical and systematic processes of distillation by means of which Marx obtains the sought-for

---

[1] *Geschichte und Kritik der Kapitalzins-Theorien*, 2nd ed., pp. 511 ff. Above, pp. 68 ff.

"common factor" in labor. They exhibit, he declares, almost as many cardinal errors as there are points in the argument. From the beginning Marx only puts into the sieve those exchangeable [should read, "interchangeable," R. H.] things which he desires finally to winnow out as "the common factor," and he leaves all the others outside. That is to say, he limits from the outset the field of his search to "commodities," considering these solely as the products of labor contrasted with the gifts of nature. Now it stands to reason, continues Böhm-Bawerk, that if exchange really means an equalization, which assumes the existence of "a common factor of the same amount," this common factor must be sought and found in every species of goods which is brought into exchange, not only in products of labor, but also in gifts of nature, such as the soil, wood in trees, water power, etc. To exclude these exchangeable goods is a gross error of method, and the exclusion of the gifts of nature is the less to be justified because many natural gifts, such as the soil, are among the most important objects of property and commerce, and also because it is impossible to affirm that in nature's gifts exchange values [this of course should be "prices"! R. H.] are always established arbitrarily and by accident. Marx is likewise careful to avoid mentioning that he excludes from investigation a part of exchangeable goods. In this case, as in so many others, he manages to glide with eel-like dialectic skill over the difficult points of his argument. He omits to call his readers' attention to the fact that his idea of "commodities" is narrower than that of exchangeable goods as a whole. Nay, more, he continually endeavors to obliterate the distinction. He is compelled to take this course, for unless Marx had confined his research, at the decisive point, to products of labor, if he had sought for the common factor in the "exchangeable" gifts of nature as well, it would have become obvious that labor cannot be the common factor. Had he carried out this limitation quite clearly and openly, the gross fallacy of method would inevitably have struck both himself and his readers. The trick could only have been performed, as Marx performed it, with the aid of the marvelous dialectic skill wherewith he glides swiftly and lightly over the knotty point.

But by means of the artifice just described, proceeds our critic, Marx has merely succeeded in convincing us that labor can in fact enter into the competition. The exclusion of other competitors is effected by two arguments, each of a few words only, but each containing a very serious logical fallacy. In the first of these Marx excludes all "geometrical, physical, chemical, or other natural qualities of the commodities," for "their physical qualities claim our attention only in so far as they affect the utility of the commodities—make them use values. On the other hand, the exchange relation of commodities is evidently characterized by the abstraction of their use values," because "within this relation (the exchange relation) one use value is as good as another provided only it be present in the proper proportion." [1]

Here, says Böhm-Bawerk, Marx falls into a grave error. He confuses the disregarding of a genus with the disregarding of the specific forms in which this genus manifests itself. The special forms under which use value may appear may be disregarded, but the use value of the commodity in general must never be disregarded. Marx might have seen that we do not absolutely disregard use value, from the fact that there can be no exchange value where there is not a use value—a fact which Marx himself is repeatedly forced to admit.

Let us for a moment interrupt our recapitulation of Böhm-Bawerk's criticism by a brief interpolation calculated to throw light upon the psychology no less than upon the logic of the leader of the psychological school.

When I disregard the "specific forms in which use value may manifest itself," disregarding, therefore, use value in its concreteness, I have, as far as I am concerned, disregarded use

[1] *Capital*, Vol. I, p. 44. [The passages are not textually quoted from the English translation.—E. & C. P.]

value in general, since, as far as I am concerned, use value exists in its concreteness solely as a thus or thus constituted use value. Having ceased for me to be a use value, it matters nothing to me that it has a use value for others, possesses utility for this or that other person. I do not exchange it until the moment arrives when it has ceased to possess a use value for me. This applies literally to the production of commodities in its developed form. Here the individual produces commodities of but one kind, commodities of which one specimen at most can possess a use value for him, whereas in the mass the commodities have for him no such use value. It is a precondition to the exchangeability of the commodities that they should possess utility for others, but since for me they are devoid of utility, the use value of my commodities is in no sense a *measure* even for my individual estimate of value, and still less is it a measure of an objective estimate of value. It avails nothing to say that the use value consists of the capacity of these commodities to be exchanged for other commodities, for this would imply that the extent of the "use value" is now determined by the extent of the exchange value, not the extent of the exchange value by the extent of the use value.

As long as goods are not produced for the purpose of exchange, are not produced as commodities, as long, that is to say, as exchange is no more than an occasional incident wherein superfluities only are exchanged, goods confront one another solely as use values.

"The proportions in which they are exchangeable are at first quite a matter of chance. What makes them exchangeable is the mutual desire of their owners to alienate them. Meantime the need for foreign objects of utility gradually establishes itself.[1] The constant repetition of exchange makes it a normal social act. In the course of time, therefore, some portion at

---

[1] A preferable translation of this sentence would be: "Meantime the need for objects of utility owned by other persons gradually establishes itself."— E. & C. P.

least of the products of labor must be produced with a special view to exchange. From that moment the distinction becomes firmly established between the utility of an object for the purposes of consumption, and its utility for the purposes of exchange. Its use value becomes distinguished from its exchange value. On the other hand, the quantitative proportion in which the articles are exchangeable becomes dependent on their production itself. Custom stamps them as values with definite magnitudes." [1]

We have in fact nothing more than a disregard by Marx of the specific forms in which the use value manifests itself. For the use value remains the "bearer of value." This is indeed self-evident, for "value" is nothing more than an economic modification of use value. It is solely the anarchy of the contemporary method of production, owing to which under certain conditions (a glut) a use value becomes a non-use-value and consequently valueless, which makes the recognition of this self-evident truth a matter of considerable importance.

Let us return to Böhm-Bawerk. The second step in the argument, he tells us, is still worse. Marx contends that if the use value of commodities be disregarded, there remains in them but one other quality, that of being products of labor. But do there not remain a number of other qualities? Such is Böhm-Bawerk's indignant inquiry. Have they not the common quality of being scarce in proportion to demand? Is it not common to them to be the objects of demand and supply, or that they are appropriated, or that they are natural products? Is it not common to them that they cause expense to their producers—a quality to which Marx draws attention in the third volume of *Capital*? Why should not the principle of value reside in any one of these qualities as well as in the quality of being products of labor? For in support of this latter proposition Marx has not adduced a shred of positive evidence. His sole argument is the

[2] Vol. I, p. 100.

negative one, that the use value, thus happily disregarded and out of the way, is not the principle of exchange value. But does not this negative argument apply with equal force to all the other common qualities overlooked [!] by Marx? This is not all. Marx writes as follows: "Along with the useful qualities of the products [of labor] we put out of sight both the useful character of the various kinds of labor embodied in them, and the concrete forms of that labor; there is nothing left but what is common to them all; they are reduced to one and the same sort of labor, human labor in the abstract." [1] But in saying this he admits that for an exchange relationship, not only one use value but also any one kind of labor "is just as good as another, provided only it be present in the proper proportion." It follows that the identical evidence on which Marx formulated his verdict of exclusion in the case of use value will hold good as regards labor. Labor and use value, says Böhm-Bawerk, have a qualitative side and a quantitative side. Just as the use value differs according as it is manifested in a table or in yarn, so also does labor differ as carpentry or spinning. And just as we may compare different kinds of labor according to their quantity, so we may compare use values of different kinds according to the varying amount of use value. It is quite impossible to understand why the very same evidence should result in the exclusion of one competitor and in the assigning of the prize to the other. Marx might just as well have reversed his reasoning process and have disregarded labor.

Such is Marx's logic, such his method of procedure, as reflected in the mind of Böhm-Bawerk. His procedure, according to the latter, was perfectly arbitrary. Although in an utterly unjustified but extremely artful manner he has managed to secure that nothing but the products of labor shall be left to be exchanged, it was impossible for him to adduce even the slightest ground for the contention that the common quality which

[1] Vol. I, p. 45.

must presumably be present in the commodities to be exchanged is to be sought and found in labor. Only by willfully ignoring a number of other qualities, only by his utterly unwarranted disregard of use value, did Marx attain the desired result. Just as little as the classical economists was Marx in a position to furnish an atom of proof on behalf of the proposition that labor is the principle of value.

Böhm-Bawerk's critical question to which Marx is alleged to have given so fallacious an answer is the question: what right had Marx to proclaim labor to be the sole creator of value? Our counter-criticism must in the first instance consist of a demonstration that the analysis of the commodity furnishes the desired answer.

To Böhm-Bawerk, the Marxist analysis establishes a contrast between utility and the product of labor. Now we fully agree with Böhm-Bawerk that no such contrast exists. Labor must be done on most things in order to render them useful. On the other hand, when we estimate the utility of a thing, it is a matter of indifference to us how much labor has been expended on it. A good does not become a commodity merely in virtue of being the product of labor. But only in so far as it is a *commodity* does a good exhibit the contrasted qualities of use value and value. Now a good becomes a commodity solely through entering into a relationship with other goods, a relationship which becomes manifest in the act of exchange, and which, quantitatively regarded, appears as the exchange value of the good. The quality of functioning as an exchange value thus determines the commodity character of the good. But a commodity cannot of its own initiative enter into relationships with other commodities; the material relationship between commodities is of necessity the expression of a personal relationship between their respective owners. As owners of commodities, these reciprocally occupy definite relationships of production. They are independent and equal producers of private "labors." But these private "labors" are of a peculiar kind, inasmuch as they are effected, not for personal use but for exchange, inasmuch as they are intended for the satisfaction, not of individual need, but of social need. Thus whereas private ownership and the division of labor reduces society into its atoms, the exchange of products restores to society its social interconnections.

The term commodity, therefore, is an *economic* term; it is the expression of social relationships between mutually independent producers in so far as these relationships are effected through the instrumentality of goods. The contrasted qualities of the commodity as use value and as value, the contrast between its manifestation as a natural form or as a value form, now appears to us to be a contrast between the commodity manifesting itself on the one hand as a *natural* thing and on the other hand as a *social* thing. We have, in fact, to do with a dichotomy, wherein the giving of the place of honor to one branch excludes the other, and conversely. But the difference is merely one of point of view. The commodity is a unity of use value and of value, but we can regard that unity from two different aspects. As a natural thing, it is the object of a natural science; as a social thing, it is the object of a social science, the object of political economy. The object of political economy is the social aspect of the commodity, of the good, in so far as it is a symbol of social interconnection. On the other hand, the natural aspect of the commodity, its use value, lies outside the domain of political economy.[1]

A commodity, however, can be the expression of social relationships only in so far as it is itself contemplated as a product of society, as a thing on which society has stamped its imprint. But for society, which exchanges nothing, the commodity is nothing more than a product of labor. Moreover, the members of society can only enter into economic relationships

[1] "That is the reason why German compilers are so fond of dwelling on use value, calling it a 'good.' . . . For intelligent information on 'goods' one must turn to treatises on commodities." Marx, *A Contribution to the Critique of Political Economy*, Kerr ed., p. 21n.

one with another according as they work one for another. This material relationship appears in its historic form as the exchange of commodities. The total product of labor presents itself as a total value, which in individual commodities manifests itself quantitatively as exchange value.

The commodity being, as far as society is concerned, the product of labor, this labor thereby secures its specific character as socially necessary labor; the commodity no longer exhibits itself to us as the product of the labor of different subjects, for these must now rather be looked upon as simple "instruments of labor." Economically regarded, therefore, the private "labors" manifest themselves as their opposites, as social "labors." The condition which gives its value-creating quality to labor is, therefore, the social determination of the labor—it is a quality of social labor.

Thus the process of abstraction whereby Marx passes from the concept of concrete private labor to the concept of abstractly human social labor, far from being, as Böhm-Bawerk imagines, identical with the process of abstraction whereby Marx excludes use value from consideration, is in fact the very opposite of that process.

A use value is an individual relationship between a thing and a human being. If I disregard its concreteness (and I am compelled to do so as soon as I alienate the thing so that it ceases to be a use value for me) I thereby destroy this individual relationship. But solely in its individuality can a use value be the measure of my personal estimate of value. If, on the other hand, I disregard the concrete manner in which I have expended my labor, it nevertheless remains a fact that labor in general has been expended in its universal human form, and this is an objective magnitude the measure of which is furnished by the duration of the effort.

It is precisely this objective magnitude with which Marx is concerned. He is endeavoring to discover the social nexus between the apparently isolated agents of production. Social production, and therewith the actual material basis of society, is, according to its nature, qualitatively determined by the nature of the organization of social labor. This organization, causally determined by economic need, soon acquires a legal, a juristic fixation. An "external regulation" of this character constitutes a logical premise of the economic system, and furnishes the framework within which the separate elements of the society, the elements which labor and the elements which control labor, mutually influence one another. In a society characterized by the division of property and by the division of labor, this relationship appears in the form of exchange, expresses itself as exchange value. The social nexus manifests itself as the outcome of private relationships, the relationships not of private individuals but of private things. It is precisely this which involves the whole problem in mystery. Inasmuch, however, as the things enter into mutual relations, the private labor which has produced them acquires validity solely in so far as it is an expenditure of its own antithesis, socially necessary labor.

The outcome of the social process of production thus qualitatively determined is quantitatively determined by the sum total of the expended social labor. As an aliquot part of the social product of labor (and as such only does the commodity function in exchange), the individual commodity is quantitatively determined by the quota of social labor time embodied in it.

As a value, therefore, the commodity is socially determined, is a social thing. As such alone can it be subjected to economic consideration. But when our task is to effect the economic analysis of any social institution that we may discover the intimate law of motion of the society, and when we call upon the law of value to render us this service, the principle of value cannot be any other than that to whose variations the changes in the social institution must in the last instance be referred.

Every theory of value which starts from use value, that is to say from the natural qualities of the thing, whether from its finished form as a useful thing or from its function, the satisfaction of a want, starts from the individual relationship between a thing and a human being instead of starting from the social relationships of human beings one with another. This involves the error of attempting from the subjective individual relationship, wherefrom subjective estimates of value are properly deducible, to deduce an objective social measure. Inasmuch as this individual relationship is equally present in all social conditions, inasmuch as it does not contain within itself any principle of change (for the development of the wants and the possibility of their satisfaction are themselves likewise determined), we must, if we adopt such a procedure, renounce the hope of discovering the laws of motion and the evolutionary tendencies of society. Such an outlook is unhistorical and unsocial. Its categories are natural and eternal categories.

Marx, conversely, starts from labor in its significance as the constitutive element in human society, as the element whose development determines in the final analysis the development of society. In his principle of value he thus grasps the factor by whose quality and quantity, by whose organization and productive energy, social life is causally controlled. The fundamental economic idea is consequently identical with the fundamental idea of the materialist conception of history. Necessarily so, seeing that economic life is but a part of historic life, so that conformity to law in economics must be the same as conformity to law in history. To the extent that labor in its social form becomes the measure of value, economics is established as a social and historical science. Therewith the purview of economic science is restricted to the definite epoch of social evolution wherein the good becomes a commodity. In other words, it is restricted to the epoch wherein labor and the power which controls labor have not been consciously elevated to the rank of a regulative principle of social metabolism and social predominance, but wherein this principle unconsciously and automatically establishes itself as a material quality of things —inasmuch as, as the outcome of the peculiar form which social metabolism has assumed in exchange, it results that private labors acquire validity only in so far as they are social labors. *Society has, as it were, assigned to each of its members the quota of labor necessary to society; has specified to each individual how much labor he must expend.* And these individuals have forgotten what their quota was, and rediscover it only in the process of social life.

It is therefore because labor is the social bond uniting an atomized society, and not because labor is the matter most technically relevant, that labor is the principle of value and that the law of value is endowed with reality. It is precisely because Marx takes socially necessary labor as his starting point that he is so well able to discover the inner working of a society based on private property and the division of labor. For him the individual relation between human being and good is a premise. What he sees in exchange is not a difference of individual estimates, but the equation of a historically determined relationship of production. Only in this relationship of production, as the symbol, as the material expression, of personal relationships, as the bearer of social labor, does the good become a commodity; and only *as the expression of derivative relationships of production* can things which are not the products of labor assume the character of commodities.

We thus reach Böhm-Bawerk's objection as expressed in his inquiry, How can the products of nature have "exchange value"? The natural conditions under which labor is performed are unalterably given to society, and from these conditions therefore changes in social relationships cannot be derived. The only thing that changes is the manner in which labor is applied to these natural conditions. The degree to which such application is successful determines the productivity of labor. The change in productivity is effected solely by the concrete labor which creates use value; but according as the mass of products wherein the value-creating labor is embodied increases or diminishes, it results that more or less labor than before is embodied in the individual specimen. To the extent that natural energy is at an individual's disposal, so that he is thereby enabled to labor with a productivity exceeding the social average, that individual is in a position to realize an extra surplus value. This extra surplus value, capitalized, then manifests itself as the price of this natural energy (it may be of the soil) whose appurtenance it is. The soil is not a commodity, but in a lengthy historical process it acquires the characteristics of a commodity as a condition requisite to the production of commodities. The expressions "value of land" or "price of land" are therefore nothing more than irrational formulas beneath which is concealed a real relationship of production, that is to say a relationship of value. The ownership of land does not create the portion of value which is transformed into surplus profit; it merely enables the landowner to transfer this surplus profit from the manufacturer's pocket to his own. But Böhm-Bawerk, who ascribes to the gifts of nature a value peculiar to themselves, is a prey to the physiocrats' illusion that rent is derived from nature and not from society.

Thus Böhm-Bawerk continually confuses the natural and the social. This is plainly shown in his enunciation of the additional qualities common to commodities. It is a strange medley: the fact of appropriation is the legal expression of the historical relationships which must be presupposed in order that goods may be exchanged at all (it is "pre-economic" fact)—though how this should be a quantitative measure remains inexplicable. It is a natural quality of commodities to be natural products, but in no way does this render them quantitatively comparable. Inasmuch, further, as they are the objects of demand and have a relationship to demand, they acquire a use value; for relative scarcity renders them subjectively the objects of esteem, whereas objectively (from the standpoint of society) their scarcity is a function of the cost of labor, securing therein its objective measure in the magnitude of its cost.

Just as in the foregoing Böhm-Bawerk fails to distinguish the natural qualities of commodities from their social qualities, so in the further course of his criticism he confuses the outlook on labor in so far as it creates use value with the outlook on labor in so far as it creates value; and he proceeds to discover a new contradiction in the law of value—though Marx "with a masterly dialectic . . . seeks to suggest" that the facts "do not contain a contradiction of his fundamental principle, but are only a slightly different reading of it."

Marx declares that skilled labor is equivalent to a definite quantity of unskilled labor. He has however taught us, says Böhm-Bawerk, that things equated with one another by exchange "contain equal amounts of some common factor, and this common factor must be labor and working time." But the facts before us, he says, do not comply at all with this demand. For in skilled labor, for example in the product of a sculptor, there is no unskilled labor at all, and still less can we say that the unskilled labor equal to the five days' labor of the stonebreaker is embodied in the sculptor's product. "The plain truth is [very plain indeed!—R. H.] that the two products embody different *kinds* of labor in different amounts, and every unprejudiced person will admit that this means a state of things exactly contrary to the conditions which Marx demands and must affirm, namely, that they embody labor of the *same kind* and of the *same amount*."

Let me parenthetically remark that there is no question here of the "same amount," no question of *quantitative equality*. We are solely concerned with the comparability of different *kinds* of labor, that is to say with the possibility of expressing them in terms of some common measure, with the possibility of their *qualitative* equalization.

It is true, continues Böhm-Bawerk, that Marx says: "Experience shows that this reduction [from skilled to unskilled labor] is constantly being made. A commodity may be the product of the most skilled labor, but its value, by equating it to the product of simple unskilled labor, represents a definite quantity of the latter labor alone. The different proportions in which different sorts of labor are reduced to unskilled labor as their standard are established by a social process that goes on behind the backs of the producers, and, consequently, appear to be fixed by custom." [1]

Böhm-Bawerk, however, inquires, what is the meaning of the appeal to "value" and the "social process" as the determining factors of the standard of reduction? "Apart from everything else, it simply means that Marx is arguing in a circle. The real subject of inquiry is the exchange relations of commodities," why, for instance, the sculptor's work is worth five times as much as the unskilled labor of the stone-breaker. "Marx . . . says that the exchange relation is this, and no other—because one day of sculptor's work is reducible exactly to five days' unskilled work. And why is it reducible to exactly five days? Because experience shows that it is so reduced by a social process." But it is this very process which requires explanation. Were the exchange relationship 1:3 instead of 1:5, "Marx would equally bid us accept the rate of reduction of 1:3 as the one derived from experience; . . . in short, it is clear that we shall never learn in this way the actual reasons why products of different kinds of work should be exchanged in this or that proportion." In this decisive point, says the critic, the law of value breaks down.

We have here a statement of the familiar difficulty, the difficulty to which others besides Böhm-Bawerk have drawn attention. In the preface to the first volume of *Capital,* Marx, with his well-known "social optimism," presupposes "a reader who is willing to learn something new, and therefore to think for himself"—this being I believe the only unwarranted presupposition Marx ever made. But every thoughtful reader will at the outset feel that there is a gap in the argument, and the void has been indicated by "more or less Marxist" writers, as by Bernstein, C. Schmidt, and Kautsky.

[1] Vol. I, pp. 51-52.

Let us regard the matter more closely. First of all, Böhm-Bawerk himself tells us that the difference consists only in this, that in the one case we have to do with skilled and in the other with unskilled labor. It is obvious, therefore, that the difference in value of the respective products must depend upon a difference in the labor. The same natural product is in one case the object upon which skilled labor has been expended, and in the other case the object upon which unskilled labor has been expended, and it acquires a different value in the respective cases. Thus there is no *logical* objection to the law of value. The only question that arises is whether it is necessary to determine the ratio of value between the two kinds of labor, and whether the difficulty of effecting this determination may not prove insuperable. For, if we assume a knowledge of the ratio to be indispensable, in the absence of such knowledge the concept of value will be incapable of furnishing the explanation of economic processes.

Let us reconsider Marx's argument. In the passage previously quoted we read: "Its value [that is to say the value of the product of skilled labor], by equating it to the product of simple unskilled labor, represents a definite quantity of the latter labor alone." For this process to be comprehensible, however, value theory must regard the labor available for society at any given moment as composed of homogeneous parts—individual labor, in so far as it creates value, being merely an aliquot part of this quantitative whole. But only if I am able to express this whole in terms of some common unit of measurement can I regard it as qualitatively homogeneous. The required unit of measurement is furnished by "simple average labor," and this "is the expenditure of simple labor power, that is, of the labor power which on the average, apart from any special development, exists in the organism of every ordinary individual." [1] Skilled labor counts as a multiple of this unit of simple average labor. But what multiple? This, says Marx, is established by a social process that

[1] Vol. I, p. 51.

goes on behind the backs of the producers. Now Böhm-Bawerk will not admit that this appeal to experience is valid, and declares that here the theory of value breaks down utterly. For "in what proportions skilled is to be translated into terms of unskilled labor in the valuation of their respective products is not determined, nor can it be determined, a priori, by any property inherent in the skilled labor itself, but it is the actual result alone which decides the actual exchange relations."[1] Thus Böhm-Bawerk demands that the ratio should enable him to determine in advance the absolute height of prices, for in his view, as he elsewhere tells us, the essential task of economics is to explain the phenomenon of price.

Is it really true, however, that in default of a knowledge of the ratio, the law of value becomes unworkable? In striking contrast with Böhm-Bawerk, Marx looks upon the theory of value, not as the means for ascertaining prices, but as the means for discovering the laws of motion of capitalist society. Experience teaches us that the *absolute* height of prices is the starting point of this movement, but, for the rest, the absolute height of prices remains a matter of secondary importance, and we are concerned merely with studying the law of their variation. It is a matter of indifference whether any specific kind of skilled labor is to be reckoned the fourfold multiple or the sixfold multiple of unskilled labor. The important point is that a doubling or trebling of productive power in the sphere of skilled labor would lower the product of skilled labor twofold or threefold vis-à-vis the product of unskilled labor (by hypothesis unchanged).

The *absolute* height of prices is given us by experience; what interests us is the *law-abiding variation* that these prices undergo. Like all variations, this variation is brought about by a force; and since we have to do with changes in social phenomena, these changes must be effected by variations in the magnitude of a social force, the social power of production.

Since, however, the law of value discloses to us that in the

1 Above, p. 83.

final analysis this development of productive power controls variations in prices, it becomes possible for us to grasp the laws of these changes; and since all economic phenomena manifest themselves by changes in prices, it is further possible to attain to an understanding of economic phenomena in general. Ricardo, aware of the incompleteness of his analysis of the law of value, therefore declares in so many words that the investigation to which he wishes to direct the reader's attention concerns variations in the relative value of commodities and not variations in their absolute value.

It follows that the lack of a knowledge of the ratio in question by no means restricts the importance of the law of value as a means by which we are enabled to recognize the conformity to law displayed by the economic mechanism. In another respect, however, this lack would be serious. If in practice the absolute height of price had in the first instance to be established by the social process, the concept of value would have to contain all the elements which *theoretically* allow us to apprehend the process whereby society effectuates the reduction of skilled labor to unskilled. Otherwise this process, which exercises a decisive influence upon the magnitude of value, though it would indeed positively exist and would not involve any contradiction to the law of value, would nevertheless afford an explanation of a part only (and that the most important) of economic phenomena, but would leave unexplained another part, namely the starting point of these variations.

When, however, Böhm-Bawerk inquires, what is the quality *inherent* in skilled labor which gives that labor its peculiar power to create value, the question is wrongly stated. The value-creating quality is not per se inherent in any labor. Solely in conjunction with a definite mode of social organization of the process of production does labor create value. Hence, we cannot attain to the concept of value-creating labor merely by contemplating isolated labor in its concreteness. Skilled labor, therefore, if I am to regard it as value-creating, must not be contemplated in isolation, but as part of social labor.

The question consequently arises, what is skilled labor from the social standpoint? Only when we can answer this can we expect to attain to a position from which we shall be able to recognize the principles according to which the aforesaid social reduction can be effected. Manifestly these principles can be none other than those which are contained in the law of value. But here we encounter a difficulty. The law of value applies to commodities, whereas labor is not a commodity even though it appears as such when we speak of the wage of labor. Only labor *power* is a commodity and possesses value; labor *creates* value, but does not itself possess value. It is not difficult to calculate the value of a labor *power* engaged on skilled work; like every other commodity it is equal to the labor requisite for its production and reproduction, and this is composed of the cost of maintenance and the cost of training. But here we are not concerned with the value of a skilled labor power, but with the question how and in what ratio skilled labor creates more value than unskilled.

We must not deduce the higher value which skilled labor creates from the higher wage of skilled labor power, for this would be to deduce the value of the product from the "value of labor." It is true that Bernstein [1] proposes to do this, and believes that he can justify himself by a quotation from Marx. But if we read the sentence in the context from which Bernstein has torn it, we see that it conveys the precise opposite of that which Bernstein wishes to deduce from it. Marx writes: "It has previously been pointed out that, as far as the process of producing surplus value is concerned, it is a matter of absolutely no moment whether the labor appropriated by the capitalist be average unskilled social labor or comparatively skilled labor, labor of a higher specific gravity. The labor which, when contrasted with average social

[1] Eduard Bernstein, "Zur Theorie des Arbeitswerts," *Die Neue Zeit*, Vol. XVIII (1899-1900), Part 1, p. 359.

labor, counts as higher, comparatively skilled labor, is the manifestation of a labor power to the making of which higher formative costs have gone, whose production has cost more labor time,
and which consequently has a higher value than that possessed
by unskilled labor power. Now whereas the value of this power
is higher, it must also be remembered that it manifests itself in
higher work, and consequently materializes, in equal spaces of
time, in comparatively higher values. Whatever difference in
skill there may be between the labor of a spinner and that of a
jeweler, the portion of his labor by which the jeweler merely
replaces the value of his own labor power does not in any way
differ in quality from the additional portion by which he creates
surplus value. In the making of jewelry, just as in spinning, the
surplus value results only from a quantitative excess of labor,
from a lengthening out of one and the same labor process, in the
one case of the process of making jewels, in the other of the
process of making yarn." [1] We see that the question Marx here
discusses is how skilled labor can create surplus value despite
the high wage, despite, that is to say, the magnitude of the
necessary labor. Expressed in fuller detail, the thoughts in the
sentence quoted by Bernstein would read somewhat as follows:
"Even though the value of this power be higher, it can none the
less produce more surplus value, because it manifests itself in
higher work"—and so on.

Marx leaves out the intermediate clause and introduces what
follows with the word *"aber"* ["but"], whereas, if Bernstein had
been right, he would have had to use the word *"daher"* ["consequently," or "therefore"]. To deduce the value of the product
of labor from the wage of labor conflicts grossly with the Marxist theory. The value of labor power being given, I should only
be in a position to deduce the value which this labor power

1 Vol. I, p. 220.—The passage is not textually identical, except as regards the
two concluding sentences, with the English edition, for we have retranslated it
from the third German edition—the text used for the translation of the standard English edition and the one used by R. H.—E. & C. P.

newly creates if I knew what had been the rate of exploitation. But even if the rate of exploitation of unskilled labor were known to me, I should have no right to assume that the identical rate of exploitation prevailed for skilled labor. For the latter, the rate of exploitation might be much lower. Thus neither directly nor indirectly does the wage of a skilled labor power give me any information regarding the value which this labor power newly creates. The visage which the Marxist theory would assume if Bernstein's interpretation were to be accepted (and Bernstein himself tells us that in his view the theory would assume an utterly different visage) would possess ironical lineaments which could hardly be concealed. We must, therefore, endeavor to approach the solution of the problem in a different manner.[1]

[1] The translators had hoped to avoid burdening Hilferding's text with any extended notes of their own, but they find it necessary to draw attention to a strange discrepancy between the text of the fourth (German) edition of *Capital,* finally revised by Engels in 1890, and the third edition, that of 1883, the one quoted above by Hilferding. In the third edition, the sentence about which the trouble arises runs as follows (p. 178): *"Ist der Wert dieser Kraft höher, so äussert sie sich aber auch in höherer Arbeit und vergegenständlicht sich daher, in denselben Zeiträumen, in verhältnissmässig höheren Wert."* Our translation of this, which we prefer to that found on page 179 of Moore & Aveling's version, runs as follows: "Now whereas the value of this power is higher, it must also be remembered that it manifests itself in higher work, and consequently materializes, in equal spaces of time, in comparatively higher values." The phrase "it must be remembered that" seems rather a lengthy rendering of the German *"aber,"* but in this particular context that phrase effectively presents the precise shade of meaning.

Next let us turn to Bernstein. This writer quotes from the second (German) edition of *Capital,* in which (p. 186) the passage cited is identical with that quoted from the third edition by Hilferding. But Bernstein interpolates an exclamation mark expressive almost of derision, the passage thus reading: "Now whereas the value of this power is higher, it must also be remembered that it manifests itself in higher work, and consequently [!] materializes in equal spaces of time, in comparatively higher values." Thereafter (writing in *Die Neue Zeit* of December 23, 1899) Bernstein continues: "Here the value of the labor power which materializes in the wage of labor appears to be decisive for the value of the product. Were we to accept this as universally valid, the Marxist theory of value would in my opinion assume a visage utterly different from that which, as presented by all its expositors, it has hitherto

Average unskilled labor is the expenditure of unskilled labor power, but qualified or skilled labor is the expenditure of qualified labor power. For the production of this skilled labor power, however, a number of unskilled labors were requisite. These are stored up in the person of the qualified laborer, and not until he begins to work are these formative labors made fluid *on behalf of society*. The labor of the technical educator thus transmits, not only *value* (which manifests itself in the form of the higher

---

assumed. It would differ from the theory as expounded by Marx himself, for Marx, in his essay *Value, Price, and Profit* expressly declares: 'To determine the values of commodities by the relative quantities of labor fixed in them, is, therefore, a thing quite different from the tautological method of determining the values of commodities by the value of labor, or by wages' [International Publishers' ed., p. 32]. However this may be, here is a point which still remains to be cleared up, unless it be imagined that the elucidation is to be found in the disquisitions of the third volume concerning cost price and price of production which, just like the fact of surplus value, do not require for their establishment the labor theory of value in its original form."

What Hilferding has to say of Bernstein we have seen in the text. The reader will note more particularly Hilferding's contention that were Bernstein right, Marx would have written *"daher"* in place of *"aber."* Now comes the point justifying the introduction of the present note. In the fourth (German) edition of *Capital* (p. 160) the word *"aber"* has been changed to *"daher,"* not in consequence of what Bernstein wrote in *Die Neue Zeit* in 1899, for Engels' preface to the fourth edition is dated June 25, 1890. Further, in this preface, Engels gives a detailed specification of the important alterations in the text of the fourth edition, making no direct allusion to the change on page 160, but adding: "Other trifling modifications are of a purely technical nature." We take it this means trifling improvements in literary style. In any case it would seem clear that Engels did not regard this particular alteration as important. The revised sentence may best be rendered as follows: "Now if the value of this power be higher, the result is that it manifests itself in higher work, and consequently it materializes in equal spaces of time, in comparatively higher values."

Marx and Engels are beyond our reach. For the moment we are unable to communicate with Bernstein in Berlin or with Hilferding in Vienna. We must leave the problems raised anent this disputed text to the ingenuity of the English-speaking Marxists. They must sharpen their weapons, and make ready to deal with both the German and the Austrian commentators when the foolish capitalist bickering which at present hampers communications shall at length have drawn to a close. Among other things, they will want to know why Hilferding, writing in 1903, did not consult the definitive fourth edition of *Capital*, published thirteen years earlier!—E. & C. P.

wage), but in addition its own *value-creating power*. The formative labors are therefore *latent as far as society is concerned,* and
do not manifest themselves until the skilled labor power begins
to work. Its expenditure consequently signifies the expenditure
of all the different unskilled labors which are simultaneously
condensed therein.

Unskilled labor, if applied to the production of a qualified or
skilled labor power, creates on the one hand the value of this
labor power, which reappears in the wage of the qualified labor
power ; but on the other hand by the concrete method of its application it creates a new use value, which consists in this, that there
is now available a labor power which can create value with all
those potentialities possessed by the unskilled labors utilized in
its formation. Inasmuch as unskilled labor is used in the formation of skilled labor, it thus creates on the one hand new value
and transmits on the other to its product its use value—to be the
source of new value. Regarded from the standpoint of society,
unskilled labor is latent as long as it is utilized for the formation
of skilled labor power. Its working for society does not begin
until the skilled labor power it has helped to produce becomes
active. Thus in this single act of the expenditure of skilled labor
a sum of unskilled labors is expended, and in this way there is
created a sum of value and surplus value corresponding to the
total value which would have been created by the expenditure
of all the unskilled labors which were requisite to produce the
skilled labor power and its function, the skilled labor. From the
standpoint of society, therefore, and economically regarded,
skilled labor appears as a multiple of unskilled labor, however
diverse skilled and unskilled labor may appear from some other
outlook, physiological, technical, or aesthetic.

In what it has to give for the product of skilled labor, society
consequently pays an equivalent for the value which the unskilled labors would have created had they been directly consumed by society.

The more unskilled labor that skilled labor embodies, the

more does the latter create higher value, for in effect we have numerous unskilled labors simultaneously employed upon the formation of the same product. In reality, therefore, skilled labor is unskilled labor multiplied. An example may make the matter clearer. A man owns ten storage batteries wherewith he can drive ten different machines. For the manufacture of a new product he requires another machine for which a far greater motive power is requisite. He now employs the ten batteries to charge a single accumulator, which is capable of driving the new machine. The powers of the individual batteries thereupon manifest themselves as a unified force in the new battery, a unified force which is the tenfold multiple of the simple average force.

A skilled labor may contain, not unskilled labors alone, but in addition skilled labors of a different kind, and these in their turn are reducible to unskilled labor. The greater the extent to which other skilled labors are incorporated in a skilled labor, the briefer will be its formative process.

Thus the Marxist theory of value enables us to recognize the principles in accordance with which the social process of reducing skilled labor to unskilled labor is effected. It therefore renders the magnitude of value *theoretically measurable*. But when Böhm-Bawerk insists that Marx ought to have furnished the empirical proof of his theory, and when he contends that the requisite proof would have consisted in demonstrating the relationship between exchange values or prices and quantities of labor, he is confusing theoretical with *practical* measurability. What I am able to determine by experience is the concrete expenditure of labor requisite for the production of a specified good. How far this concrete labor is socially necessary labor, how far, that is to say, it has a bearing on the formation of value, I am only able to determine if I know the actual average degree of productivity and intensity which the productive power has required, and if I also know what quantum of this good is demanded by society. This means that we are asking from the individual that which society performs. For society is the only accountant competent to calculate the height of prices, and the method which society employs to this end is the method of competition. Inasmuch as, in free competition on the market, society treats as a unity the concrete labor expended by all producers for the production of a good, and inasmuch as society only pays for labor in so far as its expenditure was socially necessary, it is society which first shows to what degree this concrete labor has actually collaborated in the formation of value, and fixes the price accordingly. The utopia of "labor notes" and "constituted value" was based upon this very illusion that the theoretical standard of measurement is at the same time an immediately practical standard of measurement. This is the conception in accordance with which the theory of value is regarded, not as a means "for detecting the law of motion of contemporary society," but as a means of securing a price list that shall be as stable and as just as possible.

The search for such a price list led von Buch[1] to a theory which, in order to determine price, needs nothing more than this —a knowledge of the price. But the psychological theory of "value" is in no better case.

That theory indicates the various degrees of satisfaction of needs with definite but arbitrarily selected figures, and arranges that these figures shall signify the prices which people are willing to pay for the means wherewith needs are satisfied. This more effectually conceals the process whereby a number of arbitrary prices are assumed instead of a single arbitrary price.

The empirical proof of the accuracy of the theory of value lies in a very different direction from that towards which Böhm-Bawerk directs his inquiries. If the theory of value is to be the key for the understanding of the capitalist mode of production, it must be able to explain the phenomena of that mode of production in a manner free from contradictions. The actual processes of the capitalist world must not conflict with the theory

[1] *Die Intensität der Arbeit,* Leipzig, 1896.

but must confirm it. According to Böhm-Bawerk the theory fails in this respect. The third volume of *Capital,* in which Marx has no longer been able to ignore the actual processes, shows that these actual processes could not be harmonized with the presuppositions of the theory of value. The data of the third volume are in crass contradiction with those of the first volume. The theory is shipwrecked on the rocks of reality. For reality, says Böhm-Bawerk, shows that the law of value has no validity for the process of exchange, seeing that commodities are exchanged at prices which permanently diverge from the value of the commodities. In the discussion of the problem of the average rate of profit the contradiction becomes obvious. Marx can solve this problem only by the simple abandonment of his theory of value. This reproach of self-contradiction has become a commonplace of bourgeois economics since it was made by Böhm-Bawerk. When we are criticizing Böhm-Bawerk we are criticizing the representatives of bourgeois criticism of the third volume of *Capital.*

Chapter Two

VALUE AND AVERAGE PROFIT

THE problem with which we are now concerned is familiar. In the various spheres of production the organic composition of capital, the ratio between *c* (constant capital, expended on the means of production) and *v* (variable capital, expended in paying the wage of labor), varies. Since, however, only variable capital produces new value, and since, therefore, it alone produces surplus value, the amount of surplus value produced by two capitals of equal size varies in accordance with the organic composition of these respective capitals, varies, that is to say, in accordance with variations in the ratio between the constant capital and the variable capital in the respective enterprises. But, therewith, also, the rate of profit, the ratio between the surplus value and the total capital, varies. Thus according to the law of value equal capitals yield different profits proportionate to the magnitudes of the living labor which they set in motion. This conflicts with reality, for in the real world equal capitals bring identical profits, whatever their composition. How can the "contradiction" be explained?

Let us first hear what Marx has to say.

"The whole difficulty arises from the fact that commodities are not exchanged simply as *commodities*, but as *products of capital* which claim equal shares of the total amount of surplus value, if they are of equal magnitude, or shares proportional to their different magnitudes." [1]

The capital advanced for the production of a commodity constitutes the cost price of this commodity. "The cost price [= c + v] does not show the distinction between variable and constant capital to the capitalist. A commodity, for which he must advance £100 in production, costs him the same amount whether he invests 90c + 10v, or 10c + 90v. He always spends £100 for it, no more no less. The cost prices are the same for investment of the same amounts of capital in different spheres, no matter how much the produced values and surplus values may differ. The equality of cost prices is the basis for the competition of the invested capitals, by which an average rate of profit is brought about." [2]

To elucidate the working of capitalist competition Marx presents the following table, wherein the rates of surplus value $\frac{s}{v}$ are assumed to be identical, while as regards the constant capital varying proportions are incorporated into the product according as the wear and tear varies.

Capitals	Rate of Surplus Value, Percent	Surplus Value	Rate of Profit, Percent	Used-up C	Value of Commodities
I 80c + 20v	100	20	20	50	90
II 70c + 30v	100	30	30	51	111
III 60c + 40v	100	40	40	51	131
IV 85c + 15v	100	15	15	40	70
V 95c + 5v	100	5	5	10	20

In this table we see five instances in which the total capital is identical, and in which the degree of exploitation of labor is the same in every case, but the rates of profit vary widely, according to the differing organic composition. Let us now look upon these

[1] Vol. III, p. 206.
[2] Vol. III, p. 182.

capitals, invested in various fields, as a single capital, of which
numbers I to V merely constitute component parts (more or less
analogous to the different departments of a cotton mill which
has different proportions of constant and of variable capital in
its carding, preparatory spinning, spinning, and weaving rooms,
on the basis of which the average proportion for the whole factory is calculated), then we should have a total capital of 500, a
surplus value of 110, and a total value of commodities of 610.
The average composition of the capital would be 500, made up
of 390c and 110v, or in percentages, 78c and 22v. If each of the
capitals of 100 were to be regarded simply as one fifth of the
total capital, the average composition of each portion would be
78c and 22v, and in like manner to each 100 of capital would be
allotted a mean surplus value of 22, so that the mean rate of
profit would be 22 percent. The commodities must, then, be sold
as follows:

Capitals	Surplus Value	Used-up C	Value of Commodities	Cost Price of Commodities	Price of Commodities	Rate of Profit Percent	Deviation of Price from Value
I 80c + 20v	20	50	90	70	92	22	+ 2
II 70c + 30v	30	51	111	81	103	22	− 8
III 60c + 40v	40	51	131	91	113	22	−18
IV 85c + 15v	15	40	70	55	77	22	+ 7
V 95c + 5v	5	10	20	15	37	22	+17

The commodities are thus sold at 2 + 7 + 17 = 26 above, and
8 + 18 = 26 below, their value, so that the deviations of prices
from values mutually balance one another by the uniform distribution of the surplus value, or by the addition of the average
profit of 22 percent of advanced capital to the respective cost
prices of the commodities of I to V. One portion of the commodities is sold in the same proportion above in which the other is

sold below value. Only the sale of the commodities at such prices renders it possible that the rate of profit for all five capitals shall uniformly be 22 percent, without regard to the organic composition of these capitals.

"Since the capitals invested in the various lines of production are of a different organic composition, and since the different percentages of the variable portions of these total capitals set in motion very different quantities of labor, it follows that these capitals appropriate very different quantities of surplus labor, or produce very different quantities of surplus value. Consequently the rates of profit prevailing in the various lines of production are originally very different. These different rates of profit are equalized by means of competition into a general rate of profit, which is the average of all these special rates of profit. The profit allotted according to this average rate of profit to any capital, whatever may be its organic composition, is called the average profit. That price of any commodity which is equal to its cost price plus that share of average profit on the total capital invested (not merely consumed) in its production which is allotted to it in proportion to its conditions of turnover, is called its price of production. . . . While the capitalists in the various spheres of production recover the value of the capital consumed in the production of their commodities through the sale of these, they do not secure the surplus value, and consequently the profit, created in their own sphere by the production of these commodities, but only as much surplus value, and profit, as falls to the share of every aliquot part of the total social capital out of the total social surplus value, or social profit produced by the total capital of society in all spheres of production. Every 100 of any invested capital, whatever may be its organic composition, draws as much profit during one year, or any other period of time, as falls to the share of every 100 of the total social capital during the same period. The various capitalists, so far as profits are concerned, are so many stockholders in a stock company in which the shares of profit are uniformly divided for every 100 shares of capital, so that profits differ in the case of the individual capitalists only according to the amount of capital invested by each one of them in the social enterprise, according to his investment in social production as a whole, according to his shares" (III, 186-187). The average profit is nothing other than the profit on the average social capital; its total, like the total of the surplus values, and like the prices determined by the addition of this average profit to the cost prices, are nothing other than the values transformed into prices of production. In the simple production of commodities, values are the center of gravity round which prices fluctuate. But "under capitalist production it is not a question of merely throwing a certain mass of values into circulation and exchanging that mass for equal values in some other form, whether of money or other commodities, but it is also a question of advancing capital in production and realizing on it as much surplus value, or profit, in proportion to its magnitude, as any other capital of the same or of other magnitudes in whatever line of production. It is a question, then, of selling the commodities at least at prices which will yield the average profit, in other words, at prices of production. Capital comes in this form to a realization of *the social nature of its power*, in which every capitalist participates in proportion to his share in the total social capital. . . . If the commodities are sold at their values . . . considerably different rates of profit arise in the various spheres of production. . . . But capital withdraws from spheres with low rates of profit and invades others which yield a higher rate. By means of this incessant emigration and immigration, in a word by its distribution among the various spheres in response to a rise in the rate of profit here and its fall there, it brings about such a proportion of supply to demand that the average profit in the various spheres of production becomes the same, so that values are converted into prices of production" (III, 229-230).

In what relationship does this doctrine of the third volume stand to the celebrated law of value of the first volume?

In Böhm-Bawerk's opinion the third volume of *Capital* manifestly contains the statement of an actual and irreconcilable contradiction to the law of value, and furnishes proof that the equal average rate of profit can only become established if and because the alleged law of value does not hold good. In the first volume, declares Böhm-Bawerk,[1] it was maintained with the greatest emphasis that all value is based on labor and labor alone; the value was declared to be the common factor which appears in the exchange relation of commodities. We were told, in the form and with the emphasis of a stringent syllogistic conclusion, allowing of no exception, that to set down two commodities as equivalents in exchange implies that a common factor of the same magnitude exists in both, to which each of the two must be reducible. Apart, therefore, from temporary and occasional deviations, which are merely apparent breaches of the law of exchange of commodities, commodities which embody the same amount of labor must on principle, in the long run, exchange for each other. And now, in the third volume, we are told that what according to the teaching of the first volume must be, is not and never can be; that individual commodities do and must exchange with each other in a proportion different from that of the labor incorporated in them, and this not accidentally and temporarily, but of necessity and permanently.

But this, says Böhm-Bawerk, is no explanation and reconciliation of a contradiction, it is the naked contradiction itself. The theory of the average rate of profit and of the prices of production cannot be reconciled with the theory of value. Marx must himself have foreseen that this reproach would be made, and to this prevision is evidently due an anticipatory self-defense which, if not in form, yet in point of fact, is found in the Marxist system. He tries by a number of observations to render plausible the view that in spite of exchange relations

[1] Above, pp. 29 ff.

being directly governed by prices of production, which differ from the values, all is nevertheless moving within the framework of the law of value, and that this law, in the last resort at least, governs prices. On this subject, however, Marx does not make use of his customary method, a formal, circumscribed demonstration, but gives only a number of juxtaposed casual remarks, containing divers arguments which are summed up by Böhm-Bawerk under four heads.

Before we consider these "arguments" and the counterarguments of Böhm-Bawerk, it is necessary to say a word or two concerning the "contradiction" or the "withdrawal" which Marx is supposed to have perpetrated in the third volume. As regards the alleged withdrawal, those who use this term have forgotten that the first volume was not published until the tenth chapter of the third volume, which forms the bone of contention, had already been composed. For the draft of the last two books of *Capital* was composed by Marx during the years 1863 to 1867, and from a note by Engels (III, 209n) we learn that the tenth chapter of the third volume, the one containing the solution of the riddle, was written in 1865. To speak of a withdrawal in this connection is tantamount to saying that Marx, in order to remain at a definite point, first moved a mile forward and then a mile backward. Such is, nevertheless, the view which the vulgar economists have formed of the essence of the dialectic method, because they never see the process but only the completed result, so that the method always seems to them a mystical "hocus-pocus." Nor is there any better justification for the accusation of contradiction than for the accusation of withdrawal.

In Böhm-Bawerk's view, the contradiction is found in this, that, according to the first volume, only commodities embodying *equivalent* amounts of labor are exchanged each for the other, whereas in the third volume we are told that the individual commodities are exchanged one for another in ratios which do not correspond to the ratios between the amounts of labor respectively incorporated in them. Who denies it? If Marx had really maintained that, apart from irregular oscillations, commodities could only be exchanged one for another *because* equivalent quantities of labor are incorporated in them, or only in the ratios corresponding to the amounts of labor incorporated in them, Böhm-Bawerk would be perfectly right. But in the first volume Marx is only discussing exchange relationships as they manifest themselves when commodities are exchanged for their *values;* and solely on this supposition do the commodities embody equivalent quantities of labor. But exchange for their values is not a condition of exchange in general, even though, under certain specific historical conditions, exchange for corresponding values is indispensable, if these historical conditions are to be perpetually reproduced by the mechanism of social life. Under changed historical conditions, modifications of exchange ensue, and the only question is whether these modifications are to be regarded as taking place according to law, and whether they can be represented as modifications of the law of value. If this be so, the law of value, though in modified form, continues to control exchange and the course of prices. All that is necessary is that we should understand the course of prices to be a modification of the pre-existing course of prices, which was under direct control of the law of value.

Böhm-Bawerk's mistake is that he confuses value with price, being led into this confusion by his own theory. Only if value (disregarding chance deviations, which may be neglected because they are mutually compensatory) were identical with price, would a permanent deviation of the prices of individual commodities from their values be a contradiction to the law of value. In the first volume, Marx already refers to the divergence of values from prices. Thus, he asks: "How can we account for the origin of capital on the supposition that prices are regulated by the average price, that is, ultimately by the value of the commodities?" And he adds: "I say 'ultimately,' because average prices do not directly coincide with the values of commodities, as Adam Smith, Ricardo, and others believe" (I, 185n). Again: "We have assumed that prices = values. We shall, however, see in Volume III, that even in the case of average prices the assumption cannot be made in this very simple manner" (I, 244n).

We thus see that the Marxist law of value is not canceled by the data of the third volume, but is merely modified in a definite way. We shall make closer acquaintance with these modifications and grasp their significance better after we have further considered the course of Böhm-Bawerk's exposition.

The first "argument" adduced by Marx in favor of his view is summarized by Böhm-Bawerk as follows:[1] Even if the separate commodities are being sold either above or below their values, these reciprocal fluctuations cancel each other, and in the community itself—taking into account all the branches of production—the total of the prices of production of the commodities produced still remains equal to the sum of their values.

The first thing that strikes us here (and the observation may be repeated with regard to all that follows) is that Böhm-Bawerk denotes as an "argument" that which for Marx was no more than a logical deduction from his premises. It is then, of course, easy to demonstrate that what Marx says does not amount to an argument.

Böhm-Bawerk tells us that it is admitted by Marx that *individual* commodities do not exchange for one another at their values. Stress is laid on the fact that these individual deviations compensate or cancel each other. How much of the law of value is left? asks Böhm-Bawerk. The object of the law of value is to elucidate the actual exchange relations of commodities. We wish to know, for instance, why a coat should be worth as much in exchange as twenty yards of linen. There can clearly be a question of an exchange relationship only between *individual commodities among each other*. As soon,

---

[1] Above, pp. 32 ff.

however, as we look at *all commodities as a whole* and sum up their prices, we must studiously and perforce avoid looking at the relations existing within this whole. The relative differences of price compensate each other in the sum total. It is, therefore, no answer to our question concerning the exchange relationships of the commodities to be told the total price which they bring when taken together. The state of the case is this: to the question of the problem of value, the Marxists first reply with their law of value, telling us that commodities exchange in proportion to the labor time embodied in them. They then revoke this answer as far as it concerns the domain of the exchange of individual commodities, the one domain in which the problem has any meaning, while they maintain it in full force only for the aggregate national product, for a domain therefore in which the problem, being without object, cannot properly be put at all. As an answer to the strict question of the problem of value, the law of value is avowedly contradicted by the facts; and in the only application in which it is not contradicted by them, it is no longer an answer to the question which demanded a solution. It is no answer at all, it is mere tautology. When one penetrates the disguises due to the use of money, commodities do eventually exchange for commodities. The aggregate of commodities is thus identical with the aggregate of the prices paid for them; or the price of the entire national product is nothing else than the national product itself. In these circumstances, therefore, it is quite true that the total price paid for the entire national product coincides precisely with the total amount of value or labor crystallized therein. But this tautological utterance denotes no increase of true knowledge, neither does it prove the correctness of the law that commodities exchange in proportion to the labor embodied in them. Thus Böhm-Bawerk.

The entire train of reasoning is utterly beside the point. Marx is inquiring about the total value, and his critic complains because he is not inquiring about the value of the individual commodity. Böhm-Bawerk fails to see what Marx is aiming at in this demonstration. It is important to show that the sum total of the prices of production is identical with the sum total of the values, because thereby, first of all, it is shown that the total price of production cannot be greater than the total value; but, inasmuch as the process of the production of value is effected solely within the sphere of production, this signifies that all profit originates from production and not from circulation, not from any addition to the finished product subsequently effected by the capitalist. Secondly, we learn that, since the total price is equal to the total value, the total profit cannot be anything else than the total surplus value. The total profit is thereby quantitatively determined, and solely on the basis of this determination does it become possible to calculate the magnitude of the rate of profit.

But can we, without lapsing into absurdity, venture to speak of a total value at all? Böhm-Bawerk confounds the exchange value with the value. Value manifests itself as exchange value, as a quantitatively determined relationship, in virtue of the fact that one commodity can be exchanged for another. But whether, for example, a coat can be exchanged for twenty yards of linen cloth or for forty yards is not a matter of chance, but depends upon objective conditions, upon the amount of socially necessary labor time contained in the coat and in the linen respectively. These conditions must make themselves felt in the process of exchange, they must substantially control that process, and they must have an independent existence quite apart from exchange, if we are to be entitled to speak of the total value of commodities.[1]

Böhm-Bawerk overlooks the fact that value in the Marxist sense is an objective, quantitatively determined magnitude. He overlooks it because in reality the concept of value as determined by the marginal utility theory lacks this quantitative

[1] See Friedrich Engels, "Ergänzung und Nachtrag zum dritten Buch des 'Kapital,'" *Die Neue Zeit*, Vol. I, p. 7. [Reprinted in *Engels on Capital* (1937), p. 97.]

definiteness. Even supposing that the value as equivalent to the marginal utility of each unit in an aggregate of goods is known to me, this value being determined by the utility of the last unit in this store of goods, this does not enable me to calculate the magnitude of the value of the total store. But if the value, in the Marxist sense, of a single unit be known to me, the value of the aggregate of these units is likewise known.

In the transition from the simple to the capitalist production of commodities, the distribution of the social product is what undergoes change. The distribution of the surplus value is now no longer effected in accordance with the measure of the labor power which the individual producer has in his particular sphere expended for the production of surplus value, but is regulated by the magnitude of the capital it has been necessary to advance in order to set in motion the labor that creates the surplus value. It is obvious that the change in the distribution makes no difference in the total amount of surplus value undergoing distribution, that the social relationship is unaltered, and that the change in the distribution comes to pass solely through a modification in the price of the individual commodities. It is further obvious that if we are to determine the amount of divergence, we must know, not only the magnitude of the surplus value, but also the magnitude and indeed the *value* magnitude of the advanced capital. The law of value enables us to determine this magnitude. I can thus readily ascertain the deviations as soon as the value magnitudes are known to me. Value is consequently the necessary theoretical starting point whence we can elucidate the peculiar phenomenon of prices resulting from capitalist competition.

Böhm-Bawerk's entire polemic is therefore all the more fallacious inasmuch as Marx, when he inquires about the total value, does this solely in order to distinguish, within the total value, the individual parts which are important to the capitalist process of distribution. Marx's concern is with the value newly created within a period of production, and with the ratio in which this newly created value is distributed between the working class and the capitalist class, thus furnishing the revenues of the two great classes. It is therefore utterly false to say that Marx revokes the law of value as far as individual commodities are concerned, and maintains it in force solely for the aggregate of these commodities. Böhm-Bawerk is led to make this contention only because he fails to distinguish between value and price. The truth is, rather, that the law of value, directly valid for the social product and its parts, enforces itself only inasmuch as certain definite modifications, conformable to law, occur in the prices of the individual capitalistically-produced commodities—but these modifications can only be made comprehensible by the discovery of the social nexus, and the law of value renders us this service. Finally, it is pure gibberish for Böhm-Bawerk to say, as he does, that the aggregate of commodities is identical with the aggregate of the prices paid for them. Aggregate of commodities and aggregate of prices are incommensurable magnitudes. Marx says that the sum total of the values (not of the commodities) is equal to the sum total of the prices of production. In this case we have commensurability, inasmuch as prices and values are both expressions for different quantities of labor. For the total price of production can be compared with the total value only if, though quantitatively different, they are qualitatively homogeneous, both being the expression of materialized labor.

It is true that Böhm-Bawerk considers that in the ultimate analysis commodities exchange for commodities, and that this is why the aggregate of prices is identical with the aggregate of commodities. But here he disregards not only the price but also the value of the commodities. The question is, given an aggregate of commodities, by the piece, by weight, etc., how great is their value, or what is their price, since for the social product these are coincident. This value or price is the magnitude of a definite quantity of money, and is something completely different from the aggregate of commodities. Marx's inquiry relates to this magnitude, which must according to his theory incorporate an equal expenditure of labor with the aggregate of commodities.

The first "argument," like those that follow, is merely designed to indicate how far the law of value holds good directly, without modifications. Naturally, it is easy for Böhm-Bawerk to show that the modification of the law of value which Marx had previously indicated as a necessary outcome of the nature of capitalist competition, and which he here invariably presupposes, is not proved.

In his criticism of the second argument, Böhm-Bawerk proceeds as follows. Marx, he says, claims for the law of value that it governs the variation of prices, inasmuch as, if the labor time required for the production of commodities be reduced, prices fall; if it be increased, prices rise (III, 208, 211). But Böhm-Bawerk has omitted the condition which Marx attaches to this proposition, for Marx begins by saying: "Whatever may be the way in which the prices of the various commodities are first fixed or mutually regulated, the law of value always dominates their movements." Böhm-Bawerk overlooks this, and reproaches Marx with ignoring the fact that labor, while it is *one* of the determinants of price, is not the sole determinant, as Marx's theory demands. This conclusion, says Böhm-Bawerk, rests on an oversight so obvious that it is amazing Marx failed to perceive it. But what Marx said, and the only thing he wanted to say, was that changes in the expenditure of labor entail changes in prices, that is to say that, the prices being given, the variation in prices is determined by the variation in the productivity of labor. The oversight is here committed by Böhm-Bawerk, who could not have raised the objection he does had he quoted the passage in full.

More important, however, are Böhm-Bawerk's subsequent objections to the Marxist exposition. Marx conceives the transformation of value into price of production as an historical process, which is summarized by Böhm-Bawerk as the "third argument" in the following terms: "The law of value, Marx affirms, governs with undiminished authority the exchange of commodities in certain primary stages in which the change of values into prices of production has not yet been accomplished." The argument, we are told, has not been developed by Marx with precision and clearness, but the substance of it has been interwoven into his other disquisitions.

The conditions which are requisite in order that commodities shall be exchanged for their values are developed by Marx as follows: He assumes that the workers themselves own their respective means of production, that they labor on the average for an equal time and with equal intensity, and that they exchange their commodities directly. Then two workmen in any one day will by their labor have added to their product equal amounts of new value, but the respective products will vary in value in accordance with variations in the amount of labor previously incorporated in the means of production. This latter portion of value will correspond to the constant capital of the capitalist economy; the portion of the new value expended upon the workers' means of subsistence will correspond to the variable capital; while the portion of the new value which remains will correspond to the surplus value, which will accrue to the laborer. Thus both the laborers receive equal values after the value of the invested "constant" capital has been deducted; but the relationship between the portion of value representing surplus value and the value of the means of production—that which corresponds to the capitalist rate of profit—will differ in the respective cases. Since, however, each of them has the value of the means of production made good to him in exchange, the circumstance is completely immaterial. "The exchange of commodities at their values, or approximately at their values, requires, therefore, a much lower stage than their exchange at their prices of production, which requires a relatively high development of capitalist production. . . . Aside from the fact that prices and their movements are dominated by the law of value, it is quite appropriate, under these circumstances, to regard the value of commodities, not only theoretically, but also historically, as existing prior to the prices of production. This applies to conditions in which the laborer owns his means of production, and this is the condition of the land-owning farmer and of the craftsman in the old world as well as the modern world. This agrees also with the view formerly expressed by me that the development of product into commodities arises through the exchange between different communes, not through that between the members of the same commune. It applies not only to this primitive condition, but also to subsequent conditions based on slavery or serfdom, and to the guild organization of handicrafts, so long as the means of production installed in one line of production cannot be transferred to another line except under difficulties, so that the various lines of production maintain, to a certain degree, the same mutual relations as foreign countries or communistic groups" (III, 206-209).

Against this reasoning, Böhm-Bawerk tells us, "the gravest doubts arise, whether we regard it from within or without." It is inherently improbable, and experience also is against it. To demonstrate the improbability, Böhm-Bawerk illustrates Marx's example arithmetically. Laborer I, he says, represents a branch of production which requires technically a relatively large and costly preparatory means of production, for the installation of which he has required five years' labor, while the formation of the finished product needs an additional year. Let us assume that the laborer furnishes the means of production. In that case it will be six years before he secures a return for the value of his labor. Laborer II, on the other hand, can provide the necessary means of production and complete the finished product in a single month, and will therefore secure his yield after one month. But in the Marxist hypothesis absolutely no attention is paid to this difference in point of time as regards the receipt of payment, whereas a year's postponement of the remuneration of labor is assuredly a circumstance demanding compensation. Unquestionably, says Böhm-Bawerk, the different branches of production are not equally accessible to all producers. Those branches which demand an extensive outlay of capital are accessible only to a dwindling minority. Hence, in these latter branches, there ensues a certain restriction in supply, and this ultimately forces the price of their products above the level of those branches which can be carried on without vexatious delays. Marx himself recognizes that in such cases exchange for values would lead to a disproportion. He records the admission by saying that the equivalent surplus values represent unequal rates of profit. But the question naturally arises, why this inequality should not be neutralized by competition just as it is in capitalist society. Marx answers the question by saying that the only thing which matters to the two laborers is that for equal labor time they shall, when the values of the invested constant elements have been deducted, receive equal values, whereas the difference in the rates of profit is a matter of no moment to them, just as the modern wage earner is indifferent as to what rate of profit the quantum of surplus value extorted out of him may represent.

But the comparison is fallacious. For, says Böhm-Bawerk, the laborers of our day do not receive the surplus value, whereas in the supposed case the two laborers do receive it. It is therefore not an indifferent matter whether it be allotted to them by one measure or by another, by the measure of the work done or by the measure of the invested means of production. Consequently the inequality in the rates of profit cannot depend on the fact that the magnitude of the rate of profit is of no moment to the persons concerned.

These last sentences are a salient example of Böhm-Bawerk's polemic method. He completely ignores his opponent's actual line of argument, and quotes an illustrative example (which he proceeds to interpret falsely) as if it had been alleged to be a proof; he then triumphantly announces that an example is not a proof. The difference with which we have to do is the difference between pre-capitalist and capitalist competition. In the local market which it dominates, pre-capitalist competition effectuates the equalization of the different individual values to produce a single market value; capitalist competition effectuates the transformation of value into price of production. This, however, is only possible because capital and labor can remove at will from one sphere of production to another; this removal cannot take place freely until all legal and material obstacles to the transfer have ceased to exist, cannot take place until (disregarding minor considerations) there exists absolute liberty of movement for capital and for labor. But in pre-capitalist conditions this *competition for spheres of investment* is impossible, and consequently the equalization of the different rates of profit is impossible. Since this is so, since the laborer who produces on his own account cannot change his sphere of production at will, the difference in the profit rates conjoined with equal masses of profit (= surplus value), is indifferent to him, just as to the wage laborer it is of no moment what rate of profit is represented by the amount of surplus value extorted from him. The *tertium comparationis* [the third term in the comparison] is in both cases that the laborers' chief concern is with the amount of surplus value. For whether they get the surplus value or not, in both cases they have to do the work which produces it. It depends strictly upon the duration of their labor. The matter may be expressed in arithmetical terms as follows. Let us suppose that there are two producers each of whom works on his own account, that one of them makes use of means of production amounting to 20 shillings daily, and that the other makes use of means of production amounting to 10 shillings daily. Let us further suppose that each of them daily produces new value to the amount of 20 shillings. The first laborer will receive 40 shillings for his product, the second will receive 30 shillings; of the 40 shillings 20, and of the 30 shillings 10, will be reconverted into means of production, so that there will remain for each laborer 20 shillings. Since they are not free to change the sphere of production at will, the inequality of the rates of profit is of no consequence to them. Of the 20 shillings which remain at the disposal of each, let 10 shillings represent the portion used to provide the laborer's means of subsistence, or (in capitalist phraseology) let 10 shillings represent their variable capital, then for each of them the remaining 10 shillings will constitute surplus value. For a modern capitalist the affair would assume a very different complexion. In the first sphere he would have to disburse capital amounting to 30 shillings in the form of 20c = 10v in order to gain 10 shillings surplus value; in the second sphere, if he invested an equal amount of capital, it would be in the form of 15c + 15v and he would gain 15 shillings surplus value in return for his outlay. Since capital is transferable at will there will be competition between the investments until the profits are equalized, which will ensue when the prices are no longer 40 shillings and 30 shillings respectively, but 35 shillings in each case.

But Böhm-Bawerk's polemic secures its triumph in the "arithmetical exposition" of the example given by Marx. In this exposition the simple production of commodities presupposed by Marx is in the twinkling of an eye transformed into capitalist production. For with what else than capitalist production have we to do when Böhm-Bawerk equips one of the laborers with means of production requiring five years to furnish, while the means of production required by the other laborer can be furnished in a time measured in days? Does not this imply differences in the organic composition of capital, differences which, when so extensive, can arise only as the outcome of capitalist development? In the case of the laborer who works on his own account, such a laborer as Marx had in view, the means of production are tools of a comparatively simple kind, and there is no very notable difference in value between the tools used in the different spheres of production. Where tools of considerable value are employed (a fulling mill, for instance) these are usu-

ally the property of the guild or of the city, and each guilds-
man's share therein is insignificant. Speaking generally, in
pre-capitalist conditions dead labor plays a modest part as compared with living labor. Although, however, the differences in
question are inconsiderable, they do in fact suffice to determine
certain differences in the rates of profit, differences whose
equalization is hindered by the artificial barriers surrounding
every sphere of production. But wherever the means of production bulked largely in comparison with labor, co-operative industry made its appearance at an early date, was speedily
transformed into capitalist industry, and as a rule culminated
in legalized or virtual monopoly (as in the mining industry).

Marx further assumes that the laborers in his illustration
mutually exchange their respective products. Böhm-Bawerk
complains of the injustice involved, in that one of the laborers,
after working for six years, should receive merely an equivalent
for his labor time, and not be allotted in addition some compensation for the time he has had to wait. But if one of them has
had to wait six years for the return, the other has had to wait
six years for the product, has had to store up his own products
for six years that he may be able at last to exchange them for
the former's product, now at length completed. Hence there is
no occasion for allotting a special compensation to one of the
two. But in reality there is no more historical warrant for the
assumption of so great a divergence between the times when re-
turns can be expected, than there is for the similar assumption
of an extensive variation in the organic composition of the
"capital."

Böhm-Bawerk, however, is not content with the Middle Ages.
In the "modern world," too, relationships exist which correspond
to those of the Marxist hypothesis. They are found, says our critic,
as Marx himself indicates, in the case of the land-owning peasant
farmer and of the handicraftsman. These ought to secure equal
incomes whether the capital they have invested in means of production amounts to 10 shillings or to 10,000 shillings, a supposi-

tion which manifestly conflicts with the facts. Certainly it conflicts with the facts. But Marx never maintained that in the "modern" world two distinct prices obtain for an article according as it has been produced by capitalists or by handicraftsmen. As far as the "modern" world is concerned, Marx is referring, not to capitalist conditions, but to the medieval system as contrasted with the classical. This is manifest from the context, and it seems almost incredible that Böhm-Bawerk should have misunderstood the passage as he has done.

However, Böhm-Bawerk assures us that Marx's views as to the equalization of the rates of profit are historically untenable, and refers in this connection to an objection raised by Werner Sombart in the latter's criticism of Marx's third volume. But in actual fact Sombart makes no reference to the question of the validity of the law of value in pre-capitalist conditions. All he does is to oppose the contention that during the transition from the medieval to the capitalist economy, the equalization of the rates of profit has been brought about by the leveling of the originally unequal rates of surplus value. He holds, rather, that the starting point of capitalist competition is from the very outset to be found in the pre-existing commercial rate of profit. Had surplus value been the starting point, capitalism would first have seized upon the spheres in which living labor predominated, and only gradually would it have proceeded to exploit other spheres of production, in proportion as in those spheres prices had fallen owing to a great increase in production. In truth production develops with especial vigor in spheres wherein there is much constant capital, as for example in the mining industry. Capital would have had no reason to transfer itself from one sphere of production to another without a prospect of a "customary profit" such as existed in commercial profit. But, continues Sombart, the error can be shown in yet another way. If, at the outset of capitalist production, exorbitant profits had been obtainable in spheres where variable capital preponderated, this would imply that all at once capital had made use as wage earners of those who had hitherto been independent producers, had employed them at half the amount which they had previously earned for themselves, and had pocketed all the difference realizable by the sale of the commodities at prices corresponding to their values. In actual fact, says Sombart, capitalist production began with the exploitation of declassed individuals, and in spheres of production some of which were completely new creations; unquestionably, therefore, capitalist production started from the fixing of prices directly in relation to the amount of capital invested.[1]

In opposition to Sombart, my own opinion is that equalization of the different rates of surplus value to form a single rate of profit was the outcome of a process long drawn out. In Sombart's opinion it would be incomprehensible that the capitalist should have troubled to gain control of production unless he had a prospect of securing as industrial capitalist the same profit which he had been in the habit of securing as a merchant. It seems to me, however, that Sombart overlooks the consideration that the merchant did not in the first instance cease to be a merchant when he became a manufacturer. The capital he employed in export was still his main concern. But by employing his extra capital (and in view of the comparatively small amount of constant capital then requisite, no considerable sum would be needed) for the production of commodities on his own account, he was enabled to provide the necessary articles more regularly and in larger quantities—important considerations in a rapidly expanding market. In the second place, inasmuch as he appropriated part of the surplus value produced by the handicraftsmen he transferred to the new industry, he realized an extra profit. Even if the profit rate he could secure on the capital invested in industry was lower than that obtainable on his commercial capital, nevertheless the total rate of profit was henceforth greater. However, a rapid increase in his industrial profit

[1] Sombart, *op. cit.*, p. 585.

rate occurred when, through the utilization of new technical methods (the association of labor, and factory production), he was enabled to produce articles more cheaply than his competitors, who were still satisfying their demand with commodities produced by independent handicraftsmen. Competition then forced his rivals to adopt the new method of production and to disregard the products of the handicraftsmen's labor. With the further progress of capitalism, when production no longer took place mainly for the purposes of the mercantile exporter, and when the capitalist began to effect a conquest of the whole market, his profit was chiefly dependent upon the following factors: His technical methods of production were superior, so that he could produce more cheaply than the handicraftsmen. Since for the time being the market value of the handicraftsman's products determined prices, the capitalist was able to realize extra surplus value or extra profit, which was greater in proportion as his technical superiority was more marked. For the most part, through special legal privileges, the exploitation of superior technical methods was a monopoly of individual capitalists. Not until the days of monopoly were over, not until the restrictions upon the transferability of capital had been abolished, not until the shackles of the laborer had been removed, was the equalization of the varying rates of profit, originally so divergent, rendered possible.

First of all, by the supplanting of handicraftsmanship and by the increase of competition within the sphere of capitalist production, the extra profit realizable by capital was reduced; and subsequently freedom of transference from one sphere of production to another effectuated the equalization of profit to become average profit.

The expansion of the market creates a need for enhanced and more regular supply, and this in turn impels commercial capital to acquire control of production as well. The profit which capital thus realizes may be less than commercial profit. For to capital it assumes the form of extra profit, which is made because the commodities which capital produces are obtainable by it more cheaply than those purchasable from independent handicrafts-men. In the further course of economic evolution, the extra profit made with the aid of superior technical equipment by the capitalist who is competing with the handicraftsman for the home market becomes the motive force for the exclusive seizure of a sphere of production by capital. The organic composition of capital plays here a minor part; and in any case, as far as pre-capitalist conditions are concerned, Böhm-Bawerk and Sombart overestimate the extent of differences in the organic composition of capital.

Only where, as a matter of actual fact, the means of produc-tion bulk large in importance, as is the case in the mining in-dustry, does the great preponderance of constant capital become a reason for capitalization, for which co-operation constitutes a preliminary stage. For the most part such industries are likewise monopolies, the yield of which has to be dealt with by special laws.

As soon, however, as capitalist competition has definitively established the equal rate of profit, that rate becomes the start-ing point for the calculations of the capitalists in the investment of capital in newly-created branches of production. The prices here fluctuate on either side of that price of production whose attainment makes the particular branch of production appear profitable. At the same time, the capitalist goes halfway to meet competition, for he himself accepts average profit as a regulative principle, and the sole effect of competition is to prevent his deviating from the norm and from securing an above-average profit for any considerable period.

It is obvious, moreover, that the formation of price in capital-ist society must differ from the formation of price in social con-ditions based upon the simple production of commodities. We shall now pursue our examination of the change in the character of the formation of price by considering the "fourth argument."

Böhm-Bawerk tells us that, according to Marx, in a complex economic system the law of value regulates the prices of production, at least indirectly and in the last resort, since the total value of the commodities determined by the law of value determines the total surplus value, while this last regulates the amount of the average profit and therefore the general rate of profit (III, 211-212). The average profit determines the price of production. In the sense of the Marxist doctrine, says Böhm-Bawerk, this is correct, but the statement is incomplete, and our critic attempts to "complete" it as follows: The price of production is equal to cost price plus average profit. The cost price of the means of production consists, again, of two components: first the outlay on wages; and secondly the outlay upon means of production whose values have already been transformed into prices of production. If we continue this analysis we come at last—as does Adam Smith in his "natural price," with which, indeed, Marx expressly identifies his price of production —to resolve the price of production into two components or *determinants* [!]: (1) the sum total of the wages paid during the different stages of production, which taken together represent the actual cost price of the commodities; (2) the sum total of the profits calculated on all these disbursements upon wages. Consequently *one* determinant of the price of a commodity is the average profit incidental to its production. Of the other determinant, the wages paid, Marx speaks no further in this passage. But it is evident, says Böhm-Bawerk, that the total expended outlay upon wages is a product of the quantity of labor employed, multiplied by the average rate of wages. Since, however, according to the law of value the exchange relations must be determined solely by the *quantity* of labor expended, and since Marx denies that the rate of wages has any influence upon the value of the commodities, it is also evident that, of the two components of the factor "outlay upon wages," only the amount of labor expended is in harmony with the law of value, while in the second component, rate of wages, a determinant alien to the law of value enters among the determinants of the prices of production.

It is almost incredible, the way in which Böhm-Bawerk deduces as a self-evident inference from Marx's train of thought the very conclusion which Marx has in so many words stigmatized as a gross fallacy. Let Marx speak for himself. "The value of the annual product in commodities, just like the value of the commodities produced by some particular investment of capital, and like the value of any individual commodity, resolves itself into two parts: Part A, which replaces the value of the advanced constant capital, and Part B, which presents itself in the form of revenue as wages, profit, and rent. This last part of value, B, stands in opposition to Part A to the extent that this Part A, under otherwise equal circumstances, in the first place never assumes the form of revenue, and in the second place always flows back in the form of capital, and of constant capital at that. The other portion, B, however, carries within itself an antagonism. Profit and rent have this in common with wages that all three of them are forms of revenue. Nevertheless, they differ essentially from each other in that profit and rent are surplus value, unpaid labor, whereas wages are paid labor." [1]

In that he reproduces as Marx's opinion "the incredible error in analysis which permeates the whole of political economy since Adam Smith," Böhm-Bawerk makes a double mistake. First of all he ignores constant capital. Apart from all else, this is least permissible in a place in which we have to do with the transformation of value into price of production. For what is decisive for this transformation is the organic composition of the capital, that is to say, the ratio between the constant and the variable capital. To disregard the constant capital in this case is to disregard the most essential point, is to render it quite impossible to understand the formation of the price of production. Yet graver, perhaps, is the second mistake. Inasmuch as Böhm-

[1] Vol. III, p. 977.

Bawerk, in common with Adam Smith, makes variable capital and surplus value "component parts," or as he puts it more stringently, "determinants," of value, he perverts Marx's doctrine into its precise opposite. For Marx, value is the *prius,* the thing given, while v and s are no more than parts whose magnitude is limited by the new value added to the dead labor (c) and determined in accordance with the quantity of labor. How much of this new value (which can be resolved into v + s, but does not originate from them) can be assigned to v and how much to s, is determined by the value of the labor power, which is equal to the value of the means of subsistence necessary for its maintenance, the balance remaining available for surplus value. Böhm-Bawerk is still entangled in the capitalist illusion in accordance with which the cost price is regarded as a constitutive factor of the value or of the price. Precisely because he ignores c, he makes it utterly impossible for himself to gain insight into the process of the formation of value. He does not see that in the product the portion of the cost price which represents the constant capital appears reproduced with its value unchanged. It is otherwise with the portion represented by v. The value of the variable capital presents itself in the form of the means of subsistence consumed by the laborer. The value of these means of subsistence is annihilated in the process of consumption. But the new value produced by the laborers belongs to the capitalist; a portion of this new value is re-invested by him in variable capital, and seems to him to replace this again and again, just as another portion of the value which flows back to him replaces the constant capital whose value is actually transferred to the product. The distinction between c and v is thereby obliterated, and the process of the formation of value is enveloped in mystery. Labor no longer manifests itself as the source of value, for value appears to be constituted out of the cost price plus an excess over cost price coming no matter whence. Thus the "price of labor" seems to be the cause of the

price of the product, so that ultimately the whole analysis resolves itself into the circular explanation of price by price.
Instead of conceiving of value as a magnitude which, in accordance with definite laws, undergoes subdivison into two portions, one of which replaces the constant capital, while the other
becomes revenue (v + s), revenue itself is made a constituent
of price, and the constant capital is forgotten. Thus, Marx expressly insists that "it would be a mistake to say that the value
of wages, the rate of profit, and the rate of rent form independent constituent elements of value, whose composition gives
rise to the value of commodities, leaving aside the constant part;
in other words, it would be a mistake to say that they are constituent elements of the value of·commodities, or of the price of
production" (III, 994).

If, however, the wage of labor be not a constituent of value, it
naturally has no influence upon the magnitude of value. How,
then, is it possible for Böhm-Bawerk to continue to proclaim
that it has an influence upon value? To demonstrate this influence, he gives us two tables. Three commodities, A, B, and C,
have at the outset the same price of production, namely 100,
while the organic composition of the capital differs in each case.
The daily wage is 5; the rate of surplus value (s') is 100 percent; the total capital being 1,500, the average rate of profit (p)
is 10 percent.

Com- modity	Working Days	Wages	Capital Employed	Average Profit	Price of Pro- duction
A	10	50	500	50	100
B	6	30	700	70	100
C	14	70	300	30	100
Totals	30	150	1,500	150	300

Now let us assume that wages rise from 5 to 6; of the 300, 180
will now accrue to wages and 120 to profit; p' is now 8 percent;
the table, therefore, must be modified as follows:

Com- modity	Working Days	Wages	Capital Employed	Average Profit	Price of Pro- duction
A	10	60	500	40	100
B	6	36	700	56	92
C	14	84	300	24	108
Totals	30	180	1,500	120	300

The tables exhibit certain peculiarities. Namely, we are not told the magnitude of the contant capital employed in the various branches, nor do we learn how much of the constant capital is transferred to the product; thus only is Böhm-Bawerk enabled to draw the conclusion that although a notable constant capital is employed, it nowhere reappears in the product, and the prices of production are identical. Still less are we able to understand how it happens that *higher* wages can be paid with the *same* capital. It is true that these errors make little difference to the final results, for Böhm-Bawerk does in a sense allow for the organic composition, inasmuch as he calculates the profit upon varying outlays of capital; and his second survey alters only the absolute figures, not the relative ones, for the rate of profit undergoes a greater fall than Böhm-Bawerk declares, seeing that the total capital is increased. But the failure to take the constant capital into account renders it impossible to secure an insight into the actual process. If we correct Böhm-Bawerk's tables, they read as follows:

Com- modity	Total Capital $c+v$	c	v	s	p	Value	Price of Pro- duction
A	500	450	50	50	50	550	550
B	700	670	30	30	70	730	770
C	300	230	70	70	30	370	330
Totals	1,500	1,350	150	150	150	1,650	1,650= 1,500+ 150

To avoid complicating the calculation needlessly, we have assumed that c is entirely used up. If the wage now rises from 5 to 6, the total capital is increased from 1,500 to 1,530, because v increases from 150 to 180; the surplus value is reduced to 120, the rate of surplus value to 66.6 percent, and the rate of profit to approximately 7.8 percent. The new value created by the laborers remains unchanged, and is 300. But the organic composition of the capital has been modified, and therewith has been modified the factor that is decisive in the transformation of value into price of production.

Com-modity	Total Capital c+v	c	v	s	p	Value	Price of Production
A	510	450	60	40	40	550	550
B	706	670	36	24	55	730	761
C	314	230	84	56	25	370	339
Totals	1,530	1,350	180	120	120	1,650	1,650

The table shows the "effects of general fluctuations of wages on prices of production" (III, Chap. XI). We obtain the following laws [1]: (1) as far as a capital of average composition is concerned, the price of production of the commodities undergoes no change; (2) as far as a capital of lower composition is concerned, the price of production of the commodities rises, but not proportionally to the fall in the profits; (3) as far as a capital of higher composition is concerned, the price of production falls, but not as much as the profit (III, 236). What are we to deduce from this? If we are to believe Böhm-Bawerk, it appears that a rise in wages (the quantity of labor remaining unchanged) brings about a material alteration in the originally equal prices of production. This alteration can be ascribed in part only to the change in the rate of profit. Not wholly, of course, seeing that, for example, the price of production of commodity C has *risen*

[1] Rise in wages is alone considered. Naturally a fall in wages would have the contrary effect.

notwithstanding the fall in the rate of profit. This puts it beyond doubt that in the magnitude of wages we have to do with a price-determinant whose efficacy is not exhausted in the influencing of the magnitude of the profit, but which rather exercises *a direct influence of its own*. Böhm-Bawerk therefore believes that he has good reason for undertaking an independent examination of this link in the chain of determinants of price which Marx has passed over. (Marx has a special chapter on the subject!)

We have already seen that this "independence" is pushed so far as to represent Marx as saying the opposite of what he really thought. We now see how far Böhm-Bawerk's independence transcends the rules of logic. The same change in wages effects in the first case no change in the price, in the second case it causes a rise, and in the third case it causes a fall in the price. And this is what he calls having "a direct influence of its own" on price! In fact, however, the tables show clearly that wages can neither constitute components nor determinants of price; for, were it otherwise, an increase in these components must raise price and a decrease in these components must lower price. Nor can average profit constitute a magnitude independently influencing price, for if such an influence existed, whenever the profit falls the price must also fall. But by ignoring the constant portion of capital, and by thus leaving out of consideration the organic composition of capital, Böhm-Bawerk deprives himself of the possibility of explaining the process.

Speaking generally, we cannot gain an insight into the entire process from the standpoint of the individual capital, but this is the outlook to which we are restricted when we conceive the wage of labor to be an independent component of price. From this outlook it is impossible to understand how the capitalist can fail to be indemnified in the price for an increase in wages, for a greater outlay of capital. Nothing but the social relationships whose essence is disclosed by the law of value suffices to explain how the same cause, an increase in wages, can exercise so diver-

gent an effect upon the individual capitals, the effect varying
as the ratio varies in which they respectively participate in the
surplus-value-creating process of the social capital. Their participation in the social surplus-value-creating process is, however,
indicated by their organic composition.

But the changed relationship between the capitals consists in
this, that their share in the production of the total surplus value
has been altered; the surplus value has diminished; but the respective capitals have contributed in varying manners to this
diminution, according to variations in the magnitude of the
labor they have respectively set in motion. Since, however, the
reduced surplus value is to be distributed among them in like
manner, the modification of their respective parts in the production of surplus value must find expression in a modification of
the prices. The capitals, therefore, must not be regarded individually, as Böhm-Bawerk regards them, but must be apprehended in their social interconnections, as parts, that is to say,
of social capital. But the part they respectively play in the creation of the total value of the social product is only to be recognized by a knowledge of their organic composition, by a knowledge of the relationship in which the dead labor, whose value is
merely transferred, stands to the living labor which creates new
value and of which the variable capital is the index. To disregard this organic composition is tantamount to disregarding the
social relationships of the individual capital. This renders it
equally impossible to understand the process whereby value is
transformed into price of production, and to understand the
laws which regulate variations in the price of production—laws
different from those which regulate variations in value, but always traceable in the ultimate analysis to variations in the relationships of value.

"Seeing that the price of production in the second illustration
rises, while it falls in the third, it is evident from these opposite
effects brought about by a fall in the rate of surplus value or by
a general rise of wages that there is no prospect of any compen-

sation in the price for the rise in wages, since the fall of the price
of production in III cannot very well compensate the capitalist
for the fall in the profit, and since the rise of the price in II does
not prevent a fall in profit. On the contrary, in either case,
whether the price rises or falls, the profit remains the same as
that of the average capital whose price remains unchanged. . . .
It follows from this, that if the price did not rise in II and fall
in III, II would have to sell below and III above the new, recently reduced, average profit. It is quite evident that a rise of
wages must affect a capitalist who has invested one tenth of his
capital in wages differently from one who has invested one
fourth or one half, according to whether 50, 25, or 10 percent of
capital are advanced for wages. An increase in the price of production on one side, and a fall on the other, according to whether
a capital is below or above the average social composition, is
effected only by leveling to the new reduced average profit. It is
clear that when, in consequence of the establishment of a general rate of profit for the capitals of lower composition (those
wherein v is above the average), the values are lowered on the
occasion of their transformation into prices of production, for
the capitals of higher composition the values will be increased."[1]
The variation in the price of production consequent upon a
change in wages manifests itself as a direct effect of the new
average rate of profit. As we have previously seen, the establishment of this rate is an outcome of capitalist competition. Böhm-
Bawerk's polemic is therefore primarily unfortunate in this,
that it is not directed against the decisive point, but against a
phenomenon which only makes its appearance as a necessary
consequence, as a sequel, of the primary condition, which is the
formation of the price of production upon the basis of the equal
rate of profit.

It makes no difference to the regulation of the price of production by the law of value, that in the wage of labor itself,

[1] Vol. III, p. 237.

that is to say in the magnitude of the variable portion of capital which has to be advanced, the transformation of the values of the laborer's necessary means of subsistence into prices of production has already been completed. We must not attempt to prove the contention that the price of production of a commodity is not regulated by the law of value, by maintaining the same thing of another commodity, to wit, labor power. For the deviation of the variable portion of capital takes place according to exactly the same laws as are observed in the case of any other commodity; in this respect there is no difference between the variable and the constant portion of capital. Only because Böhm-Bawerk makes the "value of the labor power" a determinant of the value of the product, does he fall into the error of looking upon the deviation in the price of labor power from its value as a disturbance of the law of value. Again, the magnitude of the total surplus value is unaffected by this deviation. For the total surplus value, which is equal to the total profit and regulates the rate of profit, is calculated for the social capital, where the deviations of the prices of production from value balance each other.

One more only of Böhm-Bawerk's objections remains to be considered. Even if, as Marx declares, the total surplus value regulates the average rate of profit, this nevertheless constitutes but *one* determinant, while as a second determinant, completely independent of the first, and *likewise completely independent of the law of value*, there operates the magnitude of the capital existing in society. Now, apart from the fact that the magnitude of the social capital is here assumed by Böhm-Bawerk to be known (which presupposes the law of value, since we have to do with the determination of the magnitude of a value), the objection has been expressly refuted by Marx, who writes: "The proportion of the sum of appropriated surplus values to the advanced total capital of society varies. Since the variation in this case is not due to the rate of surplus value, it must be due to the total capital, or rather to its constant part. The mass of this part, technically speaking, increases or decreases in proportion to the quantity of labor power bought by the variable capital, and the mass of its value increases or decreases with the increase or decrease of its own mass. Its mass of value, then, increases or decreases likewise in proportion to the mass of the value of the variable capital. If the same labor sets more constant capital in motion, labor has become more productive. If less, less productive. There has then been a change in the productivity of labor, and a change must have taken place in the value of certain commodities. The following rule then applies. . . . If the price of production of a certain commodity changes in consequence of a change in the average rate of profit, its own value may have remained unchanged, but a change must have taken place in the value of other commodities" (III, 240).

Chapter Three

THE SUBJECTIVIST OUTLOOK

The phenomenon of variations in the price of production has shown us that the phenomena of capitalist society can never be understood if the commodity or capital be considered in isolation. It is the social relationship which these occupy, and changes in that relationship, which control and elucidate the movements of individual capitals, themselves no more than portions of the total social capital. But the representative of the psychological school of political economy fails to see this social nexus, and he therefore necessarily misunderstands a theory which definitely aims at disclosing the social determinism of economic phenomena, a theory whose starting point therefore is society and not the individual. In apprehending and expounding this theory he is ever influenced by his own individualistic mentality, and he thus arrives at contradictions which he ascribes to the theory, while they are in truth ascribable solely to his interpretations of the theory.

This confusion may be traced in all the stages of Böhm-Bawerk's polemic. Even the fundamental concept of the Marxist system, the concept of value-creating labor, is apprehended in a purely subjective manner. To him "labor" is identical with "trouble" or "effort" ["*Mühe*"]. To make this individual feeling of distaste the cause of value naturally leads us to see in value a purely psychological fact, and to deduce the value of commodities from our *evaluation of the labor* they have cost. As is well known, this is the foundation which Adam Smith adopts for his theory of value, for he is ever inclined to abandon the objective standpoint for a subjective. Smith writes: "Equal quantities of labor must at all times and places be of equal value to the laborer. In his ordinary state of health, strength, and spirits; in the ordinary degree of his skill and dexterity, he must always lay down the same portion of his ease, his liberty, and his happiness." [1] If labor regarded as "trouble" be the basis of our personal estimate of value, then the "value of the labor" is a constituent, or a "determinant" as Böhm-Bawerk puts it, of the value of commodities. But it need not be the only one, for a number of other factors which influence the subjective estimates made by individuals take their places beside labor and have an equal right to be regarded as determinants of value. If, therefore, we identify the value of commodities with the personal estimate of the value of these commodities made by this or that individual, it seems quite arbitrary to select labor as the sole basis for such an estimate.

From the subjectivist standpoint, therefore, the standpoint from which Böhm-Bawerk levels his criticism, the labor theory of value appears untenable from the very outset. And it is because he adopts this standpoint that Böhm-Bawerk is unable to perceive that Marx's concept of labor is totally opposed to his own. Already in *A Contribution to the Critique of Political Economy* Marx had emphasized his opposition to Adam Smith's subjectivist outlook by writing "[Smith] fails to see the objective equalization of different kinds of labor which the social process forcibly carries out, mistaking it for the subjective equality of the labors of individuals." [2] In truth, Marx is entirely unconcerned with the individual motivation of the estimate of value. In capitalist society it would be absurd to make "trouble"

[1] *Wealth of Nations,* Book I, Chap. 5.
[2] Kerr ed., p. 68.

the measure of value, for speaking generally the owners of the products have taken no trouble at all, whereas the trouble has been taken by those who have produced but do not own them. With Marx, in fact, every individual relationship is excluded from the conception of value-creating labor; labor is regarded, not as something which arouses feelings of pleasure or its opposite, but as an objective magnitude, inherent in the commodities, and determined by the degree of development of social productivity. Whereas for Böhm-Bawerk, labor seems merely one of the determinants in personal estimates of value, in Marx's view labor is the basis and connective tissue of human society, and in Marx's view the degree of productivity of labor and the method of organization of labor determine the character of social life. Since labor, viewed in its social function as the total labor of society of which each individual labor forms merely an aliquot part, is made the principle of value, economic phenomena are subordinated to objective laws independent of the individual will and controlled by social relationships. Beneath the husk of economic categories we discover social relationships, relationships of production, wherein commodities play the part of intermediaries, the social relationships being reproduced by these intermediate processes, or undergoing a gradual transformation until they demand a new type of intermediation.

Thus the law of value becomes a law of motion for a definite type of social organization based upon the production of commodities, for in the last resort all change in social structure can be referred to changes in the relationships of production, that is to say to changes in the evolution of productive power and in the organization of [productive] labor. We are thereby led, in the most striking contrast to the outlook of the psychological school, to regard political economy as a part of sociology, and sociology itself as a historical science. Böhm-Bawerk has never become aware of this contrast of outlooks. The question whether the "subjectivist method" or the "objectivist method" is the sound method in economics he decides in a controversy with Sombart by saying that each method must supplement the other—whereas in truth we are not concerned at all with two different methods, but with contrasted and mutually exclusive outlooks upon the whole of social life. Thus it happens that Böhm-Bawerk, unfailingly carrying on the controversy from his subjectivist and psychological standpoint, discovers contradictions in the Marxist theory which seem to him to be contradictions solely because of his own subjectivist interpretation of the theory.

But if labor be the only measure for the estimate of value and therewith the only measure of value, it is as regards this subjectivist outlook only logical that in that case commodities should exchange solely by the measure of equal quantities of labor embodied in them, for otherwise it would be impossible to see what should induce the individuals to deviate from their personal estimates of value. If, however, the facts do not conform to these premises, then the law of value loses all significance, even if labor be no more than one determinant among several. This is why Böhm-Bawerk lays so much stress upon the contention that commodities are *not* exchanged one for another by the measure of equal quantities of labor. This necessarily appears to be a contradiction when value is conceived, not as an objective quantity, but as the outcome of individual motivation. For if labor be the measure for my personal estimate of value, then I shall not be inclined to exchange my good for another unless in that other I obtain something which, if I had to produce it for myself, would cost me at least as much labor as my own good has cost me. A permanent deviation of the exchange relationship is in fact, if the subjectivist conception of the law of value be once assumed, a contradiction per se, a suspension of the meaning (that is to say, of the subjectivist meaning) of the law of value, which here supplies the individual's motive for economic action.

Very different is Marx's outlook. In his view, that goods

contain labor is one of their intrinsic qualities; that they are exchangeable is a distinct quality, one solely dependent on the will of the possessor, and one which presupposes that they are owned and alienable. The relationship of the quantity of labor to the process of exchange does not come into consideration until they are regularly *produced* as commodities, produced that is to say as goods specifically destined for exchange; thus this relationship makes its appearance only in a definite phase of historic evolution. The quantitative ratio wherein they are now exchanged becomes thereby dependent upon the time of production, which is in its turn determined by the degree of social productivity. The exchange relationship thus loses its chance character, thus ceases to be dependent upon the caprice of the owner. The social conditions imposed upon labor become objective limitations for the individual, and the social complex controls the individual's activities.

Now the mode of the social process of production determines the social process of distribution, for this latter is no longer consciously regulated, as if in a communist community. Under capitalism the process of distribution manifests itself as the outcome of the exchanges effected by independent individual producers, exchanges controlled by the laws of competition.

The Marxist law of value starts from this, that commodities exchange at their values, this meaning that commodities exchange one for another when they embody equal quantities of labor. The equality of the quantities of labor is solely a condition for the exchange of commodities at their values. Böhm-Bawerk, entangled in his subjectivist interpretation, mistakes this condition for a condition of exchange in general. But it is obvious that the exchange of commodities at their values, while on the one hand it merely constitutes the theoretical starting point for a subsequent analysis, on the other hand directly controls a historic phase of the production of commodities, a phase to which a specific kind of competition corresponds.

But the exchange relationship of commodities is no more than the material expression of the social relationships of persons, and what in fact secures realization in the exchange relationship is the *equality of the agents of production*. Because, in the simple production of commodities, equal and independent laborers severally possessed of their means of production confront one another, exchange takes place at prices which tend to correspond to the values. Thus only can the mechanism of the simple production of commodities be maintained; thus only can the conditions requisite for the reproduction of the relationships of production be fulfilled.

In such a society the product of labor belongs to the laborer. If by permanent deviation from this rule (chance deviations are mutually compensatory) a portion of the product of labor be taken away from the laborer and assigned to another person, the foundations of the society will be modified; the former will become a wage laborer (engaged in home industry), and the latter will become a capitalist. This is actually one of the ways in which the simple production of commodities comes to an end. But it cannot come to an end unless there has occurred a modification in social relationships, carrying with it a modification in exchange, the expression of social relationships.

In the capitalist process of exchange, whose purpose is the realization of surplus value, the equality of the economic units is once more reflected. These, however, are no longer independently working producers, but owners of capital. Their equality secures expression in that the exchange is only normal when the profits are equal, when both are average profit. The exchange which gives expression to the equality of the owners of capital is of course differently determined from the exchange that is based upon an equality in the expenditure of the labor. But just as both societies have the same foundations, the division of property and the division of labor; just as capitalist society can be conceived as merely a higher modification of the earlier type of society; so also is the law of value unchanged in its foundation, for it has merely undergone certain modifications in its realization. These are caused by the specific mode of capitalist competition, which effectuates the proportional equality of capital. The share in the total product, whose value remains directly determined by the law of value, was formerly proportional to the individual's expenditure of labor, but now becomes proportional to the expenditure of capital requisite to set labor in motion. Thus the subordination of labor to capital finds expression. It appears as social subordination, the whole society being subdivided into capitalists and laborers, the former being owners of the product of the latter, the total product, determined by the law of value, being divided among the capitalists. The capitalists are free and equal; their equality is displayed in the price of production $= k + p$, where p is proportional to k. The dependent position of the laborer is shown by his appearance as one of the constituents of k, side by side with machinery, lubricating oil, and dumb beasts; this is all he is worth to the capitalist as soon as he has left the market and has taken his place in the factory to create surplus value. For a moment only did he play his part in the market, as a free man selling his labor power. The brief glory in the market and the prolonged debasement in the factory—here we see the difference between legal equality and economic equality, between the equality demanded by the bourgeoisie and the equality demanded by the proletariat.

The capitalist mode of production (this is its historic significance, and this is why we can regard it as a preliminary stage on the way to socialist society) socializes mankind to a greater extent than did any previous mode of production, that is to say, capitalism makes the existence of the individual man dependent upon the social relationships amid which he is placed. It does so in an antagonistic form, by the establishment of the two great classes, making the performance of social labor the function of one of these classes, and enjoyment of the products of labor the function of the other.

The individual is not yet an "immediate" of society, that is, he does not yet possess a direct relationship to society, for his economic position is determined by his position as member of a class. The individual can only exist as a capitalist because his class appropriates the product of the other class, and his own share is solely determined by the total surplus value, not by the surplus value individually appropriated by him.

This significance of class gives expression to the law of value as a *social* law. To confute the theory of value it must be shown to lack confirmation *in the social domain.*

In capitalist society the individual appears as ruler or slave according as he is enrolled in one or other of the two great classes. Socialist society makes him free, inasmuch as it abolishes the antagonistic form of society, inasmuch as it consciously and directly installs socialization. No longer, then, are the interrelationships of society concealed behind enigmatic economic categories which seem to be the natural qualities of things; these interrelationships now manifest themselves as the freely willed outcome of human co-operation. Political economy then ceases to exist in the form we have hitherto known, and is replaced by a science of the "wealth of nations."

Competition is the power that effects the transformation of values into prices of production. But the competition with which we have to do here is capitalist competition. Competition is further necessary to secure a sale at prices which shall fluctuate round the value. In the simple production of commodities, on the other hand, we are concerned with the reciprocal competition of the finished commodities; it is this which equates the individual values to constitute a market value, thus objectively correcting the subjective errors of individuals. But here (in capitalist society) we have to do with the competition of capitals for different spheres of investment, a competition which establishes equal rates of profit, a competition which cannot become effective until after the abolition of the legal and material shackles which had previously been imposed upon the freedom of movement of capital and labor. Whereas the continually increasing diversity in the organic composition of capital, and the consequent greater and greater variations in the masses of surplus value directly created in the individual spheres of production, are in the first instance the outcome of capitalist evolution—this evolution in turn creates the possibility and the need for extinguishing these differences as far as capital is concerned, and for thus realizing the equality of human beings *qua* owners of capital.

We have previously seen what are the laws in accordance with which this equalization is effected. We have also seen that only upon the basis of the law of value was it possible to determine the magnitude of the total profit undergoing distribution as being equal to the total surplus value, and thus to determine the extent of the deviation of the price of production from its value. We have further seen how changes in the prices of production must always be referred to changes in value, and can only be explained with reference to such changes. All that we are interested in here is to note how, in this respect also, the subjectivist outlook hinders insight into Marx's train of thought.

For Böhm-Bawerk, competition is merely a collective name for all the psychical impulses and motives by which the parties in the market are influenced, and which thus affect the formation of prices. In relation to this view he has therefore no occasion to speak in a bad sense of the equilibrium between supply and demand, seeing that a number of wants always remain unsatisfied; for what this theory is concerned about is not the effective demand, but demand in general, so that certainly it remains enigmatical how the opinions and wishes of those who cannot buy are to influence the purchasing prices. Does not Marx destroy the validity of his objective law of value when he appeals to competition, appeals, that is to say, to these psychical impulses?

The relationship between supply and demand determines the price, but the height of the price determines the relationship between supply and demand. If the demand increases, the price rises, but if the price rises, the demand lessens, while if the price falls the demand increases. Further, if the demand increases and consequently the price rises, supply increases because production has become more lucrative. Thus price determines supply and demand, and supply and demand determine price; moreover, supply determines demand, and demand supply. In addition, all these fluctuations have a tendency to neutralize one another. If demand increases, so that price rises above its normal level, supply increases; this increase readily becomes greater than needful, and price then falls below the normal. Can we find no fixed point in all this confusion?

In Böhm-Bawerk's opinion, demand and supply invariably balance one another, whether exchange be effected at a normal price or at an irregular one. But what is this normal price? On the basis of capitalist production the surplus-value-creating process of capital is a precondition of production. In order that the capitalist may continue to produce, he must be able to sell the commodity at a price which is equal to its cost price plus average profit. If he is unable to realize this price (the normal price of the commodity produced under capitalism), the process of reproduction is arrested, and the supply is reduced to a point at which the relationship between supply and demand renders it possible to realize this price. Thus the relationship between supply and demand ceases to be a mere matter of chance; we perceive that it is regulated by the price of production, which constitutes the center around which market prices fluctuate in directions which are perpetually opposed, so that the fluctuations compensate one another in the long run. Thus the price of production is a condition of the supply, of the reproduction, of commodities. And not of this alone. It is necessary to secure such a relationship between supply and demand that the normal price, the price of production, can be realized, for then only can the course of the capitalist mode of production continue undisturbed, then only can occur the perpetual reproduction, through the very course of the process of circulation, of the social preconditions of a mode of production whose motive force is the need of capital for the creation of surplus value.

In the long run, therefore, the relationship between supply and demand must be of such a kind that that price of production (brought about independently of this relationship) may be attained which shall yield the capitalist the cost price plus the profit for the sake of which he has undertaken the production. Then we speak of the equilibrium of supply and demand.

If, on the other hand, we consider demand, we find that it is "essentially conditioned on the mutual relations of the different economic classes and their relative economic positions, that is to say, first, on the proportion of the total surplus value to the wages, and secondly, on the proportion of the various parts into which surplus value is divided (profit, interest, ground rent, taxes, etc.). And this shows once more that absolutely nothing can be explained by the relation of supply and demand, unless the basis has first been ascertained on which this relation rests" (III, 214). Thus Marx supplies the objective laws which are realized by and control the "psychical impulses" of individuals. The psychological school can attempt to elucidate but one side of the question, demand. The members of that school believe that they have explained the matter when they have classified the individual needs which manifest themselves as demand. They fail to recognize that the fact that a need exists does not convey any implication of the possibility for satisfying this need. The possibility of satisfaction does not depend upon the good will of the person feeling the need; it depends upon his economic power, upon the share of the social product of which he is able to dispose, upon the magnitude of the equivalent he is able to give for products owned by other persons.

Inasmuch as the productive power of human society in the specific form of organization which society confers upon that productive power is for Marx the fundamental idea of political economy, Marx demonstrates economic phenomena and their modifications as they manifest themselves in conformity to law, and *causally* dominated by the modifications in productive power. In this demonstration, in accordance with the dialectic method, conceptual evolution runs parallel throughout with historical evolution, inasmuch as the development of the social power of production appears in the Marxist system, on the one side as a historical reality, and on the other side as a conceptual reflex. Moreover, this parallelism furnishes the strictest empirical proof of the accuracy of the theory. The commodity form is necessarily the starting point; the commodity form is the simplest form, and becomes the object of economic contemplation, as the object of a specific scientific contemplation. For in the commodity form there already comes into being that delusive appearance which results from the fact that the social relationships of individuals assume the aspect of material qualities of things. It is this delusively material appearance which so greatly confuses the issues of economics. The social functions of individuals masquerade as material qualities of things, just as time and space, the subjective forms of perception, masquerade as objective qualities of things. Inasmuch as Marx dispels this illusion, inasmuch as he discloses personal relationships where before him material relationships had been seen, and discloses social relationships where before him individual relationships had been seen, he succeeds in furnishing a unified and consistent explanation of the phenomena which the classical economists had been unable to elucidate. The failure of the classical economists was inevitable, for they regarded bourgeois relationships of production as natural and unalterable. Marx, having demonstrated the historic conditioning of these relationships of production, was able to take up the analysis at the point where the investigations of the classical economists had been arrested.

But the demonstration of the historic transitoriness of bourgeois relationships of production signifies the close of

political economy as a *bourgeois* science and its foundation as
a *proletarian* science.

No more than two ways now remained open to the bourgeois
champions, if they desired to be anything more than mere
apologists for whom an uncritical eclecticism would provide the
crumbling pillars of their systems of harmony. They might,
like the historical school in Germany, ignore theory, and endeavor to fill its place with a history of economic science, but
would then be restricted, as the German historical school has
been restricted even within its own chosen field, by the lack of
any unified apprehension of economic happenings. The psychological school of economics has chosen the other path. The
members of this school have endeavored to construct a theory
of economic happenings by excluding economics itself from
their purview. Instead of taking economic or social relationships as the starting point of their system, they have chosen
for that starting point the *individual* relationship between men
and things. They regard this relationship from the psychological
outlook as one which is subject to natural and unalterable laws.
They ignore the relationships of production in their social
determinateness, and the idea of a law-abiding evolution of
economic happenings is alien to their minds. This economic
theory signifies the repudiation of economics. The last word in
the rejoinder of bourgeois economics to scientific socialism is
the *suicide of political economy.*

APPENDIX

"On the Correction of Marx's Fundamental

Theoretical Construction in the Third

Volume of *Capital*," by

Ladislaus von Bortkiewicz

Originally published in
Jahrbücher für Nationalökonomie und Statistik
July 1907

Translated by PAUL M. SWEEZY

CRITICS of Marx have hitherto shown little inclination to examine more closely the procedure which is used in the third volume of *Capital* [1] for the transformation of values into prices of production and for the determination of the average rate of profit, in order to see whether this procedure is free of contradictions.

Tugan-Baranowsky provides an exception in this respect.[2] He has shown specifically that the way Marx calculates the average rate of profit is not valid. Moreover, Tugan-Baranowsky has pointed out how with given prices of production and a given average rate of profit it is possible to calculate correctly the corresponding values and the rate of surplus value. In this case there is posed a problem which is the opposite of that which Marx tried to solve.

It is nevertheless interesting to show that Marx erred, and in what way, without reversing his way of posing the problem. For this purpose, it will be convenient, in order not to complicate the presentation, to introduce the same limiting assumption which Tugan-Baranowsky made use of, namely, that the entire advanced capital (including the constant capital) turns

[1] Vol. III, pp. 182-203.
[2] *Theoretische Grundlagen des Marxismus* (Leipzig, 1905), pp. 170-188.

over once a year and reappears again in the value or the price of the annual product.[1] Insofar as it is a question of demonstrating Marx's errors it is quite unobjectionable to work with limiting assumptions of this kind, since what does not hold in the special case cannot claim general validity.

In still another respect the procedure followed here agrees with that of Tugan-Baranowsky. The different spheres of production from which Marx composes social production as a whole can be put together into three departments of production. In Department I means of production are produced, in Department II workers' consumption goods, and in Department III capitalists' consumption goods. At the same time we shall assume that in the production of all three groups of means of production, that is, those which are used respectively in Departments I, II, and III—the organic composition of capital is the same.

Finally, we shall assume "simple reproduction."

Let c_1, c_2, c_3 stand for the constant capital, v_1, v_2, v_3 for the variable capital, and s_1, s_2, s_3 for the surplus value in Departments I, II, and III respectively. The conditions of simple reproduction are expressed in the following system of equations:

(1) $$c_1 + v_1 + s_1 = c_1 + c_2 + c_3$$
(2) $$c_2 + v_2 + s_2 = v_1 + v_2 + v_3$$
(3) $$c_3 + v_3 + s_3 = s_1 + s_2 + s_3$$

If we now designate the rate of surplus value by r, then we have

$$r = \frac{s_1}{v_1} = \frac{s_2}{v_2} = \frac{s_3}{v_3}$$

and equations (1), (2), and (3) can be rewritten as follows:

(4) $$c_1 + (1 + r)v_1 = c_1 + c_2 + c_3$$
(5) $$c_2 + (1 + r)v_2 = v_1 + v_2 + v_3$$
(6) $$c_3 + (1 + r)v_3 = s_1 + s_2 + s_3$$

[1] This assumption is also found, for example, in Kautsky, *Karl Marx' Ökonomische Lehren* (Stuttgart, 1903), p. 98.

The problem now is to convert these value expressions into price expressions which conform to the law of the equal rate of profit.

Marx's solution consists, first, in forming the sums

$$(7) \qquad c_1 + c_2 + c_3 = C$$
$$(8) \qquad v_1 + v_2 + v_3 = V$$
$$(9) \qquad s_1 + s_2 + s_3 = S$$

next, in determining the sought-for average rate of profit, which will be designated by ρ, from the formula

$$(10) \qquad \rho = \frac{S}{C + V}$$

and, finally, expressing the production prices of the commodities produced in the three departments by

$$c_1 + v_1 + \rho \, (c_1 + v_1)$$
$$c_2 + v_2 + \rho \, (c_2 + v_2)$$
$$c_3 + v_3 + \rho \, (c_3 + v_3)$$

from which it emerges that the sum of these three price expressions, or the total price, is identical with the sum of the corresponding value expressions, or the total value $(C + V + S)$.

This solution of the problem cannot be accepted because it excludes the constant and variable capitals from the transformation process, whereas the principle of the equal profit rate, when it takes the place of the law of value in Marx's sense, must involve these elements.[1]

The correct transition from value quantities to price quantities can be worked out as follows:

Suppose that the relation between the price and the value of the products of Department I is (on the average) as x to 1, in the case of Department II as y to 1, and in the case of Department III as z to 1. Furthermore let ρ be the profit rate which

---

[1] For a closer examination of this point, see the second article of my work "Wertrechnung und Preisrechnung im Marxschen System," *Archiv für Sozialwissenschaft und Sozialpolitik*, Vol. XXV, No. 1 (July, 1907).

is common to all departments (though now formula (10) can no longer be regarded as the correct expression for ρ).

The counterpart of equations (4), (5), and (6) is now the following system:

(11) $\qquad (1 + \rho)(c_1 x + v_1 y) = (c_1 + c_2 + c_3) x$

(12) $\qquad (1 + \rho)(c_2 x + v_2 y) = (v_1 + v_2 + v_3) y$

(13) $\qquad (1 + \rho)(c_3 x + v_3 y) = (s_1 + s_2 + s_3) z$

In this manner we obtain three equations with four unknowns (x, y, z, and ρ). In order to supply the missing fourth equation we must determine the relation between the price unit and the value unit.

If we were to choose the price unit in such a way that total price and total value are equal, we would have to set

(14) $\qquad Cx + Vy + Sz = C + V + S$

where

(15) $\qquad C = c_1 + c_2 + c_3$

(16) $\qquad V = v_1 + v_2 + v_3$

(17) $\qquad S = s_1 + s_2 + s_3$

If, on the other hand, the price unit and the value unit are to be regarded as identical, then we have to consider in which of the three departments the good which serves as the value and price unit is produced. If gold is the good in question, then Department III is involved and in place of (14) we get

(18) $\qquad z = 1$

Let us follow this last procedure. In this fashion the number of unknowns is reduced to three (x, y, and ρ).

To arrive at the simplest possible formulas, let us form the following expressions:

$$\frac{v_1}{c_1} = f_1 \quad , \quad \frac{v_1 + c_1 + s_1}{c_1} = g_1$$

$$\frac{v_2}{c_2} = f_2 \quad , \quad \frac{v_2 + c_2 + s_2}{c_2} = g_2$$

$$\frac{v_3}{c_3} = f_3 \quad , \quad \frac{v_3 + c_3 + s_3}{c_3} = g_3$$

and

$$1 + \rho = \sigma$$

Equations (11), (12), and (13) can be rewritten, taking account of (1), (2), and (3), as follows:

(19) $$\sigma(x + f_1 y) = g_1 x$$
(20) $$\sigma(x + f_2 y) = g_2 y$$
(21) $$\sigma(x + f_3 y) = g_3$$

From equation (19) we get:

(22) $$x = \frac{f_1 y \, \sigma}{g_1 - \sigma}$$

If we substitute this value for x in equation (20) the result is

(23) $$(f_1 - f_2)\, \sigma^2 + (f_2 g_1 + g_2)\, \sigma - g_1 g_2 = 0$$

from which it follows that

(24) $$\sigma = \frac{-(f_2 g_1 + g_2) + \sqrt{(f_2 g_1 + g_2)^2 + 4(f_1 - f_2) g_1 g_2}}{2(f_1 - f_2)}$$

or, otherwise written,

(25) $$\sigma = \frac{f_2 g_1 + g_2 - \sqrt{(g_2 - f_2 g_1)^2 + 4 f_1 g_1 g_2}}{2(f_2 - f_1)}$$

It is easy to show that in this case the quadratic equation (23) yields only one solution which is relevant to the terms of the problem. If $f_1 - f_2 > 0$, we get $\sigma < 0$ by putting a minus sign in front of the square root in formula (24). If on the other hand $f_1 - f_2 < 0$, the result of putting a plus sign in front of the square root in formula (25) is

$$\sigma > \frac{g_2}{f_2 - f_1}$$

and *a fortiori*

$$\sigma > \frac{g_2}{f_2}$$

This contradicts equation (20) which yields

$$\sigma < \frac{g_2}{f_2}$$

From equations (20) and (21) we find:

(26) $$y = \frac{g_3}{g_2 + (f_3 - f_2)\, \sigma}$$

and when we have solved for σ and y, x can be calculated according to formula (22).

Let us now see by several numerical examples how these formulas can be used to transform values into prices. Suppose for example that the given value expressions are the following:

TABLE 1: VALUE CALCULATION

Dept. of Production	Constant Capital	Variable Capital	Surplus Value	Value of Product
I	225	90	60	375
II	100	120	80	300
III	50	90	60	200
Total	375	300	200	875

From this we derive the following numerical values:

$$c_1 = 225, c_2 = 100, c_3 = 50, v_1 = 90, v_2 = 120, v_3 = 90,$$

$$s_1 = 60, s_2 = 80, s_3 = 60, \text{ and further: } f_1 = \frac{2}{5}, f_2 = \frac{5}{6},$$

$$f_3 = \frac{9}{5}, g_1 = \frac{5}{3}, g_2 = 3, g_3 = 4.$$

Formulas (25), (26), and (22) yield:

$$\sigma = \frac{5}{4}, \text{ therefore } \rho = \frac{1}{4}, y = \frac{16}{15}, x = \frac{32}{25}, \text{ and we get:}$$

TABLE 2: PRICE CALCULATION

Dept. of Production	Constant Capital	Variable Capital	Profit	Price of Product
I	288	96	96	480
II	128	128	64	320
III	64	96	40	200
Total	480	320	200	1,000

In Department I the price expression for constant capital (288) comes from multiplying the corresponding value expression (225) by $\frac{32}{25}$, and the price expression for variable capital

(96) from multiplying the corresponding value expression (90) by $\frac{16}{15}$. The profit in this department consists of the sum of the two price expressions $(288 + 96)$ multiplied by the profit rate $(\frac{1}{4})$. The figures for the other departments are calculated in exactly the same way.[1]

That the total price exceeds the total value arises from the fact that Department III, from which the good serving as value and price measure is taken, has a relatively low organic composition of capital. But the fact that total profit is numerically identical with total surplus value is a consequence of the fact that the good used as value and price measure belongs to Department III.

It is not without interest to compare the price and profit relations of Table 2 with the price and profit relations which Marx would have obtained in this case. According to formula (10) Marx would have written $\rho = \frac{200}{675} = \frac{8}{27}$, since (according to Table 1) $S = 200$, $C = 375$, $V = 300$.

We get:

TABLE 3: PRICE CALCULATION ACCORDING TO MARX

Dept. of Production	Constant Capital	Variable Capital	Profit	Price of Product
I	225	90	$93\frac{9}{27}$	$408\frac{9}{27}$
II	100	120	$65\frac{5}{27}$	$285\frac{5}{27}$
III	50	90	$41\frac{13}{27}$	$181\frac{13}{27}$
Total	375	300	200	875

[1] Table 1 is taken from the above-mentioned work of Tugan-Baranowsky, and all figures in Table 2 are related to the corresponding figures of Tugan-Baranowsky (*ibid.*, p. 171) as 8 to 5. Tugan-Baranowsky sets up his value schema in terms of labor units instead of money units. This is legitimate enough, but it turns attention away from the real difference between value calculation and price calculation.

There thus emerges a discrepancy between the prices of the quantities produced in the various departments ($408\frac{9}{27}$, $285\frac{5}{27}$, $181\frac{13}{27}$) and the numerical expressions for constant capital, variable capital, and profit. As already indicated, Marx would have had to determine the average rate of profit in this case to be $\frac{8}{27}$, or 29.6 percent, while according to the correct procedure it amounts to $\frac{1}{4}$, or 25 percent.[1]

But Marx not only failed to indicate a valid way of determining the rate of profit on the basis of given value and surplus value relations; more, he was misled by his wrong construction of prices into an incorrect understanding of the factors on which the height of the rate of profit in general depends.[2] He took the position that with a given rate of surplus value the rate of profit is greater or smaller according as the total social capital, including all spheres of production, has a lower or higher organic composition. This view follows from the fact that Marx expressed the rate of profit by formula (10). If we designate, as before, the rate of surplus value by r and the relation of the value of constant capital to total capital by q_0, according to which

$$r = \frac{S}{V} \text{ and } q_0 = \frac{C}{C + V}$$

we should then have:

(27) $$\rho = (1 - q_0)\, r$$

According to this, with a given rate of surplus value the only circumstance which affects the height of the rate of profit is whether the share of constant capital in total capital, the quotient q_0 is larger or smaller; and it would make no difference at all what differences existed between the organic composition of the capitals in the different spheres of production.

[1] See the first article of my work "Wertrechnung und Preisrechnung," in *Archiv für Sozialwissenschaft und Sozialpolitik*, Vol. XXIII, No. 1, p. 46.
[2] By rate of profit we understand here and in what follows, unless the contrary is expressly stated, the average rate of profit.

It is true that in *Capital* we read that the general rate of profit is determined by two factors: (1) the organic composition of the capitals in the different spheres of production, hence the different profit rates of the individual spheres, and (2) the distribution of the total social capital among these different spheres.[1] But the way Marx works these two factors into his calculation schema is such as to allow us to reduce them to one single factor, namely the organic composition of the total social capital.

Let q_1 represent the relation of constant capital in our Department I to the total capital of that department, γ_1 the share of the latter in the total social capital. Similarly let q_2, γ_2 and q_3, γ_3 represent the analogous quantities in Departments II and III. These designations can be expressed in the following formulas:

$$\frac{c_1}{c_1 + v_1} = q_1, \frac{c_2}{c_2 + v_2} = q_2, \frac{c_3}{c_3 + v_3} = q_3;$$

$$\frac{c_1 + v_1}{C + V} = \gamma_1, \frac{c_2 + v_2}{C + V} = \gamma_2, \frac{c_3 + v_3}{C + V} = \gamma_3$$

From these formulas it appears that:

$$\frac{c_1 + c_2 + c_3}{C + V} = \gamma_1 q_1 + \gamma_2 q_2 + \gamma_3 q_3$$

or also, since $c_1 + c_2 + c_3 = C$ and $\frac{C}{C + V} = q_0,$

(28) $$q_0 = \gamma_1 q_1 + \gamma_2 q_2 + \gamma_3 q_3$$

If one now substitutes this formula for q_0 in (27) and takes account of the fact that $\gamma^1 + \gamma^2 + \gamma_3 = 1$, one gets:

(29) $$\rho = \frac{\gamma_1 (1 - q_1) r + \gamma_2 (1 - q_2) r + \gamma_3 (1 - q_3) r}{\gamma_1 + \gamma_2 + \gamma_3}$$

This formula expresses the Marxian standpoint very clearly: the general rate of profit (ρ) appears as the arithmetic average

[1] Vol. III, pp. 191-192.

of the particular rates of profit $(1 - q_1)r$, $(1 - q_2)r$, and $(1 - q_3)r$, which contribute to the formation of the average with the respective "weights" $\gamma_1, \gamma_2, \gamma_3$. And of the two factors which in Marx's view determine the general rate of profit, one, according to formula (29), is represented by q_1, q_2, q_3 and the other by $\gamma_1, \gamma_2, \gamma_3$. It is, however, obvious from formula (28) that these two factors can be reduced to one single factor, that is to say, to the organic composition of the total social capital which is represented by q_0.

In opposition to this view we shall now show by means of a suitably constructed numerical example that, because formulas (27) and (29) are false, cases are possible in which, with a given rate of surplus value, one and the same rate of profit is compatible with different organic compositions of the total social capital. Take the following value schema as a starting point:

TABLE 4: VALUE CALCULATION

Dept. of Production	Constant Capital	Variable Capital	Surplus Value	Value of Product
I	300	120	80	500
II	80	96	64	240
III	120	24	16	160
Total	500	240	160	900

If we compare this table with Table 1 we find that the rate of surplus value is the same (66⅔ percent), while the organic composition of capital is higher. According to Table 1, $q_0 = \frac{375}{675} = .556$; while according to Table 4, $q_0 = \frac{500}{740} = .676$. Marx would say that the rate of profit must fall from 29.6 percent to 21.6 percent.

If we now apply to this table the correct method of transformation, as we did in going from Table 1 to Table 2, we find $x = \frac{32}{35}$, $y = \frac{16}{21}$, $\rho = \frac{1}{4}$, and as a complete result:

TABLE 5: PRICE CALCULATION

Dept. of Production	Constant Capital	Variable Capital	Profit	Price of Product
I	$274\frac{2}{7}$	$91\frac{3}{7}$	$91\frac{3}{7}$	$457\frac{1}{7}$
II	$73\frac{1}{7}$	$73\frac{1}{7}$	$36\frac{4}{7}$	$182\frac{6}{7}$
III	$109\frac{5}{7}$	$18\frac{2}{7}$	32	160
Total	$457\frac{1}{7}$	$182\frac{6}{7}$	160	800

The reason why Table 4 gives the same rate of profit as Table 1 (25 percent) is that according to formula (25) the rate of profit ($\rho = \sigma - 1$), given a certain rate of surplus value, depends exclusively on the organic composition of the capitals in Departments I and II (in this connection it is necessary to keep in mind the meaning of the quantities f_1, f_2, g_1, and g_2), and that in this respect Tables 1 and 4 are identical. But the circumstance that the ratio of constant capital to total capital in Department III has grown from about 36 percent to about 83 percent has no bearing on the height of the rate of profit. For the rest, however, this result is hardly surprising from the point of view of the theory of profit which sees the origin of profit in "surplus labor." Ricardo had already taught that a change in the relations of production which touches only such goods as do not enter into the consumption of the working class cannot affect the height of the rate of profit.[1]

Let us now consider a case where the rate of profit changes in spite of the fact that the organic composition of the total social capital remains the same. This happens if one contrasts with Tables 1 and 2 the following tables:

[1] For a closer examination of this point, see the third article of my work "Wertrechnung und Preisrechnung."

TABLE 6: VALUE CALCULATION

Dept. of Production	Constant Capital	Variable Capital	Surplus Value	Value of Product
I	205	102	68	375
II	20	168	112	300
III	150	30	20	200
Total	375	300	200	875

Following formulas (25), (26), and (22) we get

$$\sigma = \frac{415 - 5\sqrt{409}}{216} = 1.453, y = .432, x = .831$$

and as a complete result:

TABLE 7: PRICE CALCULATION

Dept. of Production	Constant Capital	Variable Capital	Profit	Price of Product
I	170.3	44.1	97.1	311.5
II	16.6	72.6	40.5	129.7
III	124.6	13.0	62.4	200
Total	311.5	129.7	200	641.2

Marx's method of transformation would have produced the same rate of profit again, 29.6 percent (instead of 45.3 percent), and the distribution of the total profit among the three departments would have been as follows: Department I, $90^{26}\!/_{27}$ (instead of 97.1), Department II, $55^{19}\!/_{27}$ (instead of 40.5), and Department III, $53^{9}\!/_{27}$ (instead of 62.4).

The erroneous character of Marx's transformation method comes out even more clearly in the special case where there is no constant capital in Department II. We have this case in the following table:

TABLE 8: VALUE CALCULATION

Dept. of Production	Constant Capital	Variable Capital	Surplus Value	Value of Product
I	180	90	60	330
II	0	180	120	300
III	150	30	20	200
Total	330	300	200	830

In this case we can no longer use formula (25) for the purpose of calculating ρ or σ, because $f_2 = \infty$ and $g_2 = \infty$. We have instead to go back to equations (11), (12), and (13). We find from (12), since $c_2 = 0$, that

$$1 + \rho = \frac{v_1 + v_2 + v_3}{v_2}$$

By reason of formula (2) we can also write (again because $c_2 = 0$):

$$1 + \rho = \frac{v_2 + s_2}{v_2}$$

and finally

$$\rho = \frac{s_2}{v_2}$$

or

$$\rho = r$$

The rate of profit is equal to the rate of surplus value, thus according to Table 8 equal to $\frac{2}{3}$ or $66\frac{2}{3}$ percent. If we put this value of ρ into formulas (11) and (13) we get two equations of the first degree with two unknowns (x and y), since here too $z = 1$, and we find: $x = \frac{10}{13}$, $y = \frac{2}{13}$. The conversion of values into prices and of surplus value into profit gives:

TABLE 9: PRICE CALCULATION

Dept. of Production	Constant Capital	Variable Capital	Profit	Price of Product
I	$138\frac{6}{13}$	$13\frac{11}{13}$	$101\frac{7}{13}$	$253\frac{11}{13}$
II	0	$27\frac{9}{13}$	$18\frac{6}{13}$	$46\frac{2}{13}$
III	$115\frac{5}{13}$	$4\frac{8}{13}$	80	200
Total	$253\frac{11}{13}$	$46\frac{2}{13}$	200	500

According to Marx, however, the relevant quantity relations would be as follows:

TABLE 10: PRICE CALCULATION ACCORDING TO MARX

Dept. of Production	Constant Capital	Variable Capital	Profit	Price of Product
I	180	90	$85\frac{5}{7}$	$355\frac{5}{7}$
II	0	180	$57\frac{1}{7}$	$237\frac{1}{7}$
III	150	30	$57\frac{1}{7}$	$237\frac{1}{7}$
Total	330	300	200	830

The rate of profit would be $\frac{200}{630}$ or 31.8 percent (instead of $66\frac{2}{3}$ percent!).

In this case, characterized by the absence of constant capital in Department II, the incorrectness of Marx's derivation of prices and profit is particularly obvious. For it is clear that here in Department II, where the outlay of capitalists consists solely of variable capital and indeed of the very commodities which are produced in that department, the gain of the capitalists must always remain in the same relation to their outlay whether the prices of the relevant commodities are higher or lower. There is no way, either through exchange of commodities or through "price regulation," by which this relation could be reduced from $66\frac{2}{3}$ percent to 31.8 percent.

Following Table 9 we can represent commodity exchanges as follows: [1]

The capitalists of Department

I	II	III

(1) hold commodities priced at:

$138\frac{8}{13}$	$27\frac{9}{13}$	80

[1] For the sake of simplicity it is assumed that the capitalists advance consumption goods to their workers *in natura* so that the workers take no direct part in commodity exchanges.

(2) buy commodities priced at:

from
$\begin{cases} \text{I} \\ \text{II} \\ \text{III} \end{cases}$
—	—	$115\tfrac{5}{13}$
$13\tfrac{11}{13}$	—	$4\tfrac{8}{13}$
$101\tfrac{7}{13}$	$18\tfrac{6}{13}$	—

(3) sell commodities priced at:

to
$\begin{cases} \text{I} \\ \text{II} \\ \text{III} \end{cases}$
—	$13\tfrac{11}{13}$	$101\tfrac{7}{13}$
—	—	$18\tfrac{6}{13}$
$115\tfrac{5}{13}$	$4\tfrac{8}{13}$	—

As can be seen, in the case of each group of capitalists the sum of the prices at which commodities are bought is the same as the sum of the prices at which commodities are sold. Table 10 would show a different picture:

The capitalists of Department

	I	II	III

(1) hold commodities priced at:

	I	II	III
	180	180	$57\tfrac{1}{7}$

(2) buy commodities priced at:

from
$\begin{cases} \text{I} \\ \text{II} \\ \text{III} \end{cases}$
—	—	150
90	—	30
$85\tfrac{5}{7}$	$57\tfrac{1}{7}$	—

(3) sell commodities priced at:

to
$\begin{cases} \text{I} \\ \text{II} \\ \text{III} \end{cases}$
—	90	$85\tfrac{5}{7}$
—	—	$57\tfrac{1}{7}$
150	30	—

Here the capitalists of Departments I and III would take in less than they pay out, while contrariwise the capitalists of Department II would take in more than twice what they pay out.

The case where $c_2 = 0$ is, however, useful not only for showing up very clearly to what paradoxes Marx's method of converting values into prices leads, it is also very well suited to serve as a starting point for an essential supplement to our previous exposition.

One would be inclined to conclude from the fact that in this particular special case the rate of profit is simply equal to the rate of surplus value, and also from the fact that it is entirely independent of the organic composition of capital in Departments I and III, that the organic composition in these two departments could be of any height without there ensuing a decline in the rate of profit. If this were true, and regardless of its being a special case, one could hardly suppress a strong doubt about the correctness of explaining profit by the principle of "surplus labor."

The truth of the matter, however, is that the share of constant capital in the total investment of Departments I and III cannot exceed a certain limit if the rate of profit in these two departments is also to equal r. If we substitute r for ρ in equation (11) and take account of equation (4), we get:

$$(1 + r)(c_1 x + v_1 y) = [c_1 + (1 + r)v_1]x$$

from which follow

$$c_1 x r < (1 + r)v_1 x$$

and also

$$c_1 < \frac{1 + r}{r} v_1$$

On the other hand, by reason of equation (1), with $c_2 = 0$, we have

$$c_3 = (1 + r)v_1$$

Let us introduce the new expressions

$$\frac{(1 + r)^2}{r} = \beta \qquad \text{and} \qquad \frac{c_1 + c_3}{c_1 + v_1 + c_3 + v_3} = q'$$

We now have the inequality

(30) $$c_1 + c_3 < \beta v_1$$

Therefore

$$1 + \frac{v_1 + v_3}{c_1 + c_3} > 1 + \frac{v_1 + v_3}{\beta v_1}$$

or

$$\frac{1}{q'} > \frac{(1 + \beta) v_1 + v_3}{\beta v_1}$$

and as a consequence

(31)
$$q' < \frac{\beta v_1}{(1 + \beta) v_1 + v_3}$$

We then have *a fortiori*:

$$q' < \frac{\beta}{1 + \beta}$$

or

(32)
$$q' < \frac{1 + 2r + r^2}{1 + 3r + r^2}$$

The quantity q' is, however, the expression for the organic composition of the combined capitals of Departments I and III. The independence of the rate of profit from the organic composition of the capitals in I and III, in the case where there is no constant capital in II, therefore, does not at all mean that the organic composition of capital in the other two departments can be indefinitely high. The truth of the matter is rather that if the share of constant capital in these departments, the quantity q', exceeds a certain limit, the equalization of the rate of profit becomes impossible.

In order to determine the upper limit for q_0, in other words for the share of constant capital in the total social capital, it is most convenient to start from the inequality (30) which can also be written as follows (with $c_2 = 0$):

$$C < \beta v_1$$

We have

$$q_0 = \frac{C}{C + V}$$

and therefore:

(33)
$$q_0 < \frac{\beta v_1}{\beta v_1 + V}$$

From the relation

(34)
$$\frac{V}{v_2} = 1 + r$$

we get, however,

$$V = v_2 + r v_2$$

and since on the other hand

$$V = v_1 + v_2 + v_3$$

it emerges that:

$$v_1 + v_3 = r v_2$$

and as a consequence

$$v_1 < r v_2$$

If we now substitute $r v_2$ for v_1 in (33), we get *a fortiori*

$$q_0 < \frac{\beta r v_2}{\beta r v_2 + V}$$

or also, taking account of (34),

(35)
$$q_0 < \frac{1 + r}{2 + r}$$

Hence if the rate of surplus value is 66⅔ percent, as we have assumed in the foregoing examples, then the constant capital invested in Departments I and III can in no case exceed ⅝ of the total social capital.

So much for the case in which $c_2 = 0$, that is to say in which constant capital is absent from Department II.

Likewise if $c_1 = 0$ it is impossible to determine the rate of profit by means of formulas (24) or (25), because here $f_1 = \infty$ and $g_1 = \infty$. If we take equations (11) and (12) as a basis for the determination of ρ or σ, we easily find:

(36)
$$\frac{1}{1 + r} \sigma^2 + f_2 \sigma - g_2 = 0$$

where r, as formerly, signifies the rate of surplus value$\left(\dfrac{s_1}{v_1}\right)$. This last equation can also be derived from equation (23) if one divides its coefficients by g_1. With $c_1 = 0$,

$$\frac{f_1}{g_1} = \frac{v_1}{v_1 + s_1} = \frac{1}{1 + r}$$

It would be entirely wrong to assume from the fact that r appears in (36) and not in (23) that in the case where c_1 is not zero the rate of profit is independent of the rate of surplus value. This is because the quantities g_1 and g_2 depend on r. We have:

$$g_1 = 1 + (1 + r)f_1$$

and

$$g_2 = 1 + (1 + r)f_2$$

If we eliminate the quantities f_1, f_2, g_1, g_2 from equations (23) and (36) by introducing the quantities q_1, q_2, and r, then the following relations emerge:

$$f_1 = \frac{1 - q_1}{q_1}, \; f_2 = \frac{1 - q_2}{q_2}$$

$$g_1 = \frac{1 + r(1 - q_1)}{q_1}, \; g_2 = \frac{1 + r(1 - q_2)}{q_2}$$

From this it is at once apparent that the rate of profit depends only on the rate of surplus value (r) and the organic composition of the capitals invested in Departments I and II.

The rate of profit is always smaller than the rate of surplus value, if we abstract from the special case where $c_2 = 0$. This can be proved as follows:

From equation (11) we find

$$c_1 x + v_1 y < (c_1 + c_2 + c_3)x$$

and, taking account of (4),

$$v_1 y < (1 + r)v_1 x,$$

from which it follows that

$$x > \frac{y}{1 + r}$$

Appendix

From equation (12) there thus emerges the inequality:

$$(1 + \rho)\left(\frac{c_2 y}{1 + r} + v_2 y\right) < (v_1 + v_2 + v_3)y$$

or, taking account of (9),

$$(1 + \rho)\left(\frac{c_2}{1 + r} + v_2\right) < c_2 + (1 + r)v_2$$

and finally

$$1 + \rho < 1 + r$$

and

(37) $$\rho < r$$

Another upper limit for ρ can be derived from (11) in the following way. We have:

$$(1 + \rho)c_1 x < (c_1 + c_2 + c_3)x$$

and hence

(38) $$\rho < \frac{c_2 + c_3}{c_1}$$

This inequality allows us to conclude that with a given rate of surplus value (r) and a given quantity of variable capital (V), an unlimited growth of constant capital cannot take place without bringing about a decline in the rate of profit.

It follows from (4) that:

$$c_2 + c_3 = (1 + r)v_1$$

and this means that the growth of constant capital in Departments II and III finds a limit in the height of the rate of surplus value and in the size of the total disposable variable capital. It is to be remembered, too, that v_1 forms a part of V.

We could say with equal justification that the growth of constant capital in Departments II and III finds a limit in the quantity of labor which society has at its disposal in a given economic period. Let this quantity be H. Of this h_1 belongs to Department I, h_2 to II, and h_3 to III, so that $H = h_1 + h_2 + h_3$.

If we designate the quantity of labor contained in one unit of value as η then we have:

$$h_1 = (v_1 + s_1)\eta, \; h_2 = (v_2 + s_2)\eta, \; h_3 = (v_3 + c_3)\eta, \text{ and}$$

$$H = (V + S)\eta$$

We can now write

$$(c_2 + c_3)\eta = h_1$$

and since h_1 is a part of H, it appears that the constant capital invested in Departments II and III, measured in terms of the quantity of (stored-up) labor which it contains, is limited by the quantity of (living) labor which is available for use in production during the relevant economic period.

Nevertheless, so far as the constant capital invested in Department I (c_1) is concerned, one can imagine it as growing indefinitely without disturbing the conditions of economic equilibrium as they find expression in equations (4), (5), and (6). But, as formula (38) shows, sooner or later the consequence of the growth of constant capital in Department I must be a decline in the rate of profit. For the rest, the inequality (38) is valid even in the case where $c_2 = 0$.

It follows from what has been said that it would be entirely incorrect to state in opposition to Marx that the rate of profit does not depend in general on the organic composition of the total social capital. The simple relation between ρ and q_0 with which Marx operates—see equation (27)—does not exist, and cases can be constructed in which, with a given rate of surplus value (r), the rate of profit (ρ) remains unchanged although q_0 takes on different values, just as cases are possible in which ρ assumes different values although q_0 remains unchanged. But—and this should not be overlooked—such cases are based on the supposition that the organic composition of capital is different in the three departments. If, on the other hand, the condition $q_1 = q_2 = q_3$ is fulfilled, then values and prices are identical and formula (27) comes into force.

This last remark cannot serve to excuse Marx. For if the condition which would validate formula (27) is fulfilled, then the entire operation of converting values into prices is pointless, while Marx makes use of this formula precisely in connection with this operation.

The above remark is directed only against the criticism which holds that, regardless of whether the quantities q_1, q_2, and q_3 are equal or not, the Marxian thesis of the influence of the organic composition of the total social capital on the height of the rate of profit, as this thesis finds expression in formula (27), is false.

Tugan-Baranowsky in particular makes this mistake. The two numerical examples with which he tries to refute the Marxian thesis are precisely characterized by the assumption that the organic composition of capital is equal in all three departments, in other words that $q_1 = q_2 = q_3 = q_0$.

In one example,[1] r (the rate of surplus value) falls from 1 to $\frac{7}{9}$, while at the same time q_0 increases from $\frac{2}{3}$ to $\frac{20}{29}$, from which it emerges, entirely in keeping with formula (27), that ρ (the rate of profit) declines from $\frac{1}{3}$ to $\frac{7}{29}$.[2]

In the other example,[3] r rises from 1 to $\frac{81}{44}$, while at the same time q_0 increases from $\frac{2}{3}$ to $\frac{25}{36}$, from which, once again in keeping with formula (27), ρ increases from $\frac{1}{3}$ to $\frac{9}{16}$.

Tugan-Baranowsky concludes from the fact that in the one case a growth in the share of constant capital accompanies a fall and in the other case a rise in the rate of profit, that the general

[1] *Op. cit.*, p. 177.
[2] By q_0 I always understand the relation of the *value* of variable capital to the *value* of the total capital, while in Tugan-Baranowsky's examples it is a question of *price* expressions. In the place of q_0, which equals $\frac{C}{C+V}$, there thus appears $\frac{Cx}{Cx+Vy}$. But the latter expression is identical with q_0 if one assumes, as Tugan-Baranowsky does, that the organic composition of capital is identical in all three departments. For in this case we have $x = y$ or alternatively $x = y = 1$.
[3] *Ibid.*, pp. 180-181.

rate of profit is entirely independent of the organic composition of the social capital, and that therefore the Marxian theory of profit is false.[1]

As though such numerical examples could in any way touch the Marxian theory of the influence of the organic composition of the total social capital on the rate of profit! According to Marx, this influence makes itself felt in the indicated way only if the rate of surplus value remains unchanged.[2]

[1] See the first article in my work "Wertrechnung und Preisrechnung," pp. 48-49.
[2] *Capital*, Vol. III, for example p. 75 and p. 248. The extent to which this limiting condition figures in the Marxian law of the falling rate of profit I have discussed thoroughly in the third article of my work "Wertrechnung und Preisrechnung im Marxschen System."

INDEX OF NAMES

The names of Marx, Böhm-Bawerk, Hilferding, and Bortkiewicz have been omitted from this index.

www.ingramcontent.com/pod-product-compliance
Lightning Source LLC
Chambersburg PA
CBHW020850270326
41928CB00006B/630